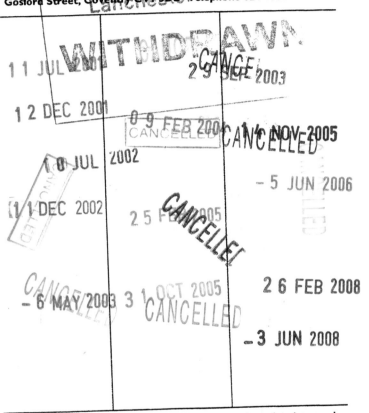

SCHEDULING OF PRODUCTION PROCESSES

SCHEDULING OF PRODUCTION PROCESSES

Editors:
JÜRGEN DORN and KARL FROESCHL
Christian Doppler Laboratory for Expert Systems
Technical University of Vienna, Austria

ELLIS HORWOOD
NEW YORK   LONDON   TORONTO   SYDNEY   TOKYO   SINGAPORE

P04286

First published in 1993 by
Ellis Horwood Limited
Market Cross House, Cooper Street,
Chichester, West Sussex, PO19 1EB, England
A division of
Simon & Schuster International Group

Printed and bound in Great Britain
by Bookcraft, Midsomer Norton

British Library Cataloguing in Publication Data

A catalogue record for this book is available from the British Library

ISBN 0–13–075136–7

Library of Congress Cataloging-in-Publication Data

Available from the publisher

List of Contributors

Eric Bensana
ONERA-CERT/DERA
2 av E. Belin, BP 4025, F-31055 Toulouse, France
E-mail: bensana@triton.cert.fr

Pauline M. Berry
AI Applications Institute, University of Edinburgh,
80 South Bridge, Edinburgh, EH1 1HN, UK
E-mail: pb@aiai.edinburgh.ac.uk

Sandford Bessler
Kapsch AG
Wagenseilgasse 1, A-1121 Wien, Austria
E-mail: Sandford.Bessler@kapsch.co.at

Atilla Bezirgan
Institut für Automation, Technische Universität Wien
Treitlstraße 3 / 183 / 1, A-1040 Wien, Austria
E-mail: aberziga@email.tuwien.ac.at

Ulrico Canzi
Centro per la Ricerca e la Formazione in Ingegneria dell'Informazione (CEFRIEL),
Politecnico di Milano
Via Emanueli, 15, I-20126 Milano, Italy
E-mail: uli@mailer.cefriel.it

Jürgen Dorn
Christian Doppler Laboratory for Expert Systems, Technische Universität Wien
Paniglgasse 16, A-1040 Wien
E-mail: dorn@vexpert.dbai.tuwien.ac.at

Bogdan Filipic
Institut "Jozef Stefan", Univerza v Ljubljani
Jamova 39, 61111 Ljubljana, Slovenia
E-mail: Bogdan.Filipic@ijs.si

Karl A. Froeschl
Institut für Statistik, Operations Research und Computerverfahren, Universität Wien
Universitätsstraße 5, A-1010 Wien, Austria
E-mail: froeschl@atlas.smc.univie.ac.at

Khaled Ghédira
ONERA - CERT,
2. avenue Edouard Belin, B.P. 4025, F-31055 Toulouse Cedex, France
E-mail: ghedira@tls-cs.cert.fr

Manfred Gronalt
Institut für Betriebswirtschaftslehre, Universität Wien,
Brünner Str. 72, A-1210 Vienna, Austria
E-mail: a4551dac@vm.univie.ac.at

Giovanni Guida
Dipartimento di Elettronica per l'Automazione, Università di Brescia
Via Branze 38, I-25123 Brescia, Italy

José Lázaro, José Maseda, Fernando Díaz, Helge Sturesson, Gonzalo Escalada
IDEIA, Investigación y DEsarrollo en Inteligencia Artificial, LABEIN.
Parque Tecnológico 101, E-48016 Zamudio Vizcaya, Spain
E-mail: josemari@labein.es

Claude Muller, Evan H. Magill, D. Geoffrey Smith
Department of Electronic and Electrical Engineering, University of Strathclyde
204 George Street, Glasgow G1 1XW, United Kingdom;
E-mail: cmuller@comms.eee.strathclyde.ac.uk

Patrick Prosser
Department of Computer Science, University of Strathclyde
26 Richmond Street, Glasgow G1 1XH, Scotland
E-mail: pat@cs.strathclyde.ac.uk

Jürgen Sauer
FB Informatik, Universität Oldenburg
Postfach 2503, D-2900 Oldenburg
E-mail: Sauer@Informatik.Uni-Oldenburg.DE

Barbara M. Smith
School of Computer Studies, University of Leeds
Leeds LS2 9JT, United Kingdom
E-mail: bms@ai.leeds.ac.uk

Gérard Verfaillie
ONERA - CERT,
2. avenue Edouard Belin, B.P. 4025, F-31055 Toulouse Cedex, France
E-mail: verfail@tls-cs.cert.fr

Table of Contents

Tables of Figures, Tables and Algorithms

Preface

Competition in the international market place requires industrial production to become structured more and more efficiently. In particular, the organization of production processes has conflicting goals: production costs have to be kept as low as possible while specific customer demands should be satisfied to a maximum degree. Consequently, modern production management aims to satisfy high standards of product quality as well as to meet delivery dates under economic conditions requiring progressively smaller lot sizes. Frequently, managerial goals also depend considerably on fluctuations of the international economy. The continuously changing objectives place increasing emphasis on the clear formulation and flexibility of production scheduling strategies.

Large-scale production is organized by means of production planning systems delivering capacity plans as well as time windows for single orders. In a further step, scheduling derives definitive assignments of the orders contained in a production plan to available resources over time. These assignments, of course, are subject to a multitude of shop floor details ignored at higher planning levels; for instance, aspects like set-up or breakdown of machines and compatibility relations between orders, have to be taken into account. Eventually, the success of manufacturing policies such as "just-in-time" or "kanban" depends on the extent to which scheduling takes care of the actual shop floor dynamics.

The first approaches to the scheduling problem were developed in the context of Operations Research. Although being theoretically sound and yielding optimal solutions, these mathematical-analytical models are applied only seldom in realistic applications. The difficulty to express all scheduling constraints, and the inherent complexity and the uncertainties present in most scheduling applications, prevent the use of these models. As a consequence, the models have been enriched with heuristics to tackle the cited problems.

Another approach that claims to cope with these problems is the use of knowledge-based techniques. These try to represent explicitly all constraints of a scheduling problem even if some of the available information is uncertain. Several techniques have been developed to master the complexity of resulting problem representations.

Sometimes both approaches are interpreted as antagonistic and the question "What is better, Operations Research or Artificial Intelligence?" is often discussed. We believe that both approaches, rather, are complementary to each other and an integrated solution will be best. From this point of view, the "Vienna Scheduling Forum" organized a workshop at the "10th European Conference on Artificial Intelligence" in Vienna. The present book contains rewritten submissions to the workshop as well as additional papers that were considered to be relevant to this context.

Jürgen Dorn and Karl A. Froeschl

1

Two Paradigms of Combinatorial Production Scheduling Operations Research and Artificial Intelligence

Karl A. Froeschl
Institut für Statistik, Operations Research und Computerverfahren, Universität Wien

INTRODUCTION

In a very general sense, *scheduling* can be defined as "… the allocation of resources over time to perform a collection of tasks." (Baker, 1974). This definition includes an encompassing variety of problems from as different fields of application as can be imagined. Ranging from the rather crude task ordering rules governing the annual cycles of prehistoric food production up to the sophisticated group technology of advanced flexible manufacturing systems in almost completely automated production plants of our modern age, scheduling has been a ubiquitous attendant of all human economic activity. As a matter of fact, at the heart of economics lies persistently the careful, if not parsimonious, usage of resources. A distinctive feature of Western culture is its endeavour to capture most of the human activities and concepts (or, in fact, all of them?) in some formal setting, viz. framing it in mathematical or, more general, rational terms. In view of the importance of economics, be it either on the small scale of a single entrepreneur or on the large scale of national or supranational economies, it is hardly surprising that scheduling has become a major object of thorough mathematical treatment. Unfortunately, it turned out that real-size scheduling problems hopelessly exceed the border of computational tractability whence the whole subject has resisted all brute-force algorithmic approaches. On the contrary, the human factor again enters the scene, thus giving the scheduling discipline the flair of a skilful art reserved for the highly qualified. Essentially, how far this art can be turned into plain, effective technology is the current quest of research. Plainly speaking, the optimal point on a scale delimited by its two extremes, the utmost formal optimization approach and the rather informal, heuristic search-and-improvement approach, is sought, conditional on the nature of individual problem instances or, rather more efficiently, classes of similar problem instances. In the history of the development of scheduling approaches these extremes have been associated, on the one hand, with *Operations Research* and, on the other hand, with *Artificial Intelligence*. It is for this reason, mainly, that the *Operations Research – Artificial Intelligence* dichotomy has been chosen as the opening contribution to this book. In particular, this initial chapter will sketch the development of scheduling as a discipline in its own right pointing out the proximity of temporary tendencies to the one or the other end of the scale, whereupon both positions – each in its idealized appearance – are contrasted with each other.

In this book, scheduling problems emanating from the realm of industrial production are considered. In particular, the focus is narrowed to a class of scheduling problems for which the relevant problem information is either specified in exact terms (at least, ideally) or entirely unknown otherwise. This point of view rules out, of course, scheduling problems involving stochastic problem information, i.e. problems concerning information varying according to some given probability distribution. In short, the main focus of the subsequent discussion is put on typical *production scheduling* problems regarding exclusively discrete objects (such as orders, machines, operations, resources, etc.) and deterministic parameters. Essentially, this type of problem is characterized by its inherent *combinatorial* nature for which reason the various methods devised for exploring combinatorial problem spaces attract special interest. In this respect, the following exposition will also include non-discrete solution approaches in addition to classical as well as "modern" methods of (partial, heuristic, etc.) enumeration.

Another decisive feature of the problem class concerned is the *short-term* planning horizon. Essentially, this amounts to maintaining the assumption of both a fixed planning environment and a given product structure. In particular, it is supposed that neither the *shop floor* nor production organization are altered in the course of planning or during the time period production is scheduled for. Likewise, *process plans* prescribing operation sequences required to bring about complete jobs or orders are assumed constant. In other words, scheduling is thought as subject to static boundary conditions, with the one exception of possible external disturbances affecting the shop floor negatively in the sense of capacity *reductions* occurring (and ending) spontaneously like, e.g., machine breakdowns, etc.

Formally, the considered class of scheduling problems belongs to the class of discrete assignment problems: as far as possible, the sum total of all operations of jobs / orders to be scheduled in some planning period shall be assigned to the available resources such that all logical, physical, temporal, etc. constraints are obeyed and, at the same time, a particular planning goal expressing the – economic – interest of the planner is achieved. The most important constraints defining problem structure pertain to

- the sequence (or network) of operations to be carried out for completing an order (i.e., process plans),
- the availability of resources required to carry out each of the operations,
- the admissibility of assigning particular operations to particular machines.

The type of constraint mentioned last is more typical for scheduling problems in *flexible manufacturing systems* (FMS); traditionally, each defined operation is assigned to just one particular machine. An essential feature of the scheduling problems treated here is the presence of resource constraints, i.e. typically resources are available only with some limited amount which may, additionally, vary over time. Although various kinds of resource constraints are conceivable (e.g., Blazewicz *et al.*, 1986), *renewable* resources are assumed in general, i.e. resources are available with constant capacity throughout. In particular, this holds for *machines* which, obviously, represent the cardinal resource concerned in scheduling; for this reason machines are distinguished from other resources generally. As to resource *contention*, during the execution of operations it is assumed regularly that – regardless of the type resource used – an executed operation consumes some constant amount of a resource's capacity during the full time of execution whereupon the resource is relieved again. Once bound to an operation, only the remaining capacity of a resource is left for other operations.

In addition to fixed constraints resulting from both production and product structure there usually are further constraints regarding the orders to be scheduled. As an example, assured due dates of orders belong to this type of constraint. In contrast to most technological or physical production constraints, such due dates – along with several other capacity restrictions (such as regular work time), are *soft - constraints* in the sense that they can be adjusted (within limits) dynamically to the requirements of the production. Violation of hard constraints renders any schedule invalid (i.e., physically useless or impossible) whereas the adjustment of soft constraints typically impinges on the degree to which economic planning goals are achieved. For instance, keeping an assured due date might cause additional labour cost due to overtime payments, although this may still be less disastrous than being late.

Schedules obeying all imposed constraints (possibly after suitable adjustments) are termed *feasible*. In addition to mere feasibility schedules may be evaluated according to some criterion of efficiency. These planning goals can be expressed either explicitly in a quantifying objective function or in terms of preference rules ordering possible schedule alternatives according to some measure of utility. As far as formal models of schedule optimization are employed, the economic goal of the planning actor is expressed in terms of performance measures which, in turn, draw upon the decision variables of the generated schedules. Typically, schedule performance refers to production time (such as overall completion time of a set of orders, mean lateness of finished orders, number of late orders) but also to other resources (like the sum total of capital bound in unfinished orders) and combinations thereof (like the value of late orders). In most instances, the objective function is going to be minimized, i.e. among all feasible schedules the one resulting in a minimal value of the objective function is preferred. In theoretical analysis particularly two types of objective criteria dominate: in scheduling problems without due dates the *makespan* (i.e. the total time used to finish a set of orders) is minimized whereas in problems with due dates, naturally, a performance measure depending on lateness (or, sometimes, tardiness) is taken instead, e.g. the averaged lateness per order etc. Especially in practical scheduling applications, however, no optimal solution is sought from the outset; in view of omnipresent shop floor dynamics, asynchronous arrival of orders, etc., it is frequently almost impossible to define a performance measure reasonably. Instead, in some sense *good* feasible schedules are perfectly acceptable.

Due to both its coverage and its abstract flavour, scheduling methodology becomes related to several other theoretical disciplines. Expectedly, this results in manifold mutual influences and interactions. For the sake of brevity, only a few of these intersections will be touched upon. For obvious reasons, mathematically oriented scheduling shares a good deal with classical *optimization theory* (Papadimitriou and Steiglitz, 1982) and (Nemhauser and Wolsey, 1988), but also with heuristic search methods (Pearl, 1984), graph theory (Christofides, 1975), constraint satisfaction approaches (Meseguer, 1989) and, last but not least, complexity theory (Garey and Johnson, 1979). Essentially, these disciplines provide a formal framework in which many scheduling problems can be expressed in a very concise way, although this rarely accomplishes a straightforward means of obtaining solutions efficiently. W.r.t. Artificial Intelligence, scheduling is closest to the subfield of *planning*. According to the definitions provided by (Fox and Sadeh, 1990) "... planning selects and sequences activities such that they achieve one or more goals and satisfy a set of domain constraints...", whereas "... scheduling selects among alternative plans, and assigns resources and times for each activity so that they obey the temporal restrictions of activities and the capacity of a set of shared resources." Evidently, the planning methods of Artificial Intelligence concern the derivation of *action sequences* (composed of some predetermined repertory of elementary action units) while scheduling deals with *resource contention* for already derived, or given, action sequences. Prima vista, planning and scheduling seem to have little in common unless the process of schedule generation is viewed as a planning problem in terms of the planning agent. This, however, has not been explored in depth hitherto (as an example, cf. (Shaw, 1989)) wherefore the scrutiny of planning problems in the sense of Artificial Intelligence has contributed mainly more or less specific means of *knowledge representation* useful for modelling scheduling applications.

The body of this chapter is structured as follows. Section 2 outlines the development of scheduling as a discipline, giving a survey of the variety of formal methods adopted up to now. Particularly, this includes several attempts of synthesizing scheduling methods of Operations Research and Artificial Intelligence origin. Drawing on this presentation, section 3 will try thereafter a paradigmatic comparison of the extreme approaches to scheduling by ascribing both of them a rather idealized status. The final section, eventually, gives a short account of all chapters of this book indicating also the position of each of the presented scheduling approaches w.r.t. the contrasted paradigms.

AN OUTLINE OF SCHEDULING METHODOLOGY

As is the case with most of the very profound ideas of mankind, scheduling can be traced back into the haze of ancient history. Certainly, the temporal arrangement of tasks according to plan belongs to the set of basic "technologies" of civilization. At least the huge historical monuments of cultures long past witness the high degree of organization of labour force and material logistics, as can be gleaned, e.g., from the impressive Egypt pyramids and temples erected some millennia B.C. Like any planning activity, scheduling refers to *time* and, hence, presupposes at least an implicit notion of temporal flow. Historically, time has been associated with the – recurrent – celestial motions of planets and stars (e.g., cf. (Aveni, 1989)) which have been correlated with the course of terrestrial seasons of the year. In a very natural way ancient astronomy provided the perpetual calendar of human activities, as it is exemplified impressively by the writings of Hesiod in his *Works and Days* (dated 700 B.C., cf. (West, 1978)).

Despite the presence of these early roots, our story of scheduling really starts with the development of the Western sense of time. If we can believe the thesis of the social philosopher Lewis Mumford, the secularizing of time, i.e. the change from essentially subjective time – controlled by the daily rhythm of cultural custom as well as the changing states of the individual psyche – to some objective, "external" time measured in terms of inanimate matter (in particular, mechanical contrivances such as metal clockworks), first took place in medieval monasteries from the 6th century onwards (Mumford, 1934). It is this mundane notion of time which gives rise to the consideration of efficiency and the economic usage of temporal resources. Once measured – in the very modern meaning of this word – and turned into an abstract uniform linear scale, time becomes a scarce resource we can only try to make the best out of. Accordingly, time management began to occupy a position of utmost importance in the economic organization of industrial production processes spreading, after the invention of the steam engine, particularly in England during the 18th century. Since only the most effective exploitation of production factors, notably machinery, gains the highest return on invested capital, production scheduling received increasing interest in theoretical economic investigations. Apparently, it is more than mere coincidence that one of the early pioneers of computing technology, the remarkable Charles Babbage (1791–1871), was among the first to analyse the economy of industrial production in a manner close to modern Operations Research. In contrast to much of contemporary economic theory he based his conclusions on a profound empirical analysis of the industrial processes and facilities of his time. Although lacking the formal rigour of modern Operations Research treatises, it is by no means exaggerated to call his book *On the Economy of Machines and Manufactures*, published 1832, as the first dedicated specimen of Operations Research literature. Interestingly, there is also a well-documented impact of Babbage on great economists like Karl Marx and John Stuart Mill. Practically thinking a man as he was, Babbage turned his attitude into real proposals, e.g. he suggested the "penny post" as a single, weight-independent postage for shipping letters and parcels (thus outweighing the loss of postages by omitting costly postage determination) as well as a control clock used for recording actual work time of factory workers. Babbage was ahead of his time in many respects; it took almost another three quarters of a century until time was ripe for a systematic approach to the organization of production processes. Standing in a tradition dating back to the French military system of the Napoleon I. era, F.W. Taylor proposed his *Principles of Scientific Management* in 1911. In this treatise, Taylor claimed that any rational organization of production requires no less than a completely formalized analysis of all involved processes and sub-processes in a comprehensive fashion. In particular, he contrasted experience acquired empirically with scientifically derived designs proclaiming the unconditional superiority of the latter. His approach is, by and large, system-theoretic and lays the foundation of *classical* Operations Research methodology.

Taylor's seed started to grow and, mainly fostered by the logistic requirements of World War II, developed rapidly after the war. This modern stage of scheduling, concerning the system theoretic scrutiny of managerial planning and decision problems, developed parallel to the emerging computing technology which, in turn, is also known to be an offspring of the war effort. Starting with early considerations already in the pre-war era (particularly in Russia; e.g., cf. (Kantorovich, 1939)) the science of Operations

Research really took off in conjunction with the availability of high-speed electronic digital computing devices after 1950. An event of remarkable importance in this respect certainly has been the invention of the *Simplex* algorithm by Dantzig in 1947 which provided an elegant mathematical frame for expressing many optimization problems in a rigorous fashion. Rather naturally, this method was soon employed in scheduling and a variety of approaches emerged (Wagner, 1959), (Bowman, 1959), (Manne, 1960), (Bishop, 1957), etc. Linear Programming as well as its multifarious descendants (cf. (Dantzig, 1963), w.r.t. a detailed treatment) built the ground layer of Operations Research methodology to which advances in Monte Carlo simulation techniques (Hammersley and Handscomb, 1964), as general early reference including stochastic optimization, queuing theory, etc., Integer Programming (Gomory, 1958), Dynamic Programming (Bellman *et al.*, 1982) and a further couple of combinatorial methods (notably, (Balas, 1969)), and Branch-and-Bound methods, e.g. (Land and Doig, 1960), (Little *et al.*, 1963), (Barker and McMahon, 1985) contributed significantly. The spreading interest into the new mathematical discipline is documented by numerous new organizations and journals founded in the early 1950s. In Great Britain, the *Operations Research Quarterly* is published since 1950; in the USA the National Research Council initiated (stimulated by military representatives) a Committee on Operations Research which led to the foundation of the Operations Research Society of America in 1952 and the publication of the *Journal* of that society. Already at its first national meeting in November 1952, scheduling problems had been put on the agenda. The US *Naval Research Logistics Quarterly* started publication in 1954.

The mathematical analysis of scheduling algorithms was stimulated anew by various problems emanating from the field of computer science, like resource management in operating systems, processor scheduling, etc. These investigations resulted in a larger number of more or less efficient (i.e., polynomially bounded in run-time) algorithms which, unfortunately, are restricted in applicability to rather peculiar situations (e.g., preemptive operations). Occasionally, algorithms optimal w.r.t. computational complexity can be stated (as surveyed, e.g., in (Blazewicz *et al.*, 1986)). Complexity theory (Edmonds, 1965), (Cook, 1971) and (Karp, 1972) has been developed in theoretical computer science (with influences from formal logics) which allows the distinction between *easy* and *difficult* problems. Unfortunately, the set of easy problems solvable by algorithms needing only space / time resources bounded by some polynomial function of their input is sparse whereas most scheduling problems and, particularly, most relevant problems belong to the class of *NP-complete problems* which are called *intractable* since no one has ever been able to show that there is some algorithm obviating the traps of non-determinism, i.e. the necessity of searching the problem space in all of its combinatorial explosiveness.

In response to the computational complexity of combinatorial, deterministic optimization which cannot be overcome for theoretical reasons the focus shifted to the investigation of tractable methods which provably find optimal solutions only most of the time, i.e. algorithms which converge to a (global) optimum for most inputs but without any definite guarantee to do so for any particular input. In principle, such algorithms operate on the grounds of stochastic decision models (i.e., simulating the non-determinism required to cut down intractability to manageable orders of computational complexity) which can be mimicked on a deterministic device by (pseudo-)random numbers (cf. (Glover and Green-berg, 1989), for a condensed survey). This class of methods comprises several related algorithms like *Simulated Annealing* (van Laarhoven *et al.*, 1988) and its discrete com-panion, *tabu search* (de Werra and Hertz, 1989), (Widmer and Hertz, 1989), (Taillard, 1990), and *Genetic Algorithms* (Davis, 1985), (Cleveland and Smith, 1989), (Whitley *et al.*, 1989), (Tsang and Warwick, 1990) all of which have been applied to scheduling readily.

Starting around 1960, the symbol processing capabilities of digital computers have been recognized clearly. In addition to this, within computer science the role of heuristic reasoning became promoted by outstanding researchers like Herbert A. Simon. Symbol processing in conjunction with proof procedures as applied particularly by humans to proceed from facts to conclusions have become the hallmark of Artificial Intelligence since. Apparently, *heuristic search* (Hart *et al.*, 1968) and (Hart *et al.*, 1972) offers a promising approach to enumerate combinatorial search spaces efficiently by ruling out all those regions having low subjective chances of containing an optimal solution. As far as this subjective assessment of chances reflects the actual structure of the (implicit only, perhaps) objective function, heuristic search can be overwhelmingly successful. The undeniable potential of heuristic methods has led to a modified view of scheduling prob-lems: Operations Research-based scheduling models which are lacking very frequently a satisfactory correspondence to modelled reality for the sake of tractability, lose consider-able attractiveness in comparison to scheduling models based on Artificial Intelligence methodology relying heavily on substantial, application-dependent problem solving knowledge. In particular, the symbolic planning approaches offer quite a lot of very powerful, expressive means for representing model and problem knowledge formally while, simultaneously, this knowledge can be stated less rigidly (e.g., also *fuzzy* informa-tion can be taken into account rather easily).

Of like importance is the way problem representations are dealt with in the planning process. In Artificial Intelligence scheduling, problem representations are the symbolic data structures undergoing material changes in the course of schedule construction, i.e. problems are represented analogously instead of mapping information to numbers sub-jected to arithmetic computation. This holds particularly for so-called *constraint-based* approaches (Nadel, 1989), (Le Pape, 1991) and (Atabakhsh, 1991) which, from a static point of view, are hardly different from traditional constraint representation. As a specific consequence, symbolic problem representations enable an adequate logical analysis of some of the inherently non-numerical aspects of scheduling problems: by using the prob-lem information itself as the material carrier of computations, formally encoded schedul-ing knowledge can be applied to the representations as operations causing explicit state transitions. In principle, schedule construction is modelled formally by decomposing the elicited expert problem solving knowledge into elementary pieces (or *chunks*, as they are called sometimes) each of which effects a single state transition in a sequence of transi-tions starting at the initial state and traversing the search space. Practically, this traversal is governed by the expert heuristics incorporated into the conditions controlling the choice of individual state transitions. Typical examples of this approach to *knowledge-based* scheduling are, among others, the systems of (Fox, 1987), (Robbins, 1985), and (Kerr and Ebsary, 1988), in which the operations accomplishing state transitions are formulated as *production rules* whence comes the technical term of *rule-based scheduling*: each rule encodes a condition-action pair. Probably, the relative success of rule-based planning is due to the structural analogy between single rules and mental planning steps which is sensed as a rather obvious correspondence.

In order to make a heuristic exploration of search spaces possible, these very heuristics have to be known. In other words, the bottleneck is shifted one move further to the stage of eliciting empirical scheduling knowledge. It need not be repeated again here that the euphoria of knowledge-based reasoning has been dampened considerably with the growing awareness of the pitfalls of knowledge acquisition. One possible reaction towards this malady is the substitution of purely heuristic decision rules by other ones derived from an analysis of how heuristics actually work. This has resulted in several approaches to extract scheduling decisions and, in particular, to determine heuristically good sequences of such decisions, based on problem information alone (Keng *et al.*, 1988), (Bell and Park, 1990) or in conjunction with explicitly stated *evaluation rules* expressing the value of different schedules or sequencing decisions (Bel *et al.*, 1989).

Considering the pure knowledge-based scheduling proposals presented hitherto, the potential of this approach seems, by no means exhausted. As a further, though rather more complex step to approximate the internal workings of scheduling systems to the *cognitive* reality of the problem, an association of conditional *scheduling rules* with dynamically changing *patterns* in the – symbolic representation of the – planning environment is conceivable. This, of course, presupposes a certain apparatus of formal representation of dynamic temporal structures. Although there are some vague indications (e.g. referring to learning, adaptive systems) in the pertinent literature hitherto no appreciable efforts seem to have been undertaken in this direction of research.

Frequently, scheduling problems can be expressed rather naturally in terms of a combination of formal and heuristic-empirical planning methods. As far as formal planning methods are incorporated into managerial decision processes, implicitly some sort of subjective planning knowledge is assumed regularly either in the application of such planning methods or the analysis of planning results, i.e. schedules. In view of this insight, a synthesis of classical numerical and knowledge-based approaches is self-evident (O'Keefe, 1985). However, the mapping of possible syntheses onto concrete decision support systems can be conceived in different modes:

- In a very loose kind of coupling the knowledge-based part of such a system analyses or classifies the present scheduling problem instance and generates a call to some selected Operations Research method initialized appropriately whereupon computations commence in a classical fashion. The numeric part of the system can be restricted to a single, properly parameterized optimization model (as Linear Programming in system AURORA, (Yu, 1986)), or contain a *method base* (comprising several algorithms as proposed, e.g., by (Kusiak and Chen, 1988). Within such "*tandem*" *systems* the knowledge base is used for selecting an appropriate method only, and both components of the system are executed in sequence once without any further interaction. This strict separation certainly is beneficial in terms of development and maintenance of components. Furthermore, as far as ready-made algorithmic methods are available they can be taken instantly and thus contribute to quick system development. Rather disadvantageous, from a practical point of view, may well be the low degree of problem-orientation that can be achieved with the conception of method bases: presumably there are only few problem instances amenable to the unadapted application of an algorithm from the method store. In the simplest case, such a method base provides a straightforward collection of text-book algorithms; more sensible, but admittedly harder to achieve, would be the compilation of method bases such that the scheduling system actively supports the adaptation of available optimization methods to the peculiarities of actual problem instances (or vice versa).

• Another mode of coupling integrates numerical and heuristic-symbolic scheduling approaches by layering both components. As an example, (Kusiak, 1988) presents a scheduling problem from flexible manufacturing in which first a set of parts is produced; in a second step the parts are mounted into various assemblies. Now, if production and mounting times for the parts and assemblies, resp., are given, the scheduling problem on an outer layer corresponds formally to a 2-machines *flow-shop* (machine 1=part production, machine 2=part assembly); after orders are sequenced on the flow-shop level, part production can be scheduled dynamically on the inner layer of the problem by using, e.g., various heuristic rules for priority queuing of parts.

• There is also a conceivable mode of interlinking components such that the knowl-edge-based component controls the execution of the numerical optimization part. In this mode, the knowledge-based component is responsible for detecting conflicts (such as states leading to infeasible schedules) and selecting heuristically actions which keep the numerical optimization process on a feasible track all the time. In a sense, some of the proposed scheduling systems touch on this topic already (in par-ticular, this holds for the OPAL system, (Bel *et al.*, 1989).

Obviously, the type of synthesis mentioned last offers the largest potential to knowledge-based scheduling: subproblems that can be solved optimally as well as the hierarchical structure of a problem should be discovered by the system and treated accordingly in a fairly automated fashion. In all other cases requiring, for instance, some kind of problem decomposition, knowledge-based scheduling components should be applied instead.

Currently, in the scheduling discipline we are facing an impressive multitude of research lines. In addition to the efforts concerning syntheses of different approaches two particular trends can be spotted: on the one hand, new methodologies are continuously introduced to the field, while on the other hand, the modelling aspects are gaining domi-nance. As to the newer methodologies, especially *connectionism* and *case-based reason-ing* have to be mentioned. Connectionism, or neural networks, have aroused much interest in the last couple of years in that they are seen as superior to the more conventional symbol processing methods of Artificial Intelligence, in particular w.r.t. to the learning aspect. Neural nets essentially carry out an optimization task during *adaptation* (i.e. asso-ciating inputs and outputs of a given relation, e.g., cf. (Wassermann, 1989), (Knight, 1990), (Hecht-Nielsen, 1991)). Assigning a particular structure to a neural network makes it behave like a – possibly very complicated – minimizing function corresponding to some intended objective function on the feasible region (and being penalized close to infinity outside this region). Though not being exactly straightforward, classical discrete optimization problems (Hopfield and Tank, 1985) as well as more specific scheduling problems (Adorf and Johnston, 1990) and (Dagli *et al.*, 1990) can be modelled on neural networks.

Another interesting approach in scheduling takes up *case-based reasoning* (Riesbeck and Schank, 1989). Instead of deriving schedules by logical principles, for each scheduling problem instance a store of previous cases containing problem-solution pairs is searched for elements which are as similar as possible to the present one. Similarity of cases, of course, must be defined carefully. If sufficiently matching previous cases are found the associated schedules are considered as candidates to be applied again, perhaps with some modifications taking care of the peculiarities of the new case. Obviously, the method fails if unprecedented problems occur; but whenever this happens, the case base is augmented with the new case-new solution pair. Hitherto, there have been only few attempts of case-based scheduling systems reported (e.g., (Barletta and Hennessy, 1989), (Hennessy and Hinkle, 1991) and (Miyashita and Sycara, 1992)).

In contrast to concentrating on individual and isolated *production scheduling problem* instances, each being solved outside the real shop floor context, the frame of problem modelling can be extended to cover more and more of the salient features of the production environment. Consequently, entire production scheduling problems tend to become too large to be handled as just one monolithic problem. Therefore, an obvious approach considers the possibilities of *problem decomposition* (Smith and Ow, 1985), i.e. the strategy of divide-and-conquer: the initial scheduling problem is partitioned into manageable sub-problems such that individual sub-problems interact as weakly as possible the total problem solution is synthesized from the sub-problems' partial solutions. The decomposition can be accomplished either unconditionally (i.e., independent of situation) or flexibly. Apparently, a flexible decomposition presupposes some local or global analysis of the search space (to some depth) which, in turn, can proceed knowledge-based as well as heuristically. The result of this analysis phase determines roughly the space in which solutions are going to be derived in a stepwise fashion: by reducing the number of alternatives in each step on the solution path to a rather small set, search complexity is cut down considerably (Sadeh, 1991). In particular, backtracking (or, *back-jumping*) remains confined to local contexts by and large. As a consequence, construed partial solutions tend to be more stable w.r.t. their mutual dependency. A disadvantage of this approach, however, is its tendency towards sub-optimal solutions, especially in the case of decomposition schemes not depending on circumstances (Papas, 1986). Conversely, the synthetic approach offers a maximum of flexibility w.r.t. the adjustment of planning problems to the cognitive problem solving style of real scheduling experts, for which reason it is preferred strongly by developers of scheduling expert systems; in particular, the so-called blackboard system architecture is favoured (Nii, 1986). As an example, take the hierarchical decomposition of heuristic scheduling knowledge into several layers as proposed by (Grant, 1986): first order heuristics, like assignment heuristics, are controlled by schedule improvement heuristics which, in turn, are governed by even higher order decision heuristics. Another advantage of the decomposition strategy results from its economic flexibility: the degree of decomposition as well as the granularity of (partial) solutions can be adapted – even dynamically – to situation-dependent requirements.

Problem decomposition can take place in yet a different way: the overall scheduling task can be partitioned into subtasks considering different parts or aspects of the original problem. This amounts to a distribution of scheduling activity to several rather independent, though interacting local *agents* each of which takes care of its own problem slice, exchanging information with other agents in a formalized message passing procedure (Smith and Hynynen, 1987), (Sycara *et al.*, 1991) and (Burke and Prosser, 1991).

In dynamic scheduling situations the optimality properties of *predictive scheduling* methods lose their significance: even in ideal circumstances admitting anticipatory scheduling, e.g. for a complete planning period ahead, optimal schedules are inflicted with real-time influences in multifarious ways such that they are rendered rather useless at the time of actual execution. As a practical consequence, scheduling becomes a continuous activity consisting of successive modifications in an inherently partial schedule. Evidently, this favours scheduling regimes operating *incrementally*, adding new orders to a maintained schedule one by one. Incremental scheduling complies exceptionally well with the problem decomposition approach – schedule updates can be carried out on several layers of planning granularity and temporal resolution ranging from lower layers dedicated to more predictive aspects concerning rough, capacity oriented assignments without concise timing of operations, to higher layers of progressively shorter planning horizons specifying schedules more and more concretely. Furthermore, this approach lends itself also to *reactive scheduling* (Smith, 1988) and (Elleby *et al.*, 1988), i.e. the repair of schedules which become invalidated because of external effects on either the orders already on schedule (e.g., in case of changing priorities) or the shop floor (unforeseen shortage of resources; in particular, machine breakdowns, operators falling out, etc.).

In the last couple of years, the conviction has ripened that – whatever the particular approach chosen – too much automatism fails to produce satisfactory schedules anyway. The attempt to substitute entirely the human expert scheduler by a software system is not the appropriate goal of research; instead, the design of systems *supporting* schedule generation and maintenance is really demanded. It should be stressed that pure mathematical research (i.e., the scientific branch interested in finding the most general problem abstractions admitting still some very strong formal conclusions) has already been recognized as all too sterile to be of any serious practical value (Ackoff, 1979). This suggests a vigorous shift of focus towards the development of proper means to improve the quality of real-life decisions rather than a delegation of isolated, highly abstracted local problems to expert, or optimization, systems returning solutions out of overall context (Tobin *et al.*, 1980). Since the complexity of real scheduling problems quickly exceeds the human short-term memory capacities, the most powerful contributions of scheduling systems, in fact, are (i) the preparation of relevant information in an easily comprehensible format, and (ii) support in scrutinizing the possible or manifest effects of decisions (i.e., counterfactual reasoning). A very crucial aspect of scheduling productivity is the availability of pertinent information; if data are provided just as they are required to make decisions this is probably of more help than a system deciding completely on its own. Even more important than a multitude of information indexing facilities is support in decision *assessment*: it certainly is of paramount relevance to a scheduler to know in advance what the possible consequences of (major) decisions really are. Carrying out lower decisions autonomously, a scheduling support system conceivably can compute the likely effects of modifications to an existing schedule, thus pinpointing resource conflicts, critical bottlenecks, orders finished late, etc. Likewise, the system can support the consequences of abrupt changes on the shop floor, and suggest appropriate actions to straighten impaired schedules. However, although there are some scheduling systems touching upon several of these topics (particularly among the genre of distributed, multi-agent systems) no encompassing design has been achieved yet.

COMPARISON OF PARADIGMS

As has been pointed out already in the introduction, and despite the fundamental differences between the various methods surveyed in the previous section, there are two broad categories – *Operations Research* and *Artificial Intelligence* – to which each of these methods can be subsumed more or less naturally. This section tries to summarize the distinctive features of both paradigms on a rather high level of abstraction.

Roughly speaking, Operations Research scheduling emphasizes efficient algorithms while Artificial Intelligence scheduling stresses the crucial importance of efficient (problem) representation. Conversely, representation is dealt with straightforwardly in Operations Research scheduling since neither available (i.e. case-specific) knowledge nor actually applied strategies are deemed very relevant. Artificial Intelligence scheduling, however, draws on grown problem solving practice to a high degree, wherefore formal representation means receive proper attention. Due to the emphasis laid on observable expertise in real-world scheduling, Artificial Intelligence scheduling is synonymous with *knowledge-based scheduling*. As a rather direct consequence of these methodological differences, Operations Research solutions comprise (rather conventional) algorithms specific for generic problem classes whereas knowledge-based scheduling relies on rather general inference mechanisms operating on codified scheduling rules.

Occasionally, Operations Research and Artificial Intelligence approaches are considered antagonistic paradigms. Although this is true from an ideal point of judgement, the distinctions and differences in scheduling paradigms need by no means be disadvantageous in practice – quite on the contrary: there is a wide synergetic potential if it were possible to manage to combine the mathematical rigour and elegance of Operations Research scheduling with the expressivity and flexibility of knowledge-based approaches. To be more succinct, the knowledge-based paradigm will have to provide the representation capability to meet the complexity of real scheduling problems, while the Operations Research paradigm will be in charge of the development of fairly general scheduling algorithms with predictable efficiency and power.

As already indicated in Section 2, there are various possibilities of combining scheduling methods across both of the paradigms. In the sequel, the crucial differences in the methodological problem solving approaches in both paradigms are scrutinized in order to define the theoretical frame for the proposed cross-fertilization of paradigms.

Indisputably, the gravest divergence in the tenets of Operations Research and Artificial Intelligence scheduling regards the *effective way of finding solutions*. As Grant (1986), emphasizes appropriately, Operations Research favours the system-theoretic approach, i.e. a given problem is first reduced to its formal, mathematical structure for which, thereafter, an algorithm producing an optimal solution is sought such that the algorithm itself is as efficient (in terms of computational complexity) as possible. As an immediate consequence of this attitude, internal states of the scheduling procedure need not correspond to mental states of a human scheduler. Neither need intermediate planning states represent feasible (partial) schedules nor must they be intelligible at all. The Artificial Intelligence approach, however, starts its analysis with attempting to set up a (formal) model of the cognitive capabilities and the gathered experience of the *human* planner who is, or has been, carrying out the scheduling task for a long time. In particular, this also includes *subjective* factors of the human agent in the scheduling process. Bluntly speaking, Operations Research draws on mathematics, Artificial Intelligence on psychology or, more precisely, on cognitive science (although the formal foundations of Artificial Intelligence methods rely on mathematics, viz. logic). As to the field of scheduling problems, this cardinal difference gives rise to the following distinctions:

- In the scheduling models of Operations Research the structure of the planning problem is modelled by a set of constraints; within the set of feasible solutions the schedule yielding the (global) optimum – or, at least, some close approximation of it – of a defined objective function is called for. In principle, this objective function expresses the overall economic interest of the planner, but reduces practically to a single, unidimensional performance measure based directly on the decision variables of the optimization model (like, e.g., the mean weighted lateness of all scheduled orders). Though it is possible to set up formally more realistic objective functions (involving, for instance, multiple objectives), this faces considerable difficulties in the optimizing procedure: for one thing, computational expenses grow enormously and – even more prohibitive – the optimization problem is, in general, not well-defined unless additional utility or preference information is included. Particularly in problems involving multiple, *non-commensurable* goal criteria the global optimum has to be chosen among a (possibly very large) set of so-called *non-dominated* solution candidates (Hwang and Masud, 1979). A solution is called non-dominated, if a further optimization w.r.t. to one particular criterion is achievable only by accepting a loss w.r.t. to at least another one. Apparently, the difficulty of ordering the set of non-dominated solutions relates to the elicitation of consistent global preferences since – if available at all – this preference information can be stated explicitly on a local scale at best. One possible work-around is the so-called *bounded-objective* method, in which the ranges of all but one of the individual objective functions of the criteria are restricted to some specified interval ahead of time; essentially, this approach turns all goal functions, with one exception, formally into ordinary constraints. Alas, this does not preclude the involuntary specification of empty solution sets (due to incompatible bounds for the conflicting criteria).
- In the scheduling models of Artificial Intelligence a different approach is pursued from the beginning. First, there is no clear-cut distinction between objective function and constraints defining the set of feasible solutions. Second, as has been pointed out already, most of the time only a satisfactory schedule is aimed at in practical settings; occasionally, even a "solution" closest to feasibility is deemed sufficient. Moreover, in contrast to Operations Research modelling the problem as

specified initially is not taken as given in absolute terms; hat is taken as given is the examination of suitable variations of the initial problem, which, in fact, can be solved, considered as an integral part of the scheduling process. Thus, two practically most relevant aspects of scheduling are taken into account – the problem is adjusted to combined problem solving capacities, and problems suffering initially from empty solution sets can be transformed such that there is at least one feasible schedule eventually. In a sense, it could be said that knowledge-based scheduling amounts to modifying (heuristically) the original planning problem again and again until the most difficult variant is found which can just be solved. In this respect, Kanet and Adelsberger (1986) propose the term *reformulative* problem solving approach. Formally, however, also in this case – though somewhat implicitly – the necessity of preference information creeps in: the knowledge-based procedure must be capable of deciding between several competing reformulations. Altogether, the acquisition of preference knowledge is fraught with difficulties similar to those of eliciting the utility functions, or preference orderings, in the multiple objective optimization models.

A further distinction between Operations Research and Artificial Intelligence scheduling regards the position of the scheduling procedure w.r.t. an actual decision process. Operations Research-based systems produce – in the shape of *decision support systems* – solutions for completely formalized problems on which the decision maker can base his final decision; in no way do these systems try to compete with the decision maker in subject matter terms. Quite on the contrary, Artificial Intelligence-based systems *make use* of the formalized decision knowledge of a decision maker in order to make decisions, eventually, *on their own account*. This does not rule out the possibility of interaction in the problem solving process such that the scheduling (expert) system and the real (i.e., responsible, after all) decision maker cooperate. In any case, there is a marked difference in the position of the scheduling system in relation to the human actor: Operations Research-oriented scheduling stresses the optimality of obtained solutions regardless of the way the optimal solution is derived whereas Artificial Intelligence-oriented systems give particular attention to the *rationality* of the problem solving strategy (Kodratoff, 1987), i.e. to enable the outside observer of the system to reconstruct the derivation of a schedule in rational terms. Hence, it is a major concern in the design of knowledge-based systems to make them operate in a transparent way; in particular, so-called *explanation* components are added to the systems' core function to provide the facilities necessary to trace and evaluate a system's own line of reasoning (at least in formal terms). To act comprehensibly, the derivations developed in the system must obey the cognitive structure of human problem solving, particularly w.r.t. reasoning in qualitative terms. This provided, knowledge-based scheduling, in conjunction with the reformulative problem solving approach already mentioned, offers a much greater potential of integration into actual decision making processes compared to Operations Research-based scheduling. Especially in complex, dynamic planning situations, as they are typical in production scheduling, *comprehensible* decision support obviously is of higher value than optimization systems the output of which is hardly relevant at the time it is produced or, eventually, executed. Not that it would be a special merit of knowledge-based techniques; the effort invested in a smooth, intelligible user / system-interaction is a very convenient feature of knowledge-based systems. This includes, inter alia, plain support in system usage as well as careful, clearly arranged presentation of relevant outputs (in this respect, cf., e.g. (Alpar and Srikanth, 1989)). A serious economic disadvantage of knowledge-based scheduling systems, however, emanates from the necessity of their design and / or adaptation according to situation-dependent requirements. In the most extreme case a scheduling expert system represents the knowledge of a single expert useful in a single planning environment only; but even in fairly standard situations with common basic structure and functionality the compilation and maintenance of knowledge bases is a nontrivial, demanding endeavour.

THIS BOOK'S CONTRIBUTION

The Christian Doppler Laboratory for Expert Systems – located at the Technical University of Vienna – investigates, develops, and applies advanced scheduling techniques to industrial production processes. In its endeavour to address real problem instances, vital practical conditions of existing shop floors cannot be neglected arbitrarily. Instead, the adaptation of theoretical research in scheduling technology to production plant reality – as opposed to the popular mathematical practice of scrutinizing intriguing isolated problem facets – is of paramount interest. In view of these preconditions, the "Wiener Scheduling Forum" as a group of both scientists and practitioners of scheduling centred around the Christian Doppler Lab has initiated a workshop on production scheduling at the European Conference on Artificial Intelligence 1992 in order to review the state-of-the-art in scheduling methodology and to evaluate the practical potential of advanced scheduling techniques.

Reflecting the structure of that workshop which most of the following chapters originate from, the chapters of this book can be divided roughly into three sections. As the major objectives of the workshop have been a discussion and evaluation of new approaches to scheduling including, particularly, an assessment of recent proposals regarding (i) the modelling of scheduling constraints, and (ii) the design of comprehensive scheduling systems able to manage *real-life* problem instances, most of the chapters deal with either constraint representation / propagation, or with particular scheduling system architectures. Naturally, both topics intersect to a considerable degree which suggests the inclusion of contributions concerning illustrative applications as a third topic of its own.

Despite their differing aims, most of the subsequent chapters are inclined clearly to the Artificial Intelligence paradigm although none of it strictly refers to a typical *knowledge-based* approach. With few exceptions, most proposals combine more or less generalized (heuristic) scheduling methods with symbolic constraint representation techniques. Moreover, in a majority of approaches different methods are interlinked in original ways and, particularly, pure optimization models have been discarded as impracticable throughout. Considered as a methodology of its own, *constraint satisfaction* has gained much importance in recent years and most scheduling systems make use of it in some way.

Of the fourteen chapters to follow, constraint representation and handling is addressed primarily in the first three of them. Chapters 5 through 9 present several scheduling applications using various approaches, or combinations thereof. Chapters 10 through 14 are devoted to descriptions of more or less self-contained scheduling methodologies, or systems, comprising both a constraint modelling language and a scheduling strategy. Chapter 15 is of a somewhat different character; it casts some light on scheduling system creation and, in a sense, provides a kind of closing parenthesis to the material unfolded in this book.

The chapters of the first section address different approaches to constraint modelling. PROSSER surveys briefly constraint satisfaction problems illustrating the application of this method to production scheduling and, in particular, to the representation of temporal constraints. He restricts his view to classical constraint modelling, i.e. the search for feasible (and not necessarily optimal) solutions. BERRY, however, develops a probabilistic calculus, termed *preference capacity plan*, taking into account both the (relative) merits of alternative schedule decisions and the uncertainty of available decision information. An entirely different approach presents the chapter of BEZIRGAN who suggests the use of a *case-based* system such that scheduling decisions are resolved by retrieving similar previous cases meeting (most) of the imposed constraints. In fact, this chapter gives a short introduction to case-based methods indicating some specific issues emanating especially from scheduling applications. Albeit being a very stimulating contribution, this proposal hitherto lacks thorough theoretical as well as empirical scrutiny.

Due to their practical orientation, the chapters of the second section consider scheduling methods generating at least "good", if not optimal, solutions. Chapters 5, 6 and 7 all make use of stochastic optimization methods. FILIPIC suggests a specially adjusted *genetic* algorithm scheme to minimize energy consumption in a production unit. In order to enhance the efficiency of the method, a problem-specific crossover operator is introduced preventing the generation of illegal solution candidates. In an application of resource allocation in telecommunication, MULLER *ET AL.* propose a *distributed* scheduling architecture using also the technique of genetic algorithms: instead of a single evaluation criterion determining the *fitness* of candidate solutions several agents representing different criteria interact in the selection stage. Another distributed approach is reported by GHÉDIRA and VERFAILLE who assign agents to a problem's tasks and resources each of which tries to optimize its own local *satisfaction* by means of *simulated annealing* (i.e. agents tolerate perturbances decreasing their satisfaction, but less so with advancing time). BESSLER combines a well-known *Tabu search* heuristic with constraint satisfaction to achieve a kind of branch-and-bound approach to a permutation flow-shop problem with due dates. A rather pure constraint satisfaction model is used by SMITH to obtain an initial feasible solution to a rota compilation problem which is improved locally by stepwise exchange of assignments.

The chapters of the last section give descriptions of scheduling software systems providing frameworks to express and compute whole classes of scheduling problems. Typically, these systems have to be set up individually for each particular application before proper operation can commence. In the first chapter of this section, BENSANA reviews the OPAL system integrating generalized constraint satisfaction solving with fuzzy reasoning and modelling of quantified preference information. CANZI and GUIDA portray CRONOS-III as a general-purpose scheduling system based on a *blackboard* architecture which derives schedules incrementally by selecting iteratively a new sub-problem and choosing an appropriate allocation method to solve that sub-problem. Moreover, CRONOS-III has been designed to handle soft temporal constraints very flexibly. A reactive scheduling system named INTESIMPRO is presented in the chapter of LÁZARO *ET AL.*; schedules are also created incrementally by considering orders with decreasing criticality (i.e. bottleneck resource contention) and local relaxation of constraints in cases of manifest conflicts. GRONALT deals with loading and job sequencing in flexible manufacturing systems and proposes a heuristic two-stage approach to job shop scheduling in which job routes are selected among several alternatives first such that balanced machine loadings are achieved; thereupon, within individual machine queues jobs are sequenced by means of Tabu search. In Chapter 14, SAUER describes his proposal of using meta-scheduling knowledge, expressed in rule format, to select appropriate elements from a store of predefined skeletal scheduling strategies. Aimed towards *reactive* scheduling applications, this system is arranged to cooperate with a human expert by making accessible predefined scheduling algorithms, scheduling heuristics, selection heuristics for scheduling methods, and schedule evaluation facilities.

In the final chapter, DORN sketches a framework for a task-oriented design methodology applicable to scheduling systems; his proposal is gives particular emphasis to the *reuse* of scheduling knowledge compiled in the development of previous scheduling systems.

Despite the multitude of theoretical research inspired by practical motivations, the faint feedback from scientific endeavours to the realm of production shop floors cannot be overlooked. In most practical scheduling instances human experience and intuition are still applied almost exclusively. Thus, potentially, real advantages of available scheduling methodology are not exploited appropriately. In a sense, this reflects a rather general phenomenon of scientific progress: in a first, enthusiastic phase ambitious mathematical theories are developed which turn out – in a subsequent second phase – as annoyingly useless except in rather extraordinary circumstances. Taking account of this deficiency, in a third phase models and theories are revised pragmatically. As to Artificial Intelligence, scheduling theory seems to be in such a phase 3, hunting for smart models and heuristic solution approaches in order to achieve useful results with reasonable investments.

Conversely, it can be assumed that many practically proven approaches to scheduling never go public, e.g. for reasons of confidentiality to secure economic competitiveness. Obviously, there is a dispersed subculture of rather isolated solutions to scheduling problems which can hardly be assessed properly. It remains to be hoped only that theory does not lie below the level of sophistication achieved actually in applied scheduling. It is left to the readers' judgement if this book really achieves its goal of proceeding a substantial step further in approaching a unified and generalized methodology for the construction of scheduling systems.

REFERENCES

Ackoff, R.L. (1979) Resurrecting the Future of Operational Research, *Journal of the Operations Research Society* **30**, pp. 189–199.

Adorf, H.-M. and Johnston, M.D. (1990) A Discrete Stochastic Neural Network Algorithm for Constraint Satisfaction Problems, *Proceedings of the International Conference on Neural Networks* (IJCNN-90) San Diego, Ca., pp. 917–924.

Alpar, P. and Srikanth, K.N. (1989) Closed-shop Scheduling with Expert System Techniques, in *Knowledge-Based Systems in Manufacturing*, Kusiak, A. (ed.), London: Taylor & Francis, pp. 247–264.

Atabakhsh, H. (1991) A Survey of Constraint Based Scheduling Systems Using an Artificial Intelligence Approach, *Artificial Intelligence in Engineering* 6 (2), pp. 58–73.

Aveni, A. (1989) *Empires of Time – Calendars, Clocks and Cultures*, New York: Basic Books.

Baker, K.R. (1974) *Introduction to Sequencing and Scheduling*, New York: Wiley.

Balas, E. (1969) Machine Sequencing via Disjunctive Graphs: An Implicit Enumeration Algorithm, *Operations Research* 17 (6), pp. 941–957.

Barker, J.R. and McMahon, G.B. (1985) Scheduling the General Job Shop, *Management Science* 31 (5), pp. 594–598.

Barletta, R. and Hennessy, D. (1989) Case Adaptation in Autoclave Layout Design, *Proceedings of the Case-Based Reasoning Workshop*, San Mateo: Morgan Kaufmann, pp. 203–207.

Bel, G., Bensana, E., Dubois, D., Erschler, J. and Esquirol, P. (1989) A Knowledge-based Approach to Industrial Job-shop Scheduling, in *Knowledge-Based Systems in Manufacturing*, A. Kusiak (ed.), London: Taylor & Francis, pp. 207–246.

Bell, C.E. and Park, K. (1990) Solving Resource-constrained Scheduling Problems by A* Search, *Naval Research Logistics Quarterly* 37, pp. 61–84.

Bellman, R., Esogbue, A.O. and Nabeshima, I. (1982) *Mathematical Aspects of Scheduling and Applications*, Oxford: Pergamon Press.

Blazewicz, J., Cellary, W., Slowinski, R. and Weglarz, J. (1986) Scheduling under Resource Constraints - Deterministic Models, *Annals of Operations Research* 7 (1–4).

Bishop, G.T. (1957) On a Problem of Production Scheduling, *Operations Research* 5, pp. 97–103.

Bowman, E.H. (1959) The Schedule-Sequence Problem, *Operations Research* 7 (5), pp. 621–624.

Burke, P. and Prosser, P. (1991) A Distributed Asynchronous System for Predictive and Reactive Scheduling, *Artificial Intelligence in Engineering* 6 (3), pp. 106–124.

Christofides, N. (1975) *Graph Theory – An Algorithmic Approach*, New York-London: Academic Press.

Cleveland, G.A. and Smith, S.F. (1989) Using Genetic Algorithms to Schedule Flow Shop Releases, *Proceedings of the 3rd International Conference on Genetic Algorithms*, pp. 160–169.

Cook, S.A. (1971) The Complexity of Theorem Proving Procedures, *Proceedings of the 3rd ACM Symposium on Theory of Computing*, pp. 151–158.

Dagli, C.H., Lammers, S. and Vellanki, M. (1990) *Intelligent Scheduling in Manufacturing Through Neural Network and Expert Systems*, Working Paper 90-18-43, Department of Engineering Management, University of Missouri-Rolla (August 1990).

Dantzig, G.B. (1963) *Linear Programming and Extensions*, Princeton: Princeton University Press.

Davis, L. (1985) Job Shop Scheduling with Genetic Algorithms, *Proceedings of the International Conference on Genetic Algorithms and Their Applications*, Norwood: Lawrence Erlbaum, pp. 136–140.

de Werra, D. and Hertz, A. (1989) Tabu Search Techniques, *Operations Research Spektrum* **11**, pp. 131–141.

Edmonds, J. (1965) Paths, Trees, and Flowers, *Canadian Journal on Mathematics* **17**, pp. 449–467.

Elleby, P., Fargher, H.E. and Addis, T.R. (1988) Reactive Constraint-Based Job-Shop Scheduling, in *Expert Systems and Intelligent Manufacturing*, M.D. Oliff (ed.), Amsterdam: Elsevier Science, pp. 1–10.

Fox, M.S. (1987) *Constraint-Directed Search: A Case Study of Job-Shop Scheduling*, London: Pitman.

Fox, M.S. and Sadeh, N. (1990) Why is Scheduling Difficult? A CSP Perspective, *Proceedings of the 9th European Conference on Artificial Intelligence*, (ECAI-90), pp. 754–767.

Garey, M.R. and Johnson, D.S. (1979) *Computers and Intractability: A Guide to the Theory of NP-Completeness*, San Francisco: Freeman.

Glover, F. and Greenberg, H.J. (1989) New Approaches for Heuristic Search: A Bilateral Linkage with Artificial Intelligence, *European Journal on Operations Research* **39**, pp. 119–130.

Gomory, R.E. (1958) Outline of an Algorithm for Integer Solutions to Linear-Programs, *Bulletin of the American Mathematical Society* **64**, pp. 275–278.

Grant, T.J. (1986) Lessons for O.R. from A.I.: A Scheduling Case Study, *Journal of the Operations Research Society* **37** (1), pp. 41–57.

Hammersley, J.M and Handscombe, D.C. (1964) *Monte Carlo Methods*, London: Methuen.

Hart, P.E., Nilsson, N.J. and Raphael, B. (1968) A Formal Basis for the Heuristic Determination of Minimum Cost Paths, *IEEE Transactions on Systems, Science and Cybernetics* **SSC-4** (2), pp. 100–107

Hart, P.E., Nilsson, N.J. and Raphael, B. (1972) Correction to: A Formal Basis for the Heuristic Determination of Minimum Cost Paths, *SIGART Newsletter* **37** (12), pp. 28–29.

Hecht-Nielsen, R. (1991) *Neurocomputing*, Reading: Addison-Wesley.

Hennessy, D. and Hinkle, D. (1991) Initial Results from Clavier: A Case-based Autoclave Loading Assistant, *Proceedings of the Case-based Reasoning Workshop*, Morgan Kaufmann, San Mateo, Ca., pp. 225–232.

Hopfield, J.J. and Tank, D.W. (1985) 'Neural' Computation of Decisions in Optimization Problems, *Biological Cybernetics* **52** (3), pp. 141–152.

Hwang, C.-L. and Masud, A.S.M. (1979) *Multiple Objective Decision Making – Methods and Applications*, Berlin: Springer (LNEMS 164).

Kanet, J.J. and Adelsberger, H.H. (1986), Expert Systems in Production Scheduling, *European Journal on Operations Research* **29**, pp. 51–59.

Kantorovich, L.V. (1939) Mathematical Models in the Organization and Planning of Production, (English translation in) *Management Science* **3** (1), pp. 366–422.

Karp, R.M. (1972) Reducibility among Combinatorial Problems, in *Complexity of Computer Computation*, R.E. Miller and J.W. Thatcher (eds), New York: Plenum Press, pp. 85–104.

Keng, N.P., Yun, D.Y.Y. and Rossi, M. (1988) Interaction-sensitive Planning System for Job-shop Scheduling, in *Expert Systems and Intelligent Manufacturing*, D. Oliff (ed.), Amsterdam: Elsevier Science, pp. 57–69.

Kerr, R.M. and Ebsary, R.V. (1988) Implementation of an Expert System for Production Scheduling, *European Journal on Operations Research* **33**, pp. 17–29.

Knight, K. (1990) Connectionist Ideas and Algorithms, *Communications of the ACM* **33**(11), pp. 59–74.

Kodratoff, Y. (1987) Is A.I. a Sub-Field of Computer Science – or is A.I. the Science of Explanations? in *Progress in Machine Learning. Proceedings of EWSL'87*, Bratko, I., Lavrac, N. (eds), Bled, Yugoslavia, pp. 91–106.

Kusiak, A. (1988) Scheduling Flexible Machining and Assembly Systems, *Annals of Operations Research* **15**, pp. 337–352.

Kusiak, A. and Chen, M. (1988) Expert Systems for Planning and Scheduling Manufacturing Systems, *European Journal on Operations Research* **34**, pp. 113–130.

Land, A.H. and Doig A.G. (1960) An Automatic Method of Solving Discrete Programming Problems, *Econometrica* **28** (3), pp. 497–520.

Le Pape, C. (1991) *Constraint Propagation in Planning and Scheduling*, Technical Report, Deptartment of Computer Science, Stanford University, Palo Alto.

Little, J.D.C. *et al.* (1963) An Algorithm for the Traveling Salesman Problem, *Operations Research* **11** (12), pp. 972–989.

Manne, A.S. (1960) On the Job-shop Scheduling Problem, *Operations Research* **8** (2), pp. 219–223.

Meseguer, P. (1989) Constraint Satisfaction Problems: An Overview, *AICOM* **2** (1), pp. 3–17.

Miyashita, K. and Sycara K. (1992) Case-Based Interactive Scheduler, *Working Notes AAAI Spring Symposium Series, Symposium Practical Approaches to Scheduling and Planning*, pp. 47–51.

Mumford, L. (1934) *Technics and Civilization*, New York: Harcourt Brace.

Nadel, B.A. (1989) Constraint Satisfaction Algorithms, *Computational Intelligence* **5**, pp. 188–224.

Nemhauser, G.L. and Wolsey, L.A. (1988) *Integer and Combinatorial Optimization*, New York: Wiley.

Nii, P.N. (1986) Blackbord systems: The Blackboard Model of Problem Solving and the Evolution of Blackboard Architectures, *AI Magazine* **7** (2), pp. 38–53.

O'Keefe, R.M. (1985) Expert Systems and Operational Research – Mutual Benefits, *Journal of the Operations Research Society* **36** (2), pp. 125–129.

Papadimitriou, C.H. and Steiglitz K. (1982) *Combinatorial Optimization*, Englewood Cliffs: Prentice Hall.

Papas, P. (1986) ISIS – A Project in Review, *Proceedings of the Symposium on Real-Time Optimization in Automated Manufacturing Facilities*, (NBS, Washington DC), pp. 127–135.

Pearl, J. (1984) *Heuristics – Intelligent Search Strategies for Computer Problem Solving*, Reading: Addison-Wesley.

Riesbeck, C.K. and Schank, R.C. (1989) *Inside Case-Based Reasoning*, Norwood: Lawrence Erlbaum.

Robbins, Jr. J.H. (1985) PEPS: The Prototype Expert Priority Scheduler, *Proceedings of the AUTOFACT-5*, pp. 13.12–13.34

Sadeh, N. (1991) *Look-Ahead Techniques for Micro-Opportunistic Job Shop Scheduling*, Ph.D. Thesis, School of Computer Science, Carnegie Mellon University, CMU-CS-91-102.

Shaw, M.J. (1989) A Pattern-Directed Approach to FMS Scheduling, *Annals of Operations Research* **15**, pp. 353–76.

Smith, S.F. (1988) A Constraint-based Framework for Reactive Management of Factory Schedules, in *Intelligent Manufacturing*, M.D. Oliff (ed.), Menlo Park: Benjamin / Cummings, pp. 113–130.

Smith, S.F. and Hynynen, J.E. (1987) Integrated Decentralization of Production Management: An Approach for Factory Scheduling, Preprint, 15 pp.; *Proceedings of the Symposium on Integrated and Intelligent Manufacturing* (Boston, Ma.).

Smith, S.F. and Ow, P.S. (1985) The Use of Multiple Problem Decompositions in Time Constrained Planning Tasks, *Proceedings of the 9th International Conference on Artificial Intelligence* (IJCAI-85), Los Angeles, Ca., pp. 1013–1015.

Sycara, K.P. *et al.* (1991) Resource Allocation in Distributed Factory Scheduling, *IEEE Expert*, February, pp. 29–40.

Taillard, E. (1990) Some Efficient Heuristic Methods for the Flow Shop Sequencing Problem, *European Journal on Operations Research* **47**, pp. 65–74.

Tobin N.R., Rapley K. and Teather W. (1980) The Changing Role of O.R. *Journal of the Operations Research Society* **31**, pp. 279–288

Tsang, E.P.K. and Warwick, T. (1990) Applying Genetic Algorithms to Constraint Satisfaction Optimization Problems, *Proceedings of the 9th European Conference on Artificial Intelligence* (ECAI-90), Stockholm, pp. 649–654.

van Laarhoven, P.L.M., Aarts, E.H.L. and Lenstra, L.K. (1988) *Job Shop Scheduling by Simulated Annealing*, Report OS-R8809, Centre for Mathematics and Computer Science Amsterdam.

Wagner, H.M. (1959) An Integer Linear-Programming Model for Machine Scheduling, *Naval Research Logistics Quarterly* **6**, pp. 131–140.

Wasserman, P.D. (1989) *Neural Computing – Theory and Practice*, New York: Van Nostrand Reinhold.

West, M.L. (1978) *Hesiod: Works and Days*, Oxford: Clarendon Press.

Whitley, D., Starkweather, T. and Fuquay, D. (1989) Scheduling Problems and Traveling Salesman: The Genetic Edge Recombination Operator, *Proceedings of the 3rd International Conference on Genetic Algorithms*, pp. 133–140.

Widmer, M. and Hertz, A. (1989) A new Heuristic Method for the Flow Shop Sequencing Problem, *European Journal on Operations Research* **41**.

Yu, D.H. (1986) *A System for Utilizing Operations Research Techniques in a Knowledge Based Planning System*, TR Mitre Corp., Bedford Ma.

2

Scheduling as a Constraint Satisfaction Problem: Theory and Practice

Patrick Prosser
Department of Computer Science, University of Strathclyde

INTRODUCTION

It has been argued that *Artificial Intelligence* (AI) is an appropriate technology for the scheduling problem (Grant, 1986), (Phelps, 1986), (Fox and Sadeh, 1990) insofar as the scheduling problem is a knowledge-intensive activity which involves search, and AI gives us mechanisms for capturing and representing knowledge, and techniques for efficiently guiding search. In particular, we are encouraged to take a constraint-based approach to scheduling (Atabakhsh, 1991), (Burke, 1989), (Elleby *et al.*, 1989), (Fox, 1983), (Fox and Sadeh, 1990), (Le Pape, 1988), (Prosser, 1989), (Sadeh, 1991), (Smith *et al.*, 1986). By taking this approach we allow ourselves the opportunity to exploit the rich knowledge representational powers of constraints, and the large body of work reported on techniques for solving the *constraint satisfaction problem* (CSP) (and for a good overview of the CSP literature see (Meseguer, 1989) and (Kumar, 1992) and for detailed studies of tree search algorithms for the CSP see (Nadel, 1989) and (Prosser, 1991).

One measure of the strength of this conjecture (scheduling as AI / CSP) might be the number of successful Ph D's in this area over the past few years: (Berry, 1991), (Burke, 1989), (Fox, 1983), (Hynynen, 1988), (Le Pape, 1988), (Prosser, 1990), (Sadeh, 1991). However, it is my opinion, that few (if any) of us have conveyed the real difficulty associated with mapping CSP technology onto real-world scheduling problems. For example, the algorithms that have been reported for the CSP tend to look at "toy" problems such as the n-queens (Haralick and Elliott, 1980), the confused n-queens (Nadel, 1989), or the zebra problem (Prosser, 1991). These problems (n-queens, zebra) deal with variables with discrete domains, and binary constraints (involving only two variables), and the algorithms that are described make the assumption that the problems have these very same characteristics. Unfortunately, the real world can rarely be described within such a neat /

clean framework. Therefore, if we are (reasonably) familiar with the *scheduling problem*, and we are (reasonably) familiar with the CSP technology, how do we go about applying one to the other?

A SIMPLE SCHEDULING PROBLEM

Let us assume that we have the following job set as part of a larger scheduling problem. We have two jobs, job_1 and job_2, where job_1 is composed of the operations $\{op_{1,1}, op_{1,2}\}$, and job_2 is composed of the operations $\{op_{2,1}, op_{2,2}\}$. Associated with job job_i will be an earliest start time es_i, and a due date dd_i. An operation $op_{i,j}$ will have a demand for a resource, and we may have a set of possible resources that will satisfy that requirement, namely $R_{i,j}$. In addition, the processing time of an operation may be dependent upon the resource used to perform that operation. That is, if we select resource $r_{i,j}$ for operation $op_{i,j}$, where $r_{i,j} \in R_{i,j}$, we can expect a processing time of $pr_{i,j}$.

We should expect relations to exist between operations, and possibly between resources. For example, we might assume that we must perform operation $op_{1,1}$ before operation $op_{1,2}$, and that we have to start operations $op_{2,1}$ and $op_{2,2}$ at the same instant. Relations may exist between resources, and between operations on resources. For example, it may be the case that resource $r_{a,b}$ and $r_{c,d}$ cannot both be used at the same time (relations between resources) and that if $op_{i,j}$ uses resource $r_{a,b}$ then $op_{i,j+1}$ must also use resource $r_{a,b}$ (relations between operations on resources). Finally, in this example, we might assume that some resources may be shared. That is, a resource $r_{e,f}$ may be able to process a given amount of work concurrently (such as a batch process) but there is a physical limit to that capacity.

The above problem is simple. It is easy to imagine scheduling problems that are much more complex from a representational perspective. For example, we have ignored inventory, set-ups between jobs, transportation of jobs between resources, the availability of labour, and a myriad of other things.

THE (BINARY) CONSTRAINT SATISFACTION PROBLEM

In the *binary constraint satisfaction* problem, we have a set of variables, where each *variable* v_i has a discrete and *finite domain of values* d_i. We also have a set of constraints, where the *constraint* $C_{i,j}$ is a relation between variables v_i and v_j. The problem is then to find an instantiation for each of the variables, from their respective domains, such that the constraints are satisfied. Generally, we can view the CSP as a graph G where $V(G)$ is the set of variables and $A(G)$ is the set of constraints. If $n = |V(G)|$ and $m = |d_i|$ then the worst case complexity of the CSP is $O(m^n)$.

In the literature this is the most popular class of CSP reported, namely the "binary" CSP, and the techniques reported address this problem almost exclusively. There is some case for arguing that it is sufficient to study the binary CSP. For some time it was "CSP folklore" that an n-ary CSP could be mapped into a binary CSP. This is no longer folklore, as it has been formally proved by (Rossi *et al.*, 1990). Therefore, I shall make no exception here. Let us assume that we wish to search for the first solution to a CSP. Empirical evidence would suggest that we should use the *forward checking* (FC) algorithm of (Haralick and Elliott, 1980) (Note that this should not be taken as an unconditional endorsement of forward checking. As we will see in the next section, we may be unable to use forward checking). In forward checking we do as follows:

1. Select variable $v[i]$ as the "current" variable, and reset $d[i]$.
2. Instantiate $v[i]$ with a value $x \in d_i$.
3. Check forwards. That is, remove from the domains of the "future" variables (the variables that have not yet been instantiated with a value) values which are inconsistent with respect to the instantiation $v[i] \leftarrow x$.
4. If all future variables have values left in their domains then if (a) $i < n$ then increment i and go to step (1) or if (b) $i = n$ then quit with the solution.
5. If there exists a future variable with no values remaining in its domain then undo the effects of forward checking from $v[i]$ and if (a) there are values still to be tried in $d[i]$ go to step (2), or if (b) we have tried all the values in the domain $d[i]$, then if (i) $i > 1$ decrement i and return to step (2), or if (ii) $i = 1$ quit with no solution.

This algorithm generally out-performs other algorithms because of its pruning of the search tree. That is, the algorithm implicitly adopts the "fail first" principle. However, the algorithm is at heart a chronological backtracker (step 5.b.i) and is prone to thrashing (Mackworth, 1977). This malady can be overcome, to some degree, by combining FC with a more informed style of backtracking, such as backjumping (Gaschnig, 1978) or conflict-directed backjumping. These "hybrids" are described in (Prosser, 1991).

Step (3) is of particular interest. In order to check forwards from $v[i]$ to $v[j]$ (where $i < j$) we must apply the constraint $C_{i,j}$ between the current instantiation of $v[i]$ and all possible instantiations of $v[j]$ in $d[j]$. Therefore, if $m = |d[j]|$ we will apply the constraint $C_{i,j}$ m times for each instantiation of $v[i]$. For all "tentative" instantiations $v[j] \leftarrow y$, where $y \in d[j]$, that fail to satisfy $C_{i,j}$, we remove y from $d[j]$. Therefore, on reaching step (4) we know that all remaining values in the domains of the future variables are consistent with respect to the past variables (the instantiations already made). When we backtrack, from $v[i]$ to $v[i-1]$, or re-instantiate the current variable, we must return values to the domains of the future variables.

REPRESENTING THE SCHEDULING PROBLEM AS CSP

Returning to our *simple scheduling problem* (SSP), how do we represent this as a CSP, and how do we apply the forward checking algorithm to that problem?

First, let us consider how we might map the SSP into a CSP. Clearly, we can represent operations as variables. We can then cast the problem as follows: "assign to each variable a pair, where that pair is a time and a resource, such that all constraints are satisfied". Therefore, I might say that $v_{1,1}$ represents operation $op_{1,1}$ and $v_{1,2}$ represents $op_{1,2}$, and so on. I now need to associate with each operation / variable a domain. We might anticipate that the domain will be the Cartesian product of the set of possible resources for an operation with the set of possible times for that operation. More generally, we might expect an operation to have a number of domains, such as a temporal domain, a resource domain, an inventory domain, etc., and the corresponding variable to have a domain which is a set of n-tuples. Therefore, my first hurdle is to compute the temporal domain $T_{i,j}$ for operation $op_{i,j}$.

As I have said previously, the processing time for an operation may vary depending on the resources that we choose to employ. For the moment I will assume that there is no variation in processing time. The *temporal domain* $T_{i,j}$ may be represented as a sequence of *temporal intervals* (Allen, 1984), of the form $\langle\langle S_{i,1}, E_{i,1}\rangle, \langle S_{i,2}, E_{i,2}\rangle, ..., \langle S_{i,n_i}, E_{i,n_i}\rangle\rangle$, where $S_{i,j} \leq E_{i,j}$ and $E_{i,j} < S_{i,j+1}$. If we represent the precedence constraints between operations as *temporal relations* (Allen, 1984), and employ an arc consistency algorithm such as AC-3 (Mackworth, 1977) or AC-4 (Mohr and Henderson, 1986) we can compute the temporal domains of operations within a job. In job_i we initialise the temporal domain of each operation to be the sequence $\langle\langle es_i, dd_i\rangle\rangle$ Taking cognisance of the duration of each operation, and the temporal relations between operations, we can propagate this information such that we achieve 2-consistency. Furthermore, we might attempt to maintain this level of consistency during the search process. That is, whenever a (tentative) decision is made to start an operation at a given point in time we might propagate this decision through the operations in the job (through the *process plan*), and whenever we retract a decision we undo the effects of propagation.

However, allow me to retract the above assumption, and again assume that the processing time of an operation does indeed depend on the resource employed. Let us assume that $R_{1,1} = \{\alpha, \beta\}$ and $R_{1,2} = \{\gamma, \delta\}$. We are then presented with four possible scenarios for job_i:

1. $op_{1,1}$ on resource α and $op_{1,2}$ on resource γ
2. $op_{1,1}$ on resource α and $op_{1,2}$ on resource δ
3. $op_{1,1}$ on resource β and $op_{1,2}$ on resource γ
4. $op_{1,1}$ on resource β and $op_{1,2}$ on resource δ

We should propagate over each of the above scenarios. This will result in each operation having four possible temporal domains. More generally, if we have n operations in a job, and each operation may be assigned to m possible resources we will have m^n temporal domains for each operation. In anything but a trivial example we should appreciate that this is not a realistic option, as neither space nor time will permit this.

Therefore, we have a number of compromises open to us. The first is to assume that the processing time for an operation is its worst case value. That is, when we compute the temporal domain of an operation we assume that it will be allocated to the slowest resource, and when the search process actually makes a (tentative) allocation, we propagate the actual processing time. Therefore, initially we take an over-constrained / pessimistic view of the problem, and accept that a decision made by the search process may bring about the relaxation of a temporal domain. This "pessimistic" approach was used in the Distributed Asynchronous Scheduler (Burke and Prosser, 1991). A second approach is symmetric to the above, namely an "optimistic" approach that assumes that operations will be allocated to the fastest resource. Therefore, a decision made by the search process may bring about restriction of domains. In retrospect, it might appear that I have fallen at the first hurdle! Representing, and maintaining, the temporal domain is definitely non-trivial, and is in fact an open area of research in its own right (Le Pape and Smith, 1987), (Burke, 1989), (Le Pape, 1991), (Prosser *et al.*, 1993).

There is of course a third approach, and one that is sometimes adopted by researchers. That is, to simplify the problem by assuming that the processing of an operation takes constant time. In other words, we wave our hands and the problem goes away. I will do just that by returning to the simplifying assumption, namely that the processing times of operations are known "a priori", and these times are independent of the resources employed. That is, we can compute the temporal domains of operations as temporal intervals. Let me assume that operation $op_{1,1}$ has a processing time of 5 minutes, and the temporal domain $T_{1,1}$ is $\langle\langle$Monday-0900, Friday-1655$\rangle\rangle$. At what level of granularity do we make our decisions? Do we want to say (a) "Start $op_{1,1}$ at 10.45 on Tuesday" or would we prefer to say (b) "Start $op_{1,1}$ some time on Tuesday morning"? We might choose (a) if we were dealing with a tightly coupled environment which involved a high degree of automation. However (b) is a "least commitment" approach (Fox and Kempf, 1985) and might be more appropriate to a more human / manual domain.

Let me assume that I take option (a) and decide to view time at a granularity of 5 minute "ticks". $T_{1,1}$ contains 1247 possible "ticks", and if I make the domain discrete, rather than semi-continuous (interval based), I must be prepared to have a domain of size (in this case) 1247 times the number of possible resources for this operation. Therefore, in this example, I would have a discrete domain for $op_{1,1}$ of 2494 $\langle tick, resource \rangle$ pairs. Clearly, this approach is expensive. For example, imagine we have an operation that can be performed any time in the future on any possible machine. We could not represent this domain as a sequence of discrete values (but we would probably not need to represent this operation anyway, since it is totally unconstrained).

We also need to represent *resources*. We might represent a *non-sharable* resource as a "time-line". Initially we assume the resource is unoccupied, and that the available time on the resource runs from now to some time in the far future. Therefore, we may represent the available capacity on a resource (again) as a sequence of intervals. Constraints between resources, and between operations on resources, can be implemented using propagation techniques. For example, if we know that resource $r_{a,b}$ and $r_{c,d}$ cannot be in use at the same time, whenever we allocate an operation $op_{i,j}$ to resource $r_{a,b}$ we update the available capacity on $r_{a,b}$ and allocate an "idle" operation to $r_{c,d}$, where that "idle" operation has the same processing time as $op_{i,j}$. Constraints between operations on resources may be implemented as follows. Assume that $op_{i,j}$ and $op_{i,k}$ must be processed on the same resource. If we allocate $op_{i,j}$ to some resource $r_{a,b}$ we update the resource domain of $op_{i,k}$ to be $\{r_{a,b}\}$.

If we assume that certain resources are sharable, but are of limited capacity, we must extend our representations of resources. We may view such a sharable resource as being composed of a time line (a sequence of intervals) where each interval is combined with an n-tuple of capacity (such as x, y, and z dimension, weight, product type, etc.).

When we allocate an operation to a resource we may consider this as the dynamic creation of constraints between process plans. For example, assume we allocate $op_{i,j}$ to $r_{a,b}$. This will consume capacity on $r_{a,b}$, updating the time line. We might then consider the allocation of $op_{k,l}$ to that same resource. The temporal domain of that operation is then the intersection between the time line on $r_{a,b}$ and $T_{k,l}$. This is the same as saying that $op_{i,j}$ cannot be in process at the same time as op_{kl}. Therefore, there was initially no explicit relation between job_i and job_k, but this relation exists implicitly within the resource domain of operations, and is made active during a search process. This is in many ways similar to the "activity constraints" of (Mittal and Falkenhainer, 1990).

It should by now be obvious that it is difficult to map our SSP into a set of variables, with finite domains, and a set of binary constraints. We do not know "a priori" just what those domains are. We can only compute domains as we make commitments. Therefore, we need something more than a "passive" representation of our problem. We need to capture the behaviour of the system by using an "active" representation of our problem. That is, we need to maintain a representation via the use of propagation methods.

FORWARD CHECKING AND THE SCHEDULING PROBLEM

Let us make the following simplifying assumptions:

A   The problem is to allocate an operation to a point of time on a resource such that all constraints are satisfied.
B   The processing time of an operation is dependent upon the resources employed.
C   We have at our disposal a constraint maintenance system, which maintains an "active" representation of the problem.

In order to use forward checking, in its "pure" form, we need to know the domains of the variables in advance. Assumption B prevents us from using "pure" FC. However, due to C above, any decision made by the search process will initiate constraint propagation, and update the representation of the scheduling problem. In effect C gives us a limited degree of forward checking. For example, we might have a constraint maintenance system that only operates over temporal domains, but does not operate over resource / inventory / labour / etc. domains. Therefore, when the search process makes a tentative assignment of values to a variable / operation there may be a requirement to check backwards against the past variables to determine if that allocation to resource / inventory / labour / etc. is consistent. Therefore, we may be checking forwards over one domain, and checking backwards over the other domains. From a theoretical perspective this is unusual, because (as far as I am aware) there has been no report of a tree search algorithm for the CSP that simultaneously checks forwards and backwards. However, from a practical point of view I think that this appears to be quite natural, and I am sure that many of us already do this without thinking.

In practice, we may treat the domain of a variable / operation as a "stream". That is, rather than enumerate the entire domain of n-tuples, we may take a lazy approach. If we did enumerate the entire domain we need to compute the Cartesian product of a set of sets (the temporal / resource / inventory / labour / etc. domains). We can compute the Cartesian product using a breadth first approach, or a depth first approach, where the leaf nodes are n-tuples to be assigned to the variable. If we take a depth first search (DFS) approach, we need only represent, at any time, the currently active part of that DFS tree. For example, let us assume that for operation $op_{i,j}$ we have a resource domain of size R, a temporal domain of size T, and an inventory domain of size I. We might write a function called *get-next-value* that takes an operation, and an ongoing DFS tree, and delivers the next leaf node and the updated DFS tree. In this example the tree will be of depth 3 (a resource level, a resource / time level, and a resource / time / inventory level). Since we only represent the current path to the current leaf node we need only have space of the order $O(R+T+I)$. Furthermore, we only need this information when we are interested in a value for $op_{i,j}$, that is when $op_{i,j}$ is a past or current variable. This approach is similar to that described in (Zweben and Eskey, 1989).

There are a number of nice features that emerge from this approach (other than space / time efficiency). First, we have data hiding. To get the next value for a variable we use the function *get-next-value*. It may be the case that we decide to extend our system such that we take into account, let us say, an arbitrary feature called "flavour". That is, each operation has to be of a distinct flavour. We now have an additional dimension to the domains of operations. We need only enhance the *get-next-value* function to accommodate this. In fact, we might have some operations being assigned an *n-tuple* where others are assigned an *m-tuple*, where $m \neq n$. If we let operations be objects, and we have different classes of operations, we can have different *get-next-value* methods for different operations. This leads to another advantage. It may be the case that we do not want to traverse the DFS tree in the same order for all operations. A different traversal may correspond to a different ordering of the values, and may be considered as a variable ordering heuristic. This may be tailored to specific operations (each has its own heuristic). Therefore, we might take a *resource perspective* on some operations, a *temporal perspective* on others, and a *flavour perspective* on yet another, and so on.

CONCLUSION

The scheduling problem can be represented using constraints. Central to that representation should be a collection of propagation techniques to maintain an active representation of that problem. It might be argued that this "active" representation (the capture of behaviour) is more than enough for most scheduling problems, and that we might adopt a "junk box" approach as advocated by (Elleby *et al.*, 1989). That is, we do not attempt to build a system that will make scheduling decisions. Rather, we let humans make the decisions, but employ constraint maintenance techniques such that the human is made aware of the consequences of those decisions. Therefore, we should not consider constraints as "passive" objects that describe relationships between objects. Constraints, in combination with propagation techniques, capture the behaviour of the system.

In practice, scheduling systems are messy. Although we may take a constraint-based approach to the design of our scheduling system, we must compromise the algorithms that underly our system. We might be unable to employ an algorithm such as forward checking, due to practical limitations. However, due to the infra-structure of that system (the constraint maintenance systems in particular) we may discover that we are using an algorithm that is genuinely novel. If we do attempt to employ one of the CSP algorithms in all purity, we may be forced to isolate that algorithm from the system. We may do this by representing domains as functions or streams, and constraints as a call to a checking function. Isolating the algorithm from the system gives us two immediate benefits. Firstly, we can attach heuristic knowledge to objects at the finest level of granularity. Secondly, we design extensibility into our system.

The preceding sections have given us a "thumb nail" sketch of how one might go about implementing a constraint-based scheduling system. I have argued that such an approach is adequate. However, we have implicitly assumed that the scheduling problem is static. Clearly this is not the case. Real world events will tend to drive any schedule into a chaotic state. Therefore, our goal should be to create and maintain a schedule. This can only add importance to the underlying infra-structure of our scheduling system, namely the constraint maintenance system. That constraint maintenance system must be able to address non-monotonic change, and will in most likelihood embrace truth maintenance technology such as (de Kleer, 1986) or (Doyle, 1979). Therefore, when we take a constraint-based approach, we should also be prepared to take a TMS-based approach (and this is done explicitly in systems such as FlyPast (Mott *et al.*, 1988), SemiMan (Elleby *et al.*, 1989), DAS (Burke and Prosser, 1991), and the DCMS of (Prosser *et al.*, 1992).

REFERENCES

Allen, J.F. (1984) Towards a General theory of Action and Time, *Artificial Intelligence* **23**, pp. 123–154.

Atabakhsh, H. (1991) A Survey of Constraint Based Scheduling Systems Using an Artificial Intelligence Approach, *Artificial Intelligence in Engineering* **6** (2), pp. 58–73.

Berry, P.M. (1991) *A Predictive Model for Satisfying Conflicting Objectives in Scheduling Problems*, Ph. D. thesis, Department of Computer Science, University of Strathclyde, Glasgow.

Burke, P. (1989) *Scheduling in Dynamic Environments*, Ph. D. thesis, Department of Computer Science, University of Strathclyde, Glasgow.

Burke, P. and Prosser, P. (1991) A Distributed Asynchronous System for Predictive and Reactive Scheduling, *Artificial Intelligence in Engineering* **6** (3) 106–124.

Doyle, J. (1979) A Truth Maintenance System, *Artificial Intelligence* **12**, pp. 231–272.

de Kleer, J. (1986) An Assumption-based TMS, *Artificial Intelligence* **28**, pp. 127–162.

Elleby, P., Fargher, H.E. and Addis, T.R. (1989) A Constraint-based Scheduling System for VLSI Wafer Fabrication, in *Knowledge Based Production Management Systems*, J. Browne (ed.), Elsevier Science Publishers B.V. (North Holland).

Fox, M.S. (1983) *Constraint-directed Search: A Case Study of Job-Shop Scheduling* Ph. D. thesis, Department of Computer Science, Carnegie-Mellon University.

Fox, B.R. and Kempf, K.G. (1985) Opportunistic Scheduling of Robot Assembly, *Proceedings IEEE International Conference on Robotics and Automation*, St Louis, Missouri, pp. 880–889.

Fox, M.S. and Sadeh, N. (1990) Why is Scheduling Difficult? A CSP Perspective, *Proceedings of the 9th European Conference on Artificial Intelligence* (ECAI-90), pp. 754–767.

Gaschnig, J. (1978) Experimental Case Studies of Backtracking versus Waltz-type versus new Algorithms for Satisfying Assignment Problems, *Proceedings of the 2nd biennial Conference of the Canadian Society for Computational Studies of Intelligence.*

Grant, T.J. (1986) Lessons for OR from AI: A Scheduling Case Study, *Journal of the Operational Research Society* **37** (1), pp. 41–57.

Hynynen, J. (1988) *A Framework for Coordination in Distributed Production Management, Doctorial dissertation*, Helsinki (Finland), Laboratory of Information Processing, Computer Science Department, Helsinki University of Technology, Acta Polytechnica Scandanavica.

Haralick, R.M. and Elliott, G.L. (1980) Increasing Tree Search Efficiency for Constraint Satisfaction Problems, *Artificial Intelligence* **14**, pp. 263–313.

Kumar, V. (1992) Algorithms for Constraint Satisfaction Problems: A Survey, *AI Magazine* **13** (1) 32–44.

Le Pape, C. and Smith, S.F. (1987) *Management of Temporal Constraints in Factory Scheduling*, Technical Report CMU-RI-TR-87-13, Carnegie Mellon University, The Robotics Institute.

Le Pape, C. (1988) *Des Systemes d'Ordonnancement Flexibles et Opportunistes*, Ph. D. thesis, Université de Paris-Sud, Centre d'Orsay.

Le Pape, C. (1991) *Constraint Propagation in Planning and Scheduling*, Technical Report, Robotics Laboratory, Department of Computer Science, Stanford University.

Mackworth, A. K. (1977) Consistency in Networks of Relations, *Artificial Intelligence* **8**, pp. 99–118.

Meseguer,P. (1989) Constraint Satisfaction Problems: An Overview, *AICOM* **2**(1)pp.3-17.

Mittal, S. and Falkenhainer, B. (1990) Dynamic Constraint Satisfaction Problems, *Proceedings of the 8th National Conference on Artificial Intelligence* (AAAI-90), pp. 25–32.

Mohr, R. and Henderson, T.C. (1986) Arc and Path Consistency Revisited, *Artificial Intelligence* **28**, pp. 225–233.

Mott, D.H., Cunningham, J., Kelleher, G. and Gadsden, J.A. (1988) Constraint-based Reasoning for Generating Naval Flying Programmes, *Expert Systems* **5** (3), pp. 226–246.

Nadel, B.A. (1989) Constraint Satisfaction Algorithms, *Computational Intelligence* **5**, pp. 188–224.

Phelps, R.I. (1986) Artificial Intelligence - An Overview of Similarities with OR, *Journal of the Operational Research Society* **37** (1), pp. 13–20.

Prosser, P. (1989) A Reactive Scheduling Agent, *Proceedings of the 13th International Joint Conference on Artificial Intelligence*, Detroit.

Prosser, P. (1990) *Distributed Asynchronous Scheduling*, Ph. D. thesis, Department of Computer Science, University of Strathclyde, Glasgow.

Prosser, P. (1991) *Hybrid Algorithms for the Constraint Satisfaction Problem*, Technical Report AISL-46-91, Department of Computer Science, University of Strathclyde, Glasgow.

Prosser, P., Conway, C. and Muller, C. (1992) A Distributed Constraint Maintenance System, *Avignon '92*.

Rossi, F. Petrie, C. and Dhar, V. (1990) On the Equivalence of Constraint Satisfaction Problems, *Proceedings of the 9th European Conference on Artificial Intelligence* (ECAI-90), Stockholm, pp. 550–556.

Sadeh, N. (1991) *Look-ahead Techniques for Micro-opportunistic Job-shop Scheduling*, CMU-CS-1-102, School of Computer Science, Carnegie Mellon University, Pittsburgh.

Smith, S., Fox, M.S. and Ow, P.S. (1986) Constructing and Maintaining detailed Production Plans: Investigations into the Development of Knowledge-based Factory Scheduling Systems, *AI Magazine* **7** (4), pp. 45–61.

Zweben, M. and Eskey, M. (1989) Constraint Satisfaction with Delayed Evaluation, *Proceedings of the 11th International Joint Conference on Artificial Intelligence* (IJCAI-89), pp. 875–880.

3

Scheduling and Uncertainty Reasoning (an Example Described)

Pauline M. Berry
AI Applications Institute, University of Edinburgh

INTRODUCTION

In most realistic situations, the information available to the decision-maker is both incomplete and uncertain. This complicates the automation of intelligent reasoning systems in the real world. In recent years a considerable amount of effort has been directed towards the representation and manipulation of uncertain information. This chapter is a discussion of the relevance of *uncertainty reasoning* in the scheduling process. It is argued that scheduling is essentially a problem of *decision-making* under uncertainty and that, as such, uncertainty is a key factor in both schedule representation and generation. The chapter shows how uncertainty reasoning, through the use of a probabilistic model, can aid scheduling. The approach is illustrated using a small example problem.

Regardless of the way in which a decision process is characterised it will necessarily involve three primary steps (Stephanou and Sage, 1987):

1. Formulation of the decision problem, in which needs and objectives of a client group are identified and potentially acceptable alternatives identified. In scheduling the objectives could take the form of organisational goals such as increasing productivity, improving customer services or reducing operating costs.
2. Analysis of alternative decisions, in which the impact of the various options are evaluated.
3. Interpretation and selection, in which the options are compared and the client needs and objectives are used as a basis for *evaluation*. The most acceptable option will be selected.

In the presence of incomplete and uncertain information the formulation of the decision problem, the identification of alternatives and their evaluation are all made more complex.

Many paradigms have been proposed to handle uncertainty in AI based systems. Some of these paradigms are quantitative or numerical, such as subjective probability theory (Duda *et al.*, 1976), (Cheeseman, 1985), possibility theory (Zadeh, 1978) and certainty factors (Shortliffe, 1976), while others are qualitative, for example the theory of endorsements (Cohen, 1985). Other forms of uncertainty are caused by the existence of imprecise descriptive languages, by inferencing without the complete information and by combining knowledge from different experts. A slightly different approach is taken within utility theory (Buchanan, 1982), (Lagomasino and Sage, 1985). Here the decision process considers the incomplete and imperfect information available about the current decision situation and assesses the impact of various alternatives on the various value perspectives of the decision-makers. Uncertainty related problems pervade a whole system, the designer of a knowledge based system must recognise that the "expert's" knowledge is neither complete nor exact, domain concepts may be ill-defined and data inaccurate.

In the exemplar domain of scheduling the problem of uncertainty is threefold. There is uncertainty associated with the requirements of a "good" schedule, there is uncertainty associated with how a decision will effect the ultimate solution and there is executional uncertainty due to stochastic and dynamic nature of the application domain.

The first section of this chapter discusses the problem of reasoning under uncertainty and incomplete information in AI systems. It then introduces the scheduling problem and describes how uncertainty influences our ability to address the problem in the real world. The main section discusses a way to reasoning with uncertainty in the scheduling domain based on a probabilistic approach and, finally, illustrates in detail how such an approach may be implemented in an example scheduling situation.

UNCERTAINTY IN AI

Making a decision is, in principle, a very straightforward task if one has complete information (i.e. knows exactly the impact of each possible decision). For example, a production manager contemplating what raw materials to order from the stores to be delivered tomorrow would have no difficulty if he knew exactly what jobs were to be completed today and which jobs where scheduled for tomorrow. However, the manager does not know if all jobs will be completed today as expected, if any rush orders will appear or if machines will break down tomorrow. The difficulty in selection is usually due to uncertainties in the situation and due to not knowing exactly what would happen if a particular course of action were to be adopted. It is necessary, therefore, to consider the language and theories that describe uncertainty and issues such as probability, preference and consequence that affect decision-making generally.

The uncertainty in any decision-making situation can be expressed by saying that we do not know what will happen in the future. The term event is used to refer to an occurrence or happening. In the English language there are many words which express aspects of the uncertainty that is felt about events; likely, probable, plausible, possible, chance, odds are just a few. They all describe the idea that some events are more "likely" than others. In science, the concept of uncertainty can be described numerically although, as will be demonstrated, the difficulty lies in the actual measurement and manipulation of uncertainty rather than the concept of using a numerical description.

In the field of AI, researchers have addressed the problem of uncertainty from three different approaches. (Pearl, 1988) divides these approaches into three formal schools; logicist, neo-calculist and neo-probabilist. The first school, the logicists, use non-numerical techniques to deal with uncertainty, primarily, nonmonotonic logics (Touretzky, 1984). The second school uses numeric representations but considers probability calculus as inadequate so has developed its own calculi such as *Dempster-Shafer calculus* (Dempster, 1968), (Shafer, 1976), *fuzzy logic* (Yager *et al.*, 1987) and *certainty factors* (Shortliffe *et al.*, 1979). Lastly, the neo-probabilists use traditional probability theory and add extra computational facilities (Cheeseman, 1985). There is another important classification of approaches to uncertainty and that is whether they are extensional or intensional. The former treats uncertainty as truth values attached to formulas, i.e. rule-based systems, while in the latter, which is also known as declarative or model-based, uncertainty is attached to "possible" worlds. Utility theory takes the intensional view.

Utility theory is based on the development of models of normative behaviour for decision-making under uncertainty and risk (Sage and White, 1984). The reasoning methodology can be interpreted as a learning process allowing the decision-maker to incorporate new alternatives, attributes and outcomes at any time during the reasoning process. Research into the theory of utility has a long tradition and is motivated by the observation that real life decision problems are so complex and poorly understood initially that a formal process for decision support must allow and encourage learning so that there is an increased understanding of the decision situation as well as value perspectives. This is certainly true of the scheduling problem where the specification and determination of a "good" schedule is itself very difficult and complex. Different people within a manufacturing organisation look for different measures of success, such as good resource usage, increased productivity or good due date satisfaction. All these measures of performance and many more interact and conflict with one another in different ways over time. The only valid measure of a manufacturer's performance is its success in the market place over a considerable period of time.

To conclude this section on uncertainty it is important to mention the notion of probabilistic models. A *probabilistic model* is an encoding of uncertain information that permits the computation of the likelihood, or possibly the probability, of an event. In practice such models can represent continuous random variables using distribution functions based on algebraic functions (i.e. like those describing normal or exponential distributions), while discrete variables can be inferred from simple relationships. An attractive feature of probabilistic model is an encoding of uncertain information that permits the computation of the likelihood, or possibly the probability, of an event. An attractive feature of probabilistic models is the ease with which information predicting future events can be extracted.

THE SCHEDULING PROBLEM

The issue of uncertainty is an important consideration during any decision-making process and scheduling is no exception, see (Le Pape, 1991) relating to the probability of events, the desire for a particular event and the effect of a decision on future choices all play a part when reasoning with uncertainty. Within the scheduling domain there is a large degree of uncertainty both from real world influences, such as machine breakdowns, rush orders and so on (*environmental uncertainties*) and also from the consequences of scheduling decisions, the repercussions of which are exponential and thus too costly to evaluate (*scheduling uncertainties*). In addition, the problem is further complicated by the need to produce a "good" quality schedule, one which both meets the individual preferences of each customer and resource and also which best satisfies the conflicting global management objectives which may change across time.

There have been several approaches to tackling the complex problems of uncertainty and preference in scheduling. Systems such as SPIKE (Johnston, 1989) and CORTES (Sadeh and Fox, 1988), (Sycara *et al.*, 1991) have addressed the problem within probabilistic frameworks. Both systems highlight the relationship between uncertainty handling and the satisfaction of objectives. The objectives addressed include scheduling objectives, such as reduce search and backtracking, and management objectives, such as maintain low cost operations and increase productivity. However, neither of the systems described reason dynamically about the desire to satisfy global objectives, that is they cannot change perspective during the scheduling process. Both CORTES and SPIKE depend upon the user to specify local utility functions or values for particular constraints or measures of performance before scheduling can commence. Neither system allows overall management objectives to be stipulated nor do they provide a mechanism for adjusting scheduling goals when an unusual or unexpected situation arises during the scheduling process. More recent developments of CORTES (Sadeh, 1991) rely on the construction of even more complex individual models of tardiness, WIP and inventory costs and, again, result in the problem of combining diverse predictive measures of performance. Problem decomposition is a significant factor in the ability of systems to reduce uncertainty and the hierarchical architecture of systems such as DAS (Burke and Prosser, 1991) provides the opportunity to take a least commitment approach. However, none of these techniques go far enough in their recognition of scheduling as a problem of dynamic decision making under uncertainty.

THE PROBABILISTIC ARGUMENT

A possible approach, suggested by this chapter, would take the form of probabilistic-type models. As mentioned earlier, a probabilistic model is an encoding of uncertain information permitting the computation of the likely consequence of an action, or decision. This idea follows on from work involving just such a model, the *preference capacity plan* (PCP) (Berry, 1991), (Berry, 1992).

Probabilistic models can be used to represent the expected value of specific qualitative measures across time. For example, the PCP provides a continuous measure of expected resource loading across time. In a knowledge-based scheduling system such a mathematical model could be used to enrich the symbolic representations already in operation. It also provides a forum for expressing uncertainty. Our knowledge of the scheduling world is never complete or certain and it is essential that this dimension be included in a complex scheduling aid. Work with the PCP (Berry, 1990) and in CORTES (Sadeh, 1991) has shown clearly that such models can be used to influence the actual schedule construction process. In both cases the models are used to indicate the most critical decision point with respect to contention for resources. This information is used to focus the attention of the scheduler and, according to specific variable ordering and value ordering heuristics (Dechter and Pearl, 1988), to improve the efficiency of the search process. Thus, mathematical techniques can be included in the knowledge-based framework of reactive and distributed scheduling.

Finally, the probabilistic models come from the utility theory and are not only concerned with the representation of uncertainty but also with the representation of preference. In both the PCP and CORTES the probabilistic models include some form of preference. In fact, the PCP allows the desire to meet many high level scheduling goals to be incorporated in its probabilistic model. These desires are not static across time and can be dynamically altered as the global situation changes. This ability to adapt, not only to changes in the scheduling problem, but also to changes in scheduling goals is essential. Real world scheduling environments are characteristically volatile in every dimension. The incorporation of preference in the probabilistic models will influence the quality of schedules produced.

AN EXAMPLE

This section will describe how a probabilistic model may be a useful tool within a constraint-based search to reduce scheduling uncertainty. The PCP which is a form of probabilistic model will be used to aid a classic forward checking algorithm in solving a small scheduling problem. The small scheduling problem is similar to one used in (Sadeh and Fox, 1989) to illustrate their mechanism for controlling a constraint based search algorithm. At the end of this section a brief comparison of the two systems will be made.

The sample problem

The general scheduling problem consists of a set of orders, or plans, $\{P_1, P_2,..., P_n\}$ which have to be scheduled through a set of resources $\{R_1, R_2,..., R_m\}$. A Plan, P_i is the process routing for an order and can be defined as a partial ordering of operations, $\{OP_{i1}, OP_{i2},. ..OP_{ip}\}$. Each operation, OP_{ij}, has associated with it, a duration, d_{ij}, and an interval I_{ij}, which denotes possible start times. There are three types of constraint which apply to this definition and these are the temporal relation constraints, the resource capacity constraints and the *resource requirement constraints*. The *temporal relation constraints* $\{C_1, C_2, ..., C_q\}$ are used to describe precedence relations between operations within a plan. The *capacity constraints* restrict the number of operations which can be performed by a resource at any one time. Each operation, OP_{ij}, may use one or more resources $\{R_{ij1}, R_{ij2},..., R_{ijr}\}$, each of which may be selected from a set of available resources.

The actual sample problem is designed to illustrate the diverse set of situations which may arise and which can be incorporated into the PCP probabilistic model. The problem consists of three orders, P_A, P_B and P_C, which involve 3, 5 and 4 operations respectively. The temporal relation constraints are illustrated in figure 3-1.

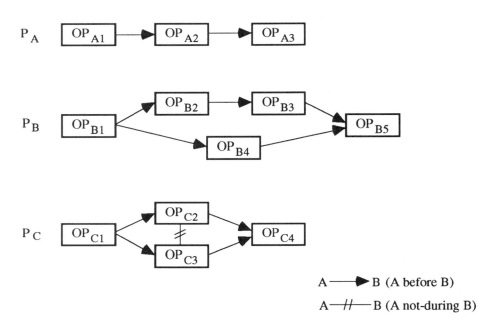

Figure 3-1: The sample problem (temporal relation constraints)

Each plan is designed to represent particular types of routing, linear, non-linear without disjunction and non-linear with disjunction. Because the sample problem does not consider secondary constraints we need only use a subset of Allen's temporal relations, namely "before", "not-during" and "after". Each operation has the same duration, namely 30 time units, and each plan has a release date of 0 and due date of 150. There are four resources each of which can process only one operation at a time. The resource requirement constraints are laid out in table 3-1. Note that a quick analysis of the problem indicates that there is competition for resource R_2 that doesn't exist for any other resource. There are five operations possibly requiring R_2, up to four of which may occur in parallel, OP_{A2}, OP_{B3}, OP_{B4} and OP_{C2}. This doesn't occur with any other resource because of the strict precedence constraints which exist. The scheduling of R_2 is therefore critical and it would be sensible to focus the attention of the scheduler on the competing operations first.

Table 3-1: The sample problem (resource requirement constraints)

Resource Requirements		
Operation	Requirement	Possible Resources
OP_{A1}	R_{A11}	R_1
OP_{A2}	R_{A21}	R_1 or R_2
OP_{A3}	R_{A31}	R_1
OP_{B1}	R_{B11}	R_2 or R_3
OP_{B2}	R_{B21}	R_3
OP_{B3}	R_{B31}	R_2
OP_{B4}	R_{B41}	R_2
OP_{B5}	R_{B51}	R_3
OP_{C1}	R_{C11}	R_4
OP_{C2}	R_{C21}	R_3 or R_2
OP_{C3}	R_{C31}	R_4
OP_{C4}	R_{C41}	R_4

Creating / maintaining the PCP

The STP Distribution:

The initial stage in the construction of a suitable probabilistic model would be to calculate the probability distributions for the possible start times of each operation. In the case of the PCP this first step ignores all resource requirement and capacity constraints. The resulting *start time preference* (STP) distributions represent the likelihood that an operation will be assigned a particular start time and takes into account both temporal precedence constraints and preference constraints since decision-making is influenced by both likelihood and desirability (probability and utility). In this context the STP distribution is defined to be a measure of belief rather than a frequency ratio or, in the language of Sadeh and Fox (1989), it can be interpreted as a measure of value goodness for possible start times assuming resource restrictions can be ignored.

The STP distribution for an operation is constructed by combining the global utility function for its order with its start time probability density function. The *probability density function* of an operation simply indicates the probability that operation k is scheduled to start a time t assuming that each possible start time is equally likely. Given that I_k is the legal interval of start times for operations k, the probability density function will be:

$$P(st_k = t) = \frac{1}{\text{No. of start times in } I_k}$$

The *global utility function* for an order indicates the preferred distribution of activity on the order over the total available time. The following preference constraints are included in the PCP approach:

1. Meet due dates
2. Minimise *WIP*
3. Adopt a global scheduling strategy (i.e. *JIT*) also called manufacturing philosophy

Examples of how these constraints are used to construct the global utility functions for the sample problem are shown in figure 3-2.

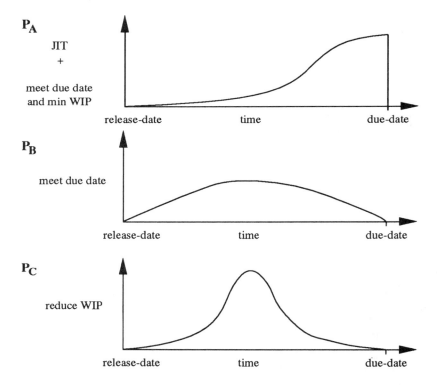

Figure 3-2: Global utility functions for the sample problem

Note that the area under each graph remains constant but the skew and kurtosis change. The Kurtosis is the degree to which a distribution is sharply peaked at its centre. For order P_A the manufacturing philosophy adopted is Just-In-Time and it is assumed the manufacturers wish to maintain a balance between meeting due dates and minimising WIP. For P_B we assume that this particular order has been given a high importance and that due dates should be met at whatever cost to WIP levels; maybe it is a new customer whom we would like to impress! The last order has been included to show the effect of a overwhelming desire to reduce the WIP level.

   The last step in the construction of the STP distribution involves imposing the desire
for the global utility function of an order onto the probability distributions for each of the
operations belonging to that order. The series of diagrams from figure 3-3 to figure 3-5
show the effect this procedure has on each operation in the sample problem. A heuristic
procedure is used to construct these distributions which uses the original start time probability functions and the skew and kurtosis of the global utility functions as inputs.

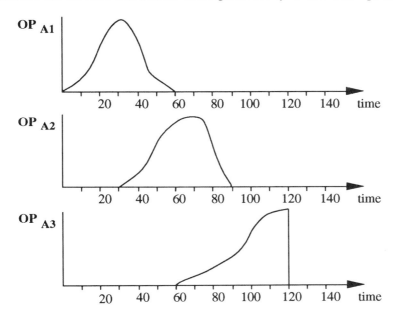

Figure 3-3: Example STP distribution for operations in P_A

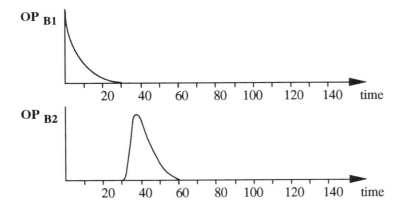

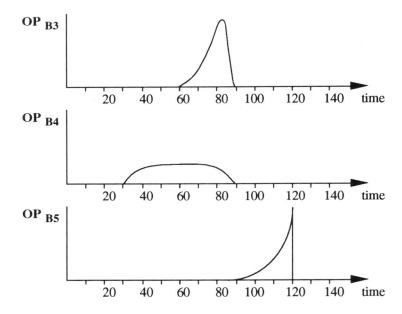

Figure 3-4: Example STP distribution for operations in P_B

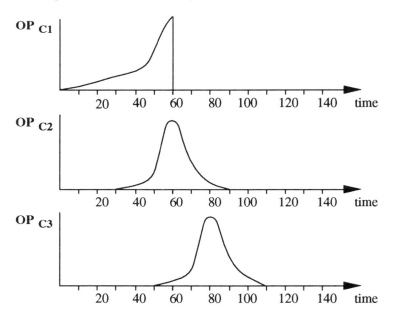

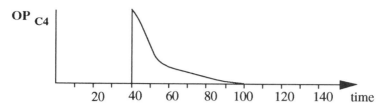

Figure 3-5: Example STP distribution for operations in P_C

Individual preference demand densities:

In order to introduce the resource constraints the PCP approach first constructs *individual preference demand* (IPD) densities for each operation. The IPD densities of an operation represent its likely demand for a set of required resources across time. There is one IPD density for each resource since duration times may vary depending on the resource. In the sample problem there are no variable durations so all the IPD densities for one operation are equal. The IPD density of OP_{ij} at time t equals the likelihood that OP_{ij} is active at time t given the current preference constraints represented in the STP distribution. This is shown in the following equation and an example is shown in figure 3-6.

$$\text{IPD-}OP_{ij}(t) = \sum_{k=(t-d_{ij})}^{t} \text{STP-}OP_{ij}(k)$$

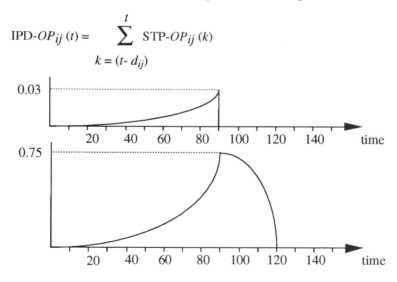

Figure 3-6: From STP distribution to IPD density

Preference capacity clan

Each resource has, associated with it, an individual *preference capacity plan* (PCP). It is produced by gathering together all the operations which might use that resource and adding together the relevant portion of their IPD densities. For example, if the operation in figure 3-6 could be performed by three resources without preference then the IPD density would be divided by three and added to the PCP of each of those resources. If preference for a particular resources is specified then the IPD density will be divided unevenly according to the resource preference constraints. The four PCP for the resources in the sample problem are shown in figure 3-7. Although three of the four resources indicate areas of high contention, resource R_2 has the largest area of demand over the available capacity. This bottleneck time interval defines R_2 as the most critical resource.

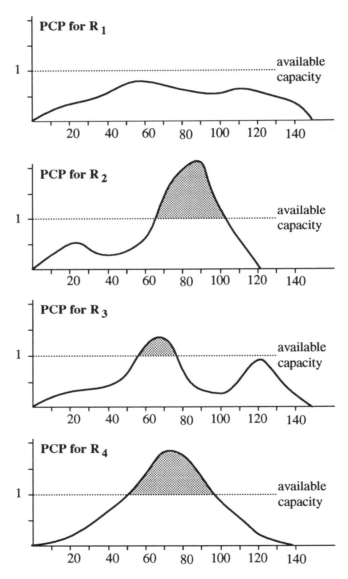

Figure 3-7: PCPs for the sample problem

Thus the construction, or rather maintenance, of the PCPs is composed of several logical steps each introducing further constraints to the probabilistic model. This process can be described diagrammatically as shown in figure 3-8. Every time a constraint changes in the problem, due to a scheduling decision being instantiated or due to an external event, that change is immediately propagated through to the PCPs.

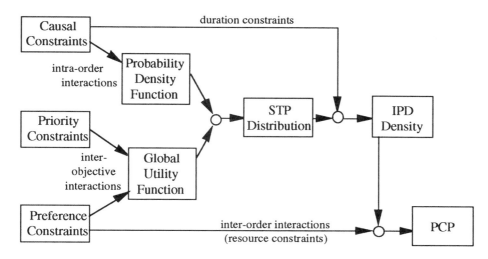

Figure 3-8: The PCP construction process (Berry, 1991)

Exploiting the probabilistic model

One approach to scheduling is to consider it as a *constraint satisfaction problem* (CSP), see (Prosser, 1993). A method for scheduling which is commonly adopted is called the incremental approach. The schedule is built incrementally by selecting an operation to be scheduled and a reservation for that operation. Every time an operation is scheduled new constraints are added to the problem and their effects propagated throughout the system. If an inconsistency is detected the system backtracks and perhaps eventually relaxes a preference constraint. Within the class of problems termed CSPs this method corresponds to the *forward checking algorithm*. There have been several analytical and experimental studies of constraint satisfaction problems and how to arrange the ordering of variables and values, (Purdom, 1983), (Freuder, 1982), (Haralick and Elliot, 1980). The efficiency of this approach and the resulting schedule quality relies on the order in which operations are considered (variable ordering) and the order of assigning reservations to those operations (value ordering). In fact, there are three principal decision points in the scheduling problem when it is modelled as a CSP: value ordering; variable ordering; and when an inconsistency is detected, whether to backtrack or relax a constraint and if so which constraint and by how much. In the worst case because the problem is NP-complete, the search may require an exponential amount of time. As (Dechter and Pearl, 1988) show, an efficient strategy for value and variable ordering would be to select the most critical operation to be scheduled first and assign to it the start time and resource which least constrain the rest of the problem. A probabilistic model, by representing uncertainties and providing a forum to evaluate uncertainties, can be used to order variables and values. This is how the CSP is used within the search process of scheduling. However, the PCP can also be used to evaluate possible *constraint relaxation* in terms of their effect on the quality of a solution and the impact on search efficiency.

Using the PCP the most constraining operation, and therefore the most critical decision point is considered to be the one which contributed the largest portion to the worst bottleneck, see OP_{B4} in figure 3-9. That is, the operation whose start time and resource reservations are most likely to become unavailable due to interactions with other constraints. In addition the quality of the resulting schedule is equally dependent on the sequence in which start times and resource reservations are considered. Because the PCP represents the likely satisfaction of global objectives the value ordering scheme can attempt to optimise the reservations. It does this by selecting the most promising resource from the PCP and the most promising start time: a compromise between search efficiency and schedule quality.

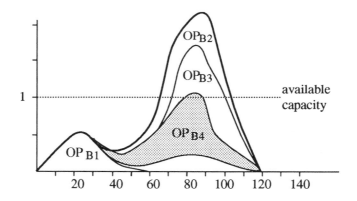

Figure 3-9: Dissection of the PCP for R_2

As was mentioned earlier the PCP can also be used to assess the impact of a *constraint relaxation* in situations where an inconsistency has been detected and backtracking has either proved futile or is considered too expensive computationally. Several possible constraint relaxation alternatives can, in turn, be tentatively made and the resulting changes in the PCPs monitored. The relaxation which causes the least disruptive, or most positive, change to the PCPs is considered the most promising relaxation. Therefore, the PCP can be used to aid decision-making at the three critical decision points in the scheduling problem.

Additionally, it must be noted that the PCPs are being continually updated. The process of building the PCPs is one of maintenance rather than construction. The PCP is also performing, continually, a self-analysis function. It is constantly monitoring itself to identify extreme or unusual orderbook conditions. This information is then used to adjust the global utility functions in order to obtain a more balanced solution. For example, if a large part of the problem becomes vastly overconstrained then it would be futile to try to achieve good due date satisfaction during this period. The PCP will identify such an unusual situation and place more emphasis on reducing WIP levels during this problematic session. Therefore this dynamic self-regulation is designed to avoid worst case measures of performance.

The PCP approach has been applied within several distinct scheduling architectures. The first was a classic blackboard-based scheduler, similar in architecture and functionality to OPIS, (Smith *et al.*, 1986), and SONIA, (Collinot *et al.*, 1988). The system and its operation with the PCP approach are described in some detail by (Berry, 1990) and (Berry, 1991). Another scheduling architecture was used to show that the PCP technique is not restricted to one architecture or scheduling philosophy but is more generally applicable. The Distributed Asynchronous Scheduler (DAS) (Burke, 1990) differs from the predictive systems like OPIS and SONIA in that it is extremely reactive by nature. The architecture and control structures are also quite different from the blackboard-based system. The aim of this second implementation was to test further the power of the PCP approach to focus search and guide decision-making in scheduling environments. DAS with the PCP is described fully in (Berry, 1991) and (Berry, 1992b).

Extensive tests on both these architectures using real factory data have shown that the PCP is effective in improving schedule quality, particularly worst case measures, while maintaining search efficiency in highly reactive environments. In the classic blackboard-based system which has a clear control structure, tests illustrated the effectiveness of the PCP in controlling schedule quality and search efficiency. In the distributed, asynchronous scheduling system (DAS), which has a less obvious control structure, the benefit of using the PCP was shown in its power to maintain a consistently high quality of solution despite a highly dynamic environment. See (Berry, 1991) for full test descriptions and results.

Comparison with other similar approaches

As mentioned earlier the method of utilising the PCP is similar to the use of texture measures in CORTES (Sadeh and Fox, 1989). However, the PCP approach allows the combination of different global preference constraints whereas the texture measure of CORTES relies on local measures of performance. Also, the goal of the variable and value ordering in CORTES is exclusively search efficiency. The result is that CORTES will minimise backtracking and be extremely efficient with respect to due date satisfaction. The cost is that WIP levels will always be maximised, see (Berry, 1991) for a full presentation of this argument.

The suitability function of SPIKE (Johnston, 1989) illustrates an alternative mechanism for representing uncertainty and encapsulates a measure of desirability. However, the suitability function uses information about local constraints only and depends on a pre-defined measure of overall quality. The PCP allows global measure of quality to be opportunistically adjusted as manufacturing situations and aims change in the real world. Analysis of the performance of several schedulers using the PCP capability have shown that this mechanism is successful in achieving a consistently high average measure of performance while also improving worst case measures of performance.

SUMMARY

Existing techniques for scheduling in complex real world environments usually fall down because they are unable to address the problems of scheduling uncertainty and environmental uncertainty. This chapter has argued that knowledge-based techniques must be augmented by mathematical methods if automatic scheduling is to succeed in the market place. One possibility presented by this chapter is the use of probabilistic models to represent uncertainty and preference.

Effective representation of uncertainty and methods to reason with uncertain information will contribute to effective schedule construction and maintenance especially in the area of schedule quality. However, this area still requires much effort.

REFERENCES

Baker, K.R. (1974) *Introduction to Sequencing and Scheduling*, New York: Wiley.

Berry, P.M. (1990) Satisfying Conflicting Objectives in Factory Scheduling, *Proceedings of the 6th IEEE Conference on Artificial Intelligence Applications*, (CAIA-90), Santa Barbara, Ca, pp. 101–107

Berry, P.M. (1991) *A Predictive Model for Satisfying Conflicting Objectives in Scheduling Problems*, Ph. D. Thesis, Department of Computer Science, University of Strathclyde, Glasgow.

Berry, P.M. (1992a) Scheduling: A Problem of Decision-making under Uncertainty, *Proceedings of the 10th European Conference on Artificial Intelligence* (ECAI-92) Vienna, pp. 638–642.

Berry, P.M. (1992b) The PCP a Predictive Model for Satisfying Conflicting Objectives in Scheduling Problems. To be published in: *Artificial Intelligence in Engineering*, Elsevier Science Publishers.

Buchanan, J.T. (1982) *Discrete and Dynamic Decision Analysis*, Chichester: Wiley.

Burke, P. and Prosser, P. (1991) A Distributed Asynchronous System for Predictive and Reactive Scheduling, *Artificial Intelligence in Engineering* **6** (3), pp. 106–124.

Cheeseman, P. (1985) In Defense of Probability, *Proceedings of the 8th International Joint Conference on Artificial Intelligence* (IJCAI-85), pp. 1002–1009.

Cohen, P.R. (1985) *Heuristic Reasoning about Uncertainty: An AI Approach*, Boston: Pitman.

Collinot, A., Le Pape, C. and Pinoteau, G. (1988) SONIA: A Knowledge-based Scheduling System, *Artificial Intelligence in Engineering* **3** (2).

Dechter, R. and Pearl, J. (1988) Network-based Heuristics for Constraint-Satisfaction Problems, *Artificial Intelligence* **34**, pp. 1–38.

Dempster, A.P. (1968) A Generalization of Bayesian Inference, *Journal Royal Statist. Soc.* **ser. B 30**, pp. 205–247.

Duda, R.O., Hart, P.E. and Nilsson, N. J. (1976) *Subjective Bayesian Methods for Rule-Based Inference Systems*, Technical Note 124, Artificial Intelligence Center, SRI International, Menlo Park, CA.

Fox, Mark. S. (1983) *Constraint-Directed Search: A Case Study Of Job-Shop Scheduling*, Ph. D. Thesis, Carnegie-Mellon University, Pittsburgh.

Freuder, E.C. (1982) A Sufficient Condition for Backtrack-free Search, *Journal of the ACM* **29** (1), pp. 24–32.

Haralick, R.M. and Elliot, G.L. (1980) Increasing Tree Search Efficiency for Constraint Satisfaction Problems, *Artificial Intelligence* **14**, pp. 263–314.

Johnston, M.D. (1989) Knowledge-based Telescope Scheduling, in *Knowledge-Based Systems in Astronomy*, A. Heck and F. Murtagh, (ed.) Springer-Verlag.

Lagomasino, A. and Sage, A.P. (1985) Representation and Interpretation of Information for Decision Support with Imperfect Knowledge, *Large Scale Systems* **5**.

Le Pape, C. (1991) *Constraint Propagation in Planning and Scheduling*, Technical Report, Robotics Laboratory, Department of Computer Science, Stanford University, Palo Alto, Ca.

Pearl, J. (1988) *Probabilistic Reasoning in Intelligent Systems: Networks of Plausible Inference*, Palo Alto: Morgan-Kaufmann.

Prosser, P. (1993) Scheduling as a Constraint Satisfaction Problem: Theory and Practice, in *Scheduling of Production Processes*, Chichester: Ellis Horwood.

Purdom, P.W. (1983) Search Rearrangement Backtracking and Polynomial Average Time, *Artificial Intelligence* **21**, pp. 117–133.

Sadeh, Norman and Fox, Mark S. (1988) *Preference Propagation in Temporal / Capacity Constraint Graphs*, CMU-CS-88-193, Computer Science Department Carnegie Mellon University, Pittsburgh.

Sadeh, Norman (1991) *Look-Ahead Techniques for Mirco-Opportunistic Scheduling*, Ph. D. Thesis, School of Computer Science, Carnegie-Mellon University, Pittsburgh.

Sage, A.P. and White, C.C. (1984) ARIADNE: A Knowledge-based Interactive System for Planning and Decision Support, *IEEE Transactions on Systems, Man and Cybernetics* **SMC-14**, pp. 35–47.

Shafer, G. (1976) *A Mathematical Theory of Evidence*, Princeton: Princeton University Press.

Shortliffe, E.H. (1976) *Computer-Based Medical Consultations: MYCIN*, New York: Elsevier.

Shortliffe, E.H., Buchanan, B.G. and Feigenbaum, E.A. (1979) Knowledge Engineering for Medical Decision Making: A Review of Computer Based Clinical Decision Aids, *Proceedings of the IEEE* **67** (9), pp. 1207-1224.

Smith, S.F., Ow, P.S., Le Pape, C., McLean, B. and Muscettola, N. (1986) Integrating Multiple Scheduling Perspectives to Generate Detailed Production Plans, *Proceedings SME Conference on AI in Manufacturing*, Long Beach, CA.

Stephanou, H. E. and Sage, A. P. (1897) Perspectives on Imperfect Information Processing, *IEEE Transactions on Systems, Man and Cybernetics* **SMC-17** (5), pp. 780–798.

Sycara, K.P., Roth, S.F., Sadeh, N. and Fox, M.F. (1991) Resource Allocation in Distributed Factory Scheduling, *IEEE Expert* February, pp. 29–40.

Touretzky, D. (1984) Implicit Ordering of Defaults in Inheritance Systems, *Proceedings of the 3rd National Conference on Artificial Intelligence*, Austin, pp. 322–325.

Yager, R., Ovchinnikov, S., Tong, R.M. and Nguyen, H.T. (1987) (eds) *Fuzzy Sets and Applications: Selected Papers* L.A. Zadeh (ed.), New York: Wiley.

Zadeh, L.A. (1978) Fuzzy Sets as a Basis for a Theory of Possibility, *Fuzzy Sets and Systems* **1** (1), pp. 3–28.

4

A Case-based Approach to Scheduling Constraints

Atilla Bezirgan
Institut für Automation, Technische Universität Wien

INTRODUCTION

In the Interuniversitary Centre for CIM (IUCCIM) in Vienna the production process for remote controlled toy cars is used to demonstrate the main ideas in CIM. In this context the problem of scheduling incoming orders for toy cars into the ongoing production process arises. The produced car consists of 60 distinct parts and is 60 cm in length. About half of the parts are produced in IUCCIM's own factory. The other half is delivered by other companies. There is a fixed set of machines available, each capable of performing several operations. For each part there are several alternative *process plans*. Scheduling in such an environment consists of selecting a plan for producing a certain part and assigning resources to the operations in the selected plan. There are several reasons for the complexity of such a scheduling task:

- Usually, there are several, *contradictory goals* which have to be kept in mind in scheduling. The goals often involve judging of alternatives and subjective decisions depending on the context of the current problem. Some goals are not or cannot be made explicit and goals change over time.
- There is a combinatorial explosion of the number of possible schedules (which must be checked for feasibility) in each problem dimension such as the number of machines and operations. This makes it necessary to use implicit representations of the search space instead of enumerative representations.
- There are a number of constraints which a valid schedule must satisfy such as due dates and constraints concerning operation sequences. Interactions of these constraints make scheduling decisions difficult.
- Scheduling decisions very often depend on context. This makes it difficult to write down an explicit goal function. What is good in one context can be bad in another.

- The kind of scheduling considered here is *dynamic*, i.e. scheduling runs in parallel with the production process and with the changing environment. The problems to be dealt with are thus real-time problems, though usually not hard real-time problems.
- Dynamic scheduling as a real-world problem takes place in an "open-world." The environment of the system changes continuously. The changes are both short term, such as the break down of a machine, and long term, such as changes in the line of products, company philosophy or effects of aging of machines. Often, problems which have not been foreseen at the time of the implementation of a scheduling system have to be dealt with.

On the other hand, in a CIM environment there is an abundance of information of various kinds available in machine readable form. Orders, prices, inventory lists, and production process logs can be stored over a long period of time. These informations represent a repository of valuable real-world experience. Today, the main user of such experience is the human scheduler, who utilises it to perform dynamic scheduling manually.

This abundance of information and its use through human schedulers is a pointer to the applicability and utility of *case-based reasoning* for such tasks. To reason from cases means using experience with earlier problems to solve the current problem rather than to solve the current problem from scratch using first principles. A case usually consists of the description of a problem, a solution to the problem as well as of knowledge used in solving the problem. A case base contains cases organised in a way to make efficient retrieval possible. In case-based reasoning, given a new problem a retrieval component retrieves the case most similar to the current problem. Using this case an adaptation component tries to generate a solution to the new problem. The work of Riesbeck and Schank (1989) and Bezirgan (1993) contain more detailed introductions to case-based reasoning.

The availability of cases or of data from which cases can be generated is a prerequisite for the applicability of case-based reasoning (Kolodner and Riesbeck, 1989). Reasoning from cases does not involve exploring the whole search space. Thus the problem of combinatorial explosion is avoided. One strength of case-based reasoning lies in its ability to deal with context dependent information. Thus constraint interaction and context dependency can be modelled efficiently in a case-based system. On the other hand case-based reasoning is not well suited for optimisation problems since it does not explore the whole search space. However, the impact of this weakness becomes smaller in a real-time environment in which a timely solution is often better than a perfect solution that misses deadlines. Further, case-based reasoning is usually faster than enumerative methods.

As can be seen from the above mentioned "reasons for the complexity of the scheduling problem" what is needed for the dynamic *job-shop* scheduling task in a real-world environment is flexibility. The system should be able to adapt to changing requirements and circumstances as quickly and easily as possible. The need for such flexibility not only in scheduling can be seen in the fact that the maintenance and revision costs often make up the largest part in the total software production costs. Ideally, a system would achieve this flexibility by using machine learning techniques to continuously acquire knowledge. A more feasible alternative in the medium term seems to be the support of the user in making the necessary changes as easily as possible.

CBS-1 is to be seen as a result of the need to provide a system architecture which

- allows more flexibility by being the basis for several machine learning techniques and
- utilises much of the scheduling know-how available in the company by using abundantly available historic data and heuristics used by human schedulers.

Case-based reasoning suits these needs well. Thus after weighing advantages and disadvantages against each other, case-based reasoning seems to have the characteristics needed for a reasoning method for dynamic scheduling tasks.

The CBS-1 (Case-Based Scheduler One) project represents an attempt to demonstrate the feasibility and utility of case-based reasoning for dynamic job-shop scheduling problems by creating a case-based reasoning system for scheduling orders for toy cars in the IUCCIM. The next section introduces the toy car production process in some detail. After that, the architecture and the components of CBS-1 are described.

TOY CAR PRODUCTION AT THE IUCCIM

The main products of the IUCCIM factory at this time are the remote controlled toy car (Ferrari Testarossa) and its parts. It is planned to allow custom designed parts to be produced in future. About 30 of the 60 parts needed for the complete Ferrari are produced in the IUCCIM factory. The other parts are delivered by other companies. The latter parts are only needed in the final assembly stage of the production process and are usually stored in sufficient amounts in the factory.

Orders are accepted for whole cars or parts. An order usually specifies the ordered part, a production deadline, an amount, quality criteria, such as the surface quality of a part, and some other requirements such as the colour of the car. Orders may arrive at any time and are to be scheduled as soon as possible. Orders also have priorities.

There is a total of twelve machines including laser cutting tools, turning machines, and drills. Each machine is capable of performing several operations. We assume that a machine cannot perform two or more operations simultaneously. Although generally one operation can be performed by more than one machine, the quality of the result of the operation and its execution time depend on the machine on which the operation is performed.

For each part there is a fixed set of alternative process plans. In the process plans the average machine preparation durations and operation execution durations are given as exact times though they may vary in real-world operation.

The IUCCIM factory is used for courses in CIM, for product demonstrations, and as a platform for trying out research ideas in CIM related technology. CBS-1 is an instance of the latter category.

THE CASE-BASED SCHEDULER CBS-1

Figure 4-1 shows the structure of CBS-1. The central knowledge store in CBS-1 is the case base. The *case base* contains information on machines, parts and subparts, processing operations, process plans, orders, and the current status of the factory. It also contains historical information on these items, i.e. a log of the temporal development of the factory. Scheduling decisions made earlier are also kept in the case base and make up the cases in CBS-1. These pieces of information are all linked together and build a semantic net organised around a time-line. One of the most important types of linking elements in this net are the so called *methods*. The methods are scheduling heuristics used in scheduling incoming orders. For example, such a method could state that incoming orders are to be scheduled as late as possible. This entails a risk of missing deadlines due to unforeseen events, but reduces storage costs. Linked to each method are cases in which the application of the method was appropriate.

The *case base manager* is responsible for keeping information in the case base about the current state of the factory up-to-date. This is done by monitoring information on the success or failure of processing steps (schedule execution report, SER) delivered by the underlying process control system. It also updates predictions about the future state of the factory by inserting newly created schedules into the case base. Since the case base can become quite large, the case base manager also realises a "forgetting" function, which removes information which is no longer needed, not used often, or not used for a long time.

Given one or more incoming orders and the knowledge structures mentioned above the *retrieval* component retrieves a set of similar previous cases from the case base. The most similar case is then passed on to the adaptation component. Similarity is judged by several means:

- Superficial features of orders, e.g. kinds of parts and amount ordered hint to relevant cases.
- Constraints on orders represent a further hint. Orders with comparable constraints, such as a certain required maximum production duration, are considered more similar than others.
- Deep and derived features, e.g. load of machines, schedulability (without changing the current schedule), and time till due date, are also used to assess similarity.
- Similarity of the current status of the factory and its state during a previous case points to further relevant cases. If machine A has a breakdown now and it had a breakdown in a previous case, then these cases are somewhat similar.

The *adaptation* component applies the method, which was used in the most similar past case to the current scheduling task. The result is a schedule which contains the operations needed for satisfying the current order, but which may not be feasible, e.g. due to collisions. The adaptation component usually does not check the schedules it generates for feasibility. This is only a design decision made to achieve faster adaptation. A simulator is used to evaluate the feasibility of the proposed schedules after adaptation is finished. These two stages could be merged, too.

Each of the three stages, namely retrieval, adaptation, and *evaluation* may signal the previous stage the need for an alternative input if the current input does not lead to success. If the evaluation signals unfeasibility of the proposed schedule, alternative adaptation strategies may be tried. If adaptation signals inadaptability, retrieval can deliver the next most similar case. If retrieval cannot find similar cases, it signals this to the order manager. There is an upper limit to this retrial mechanism. If this limit is reached without generating a feasible schedule, the order manager is informed. Note also that CBS-1 cannot process any orders for which the retrieval component cannot find a similar case. If all goes well, a schedule is passed on to process control for execution.

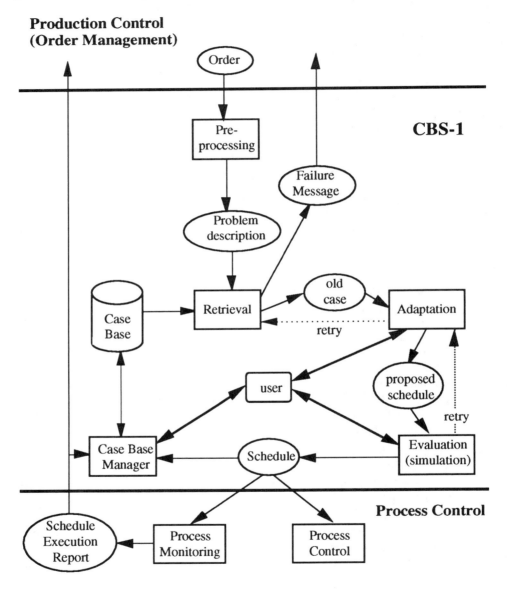

Figure 4-1: The structure of CBS-1

In the next sections some major components of CBS-1 are discussed in more detail.

CASES

One can imagine several different definitions of the term *case* in a *job-shop* scheduling environment. First, a case can be a record of information related to a single scheduling decision, e.g. which *process plan* to select for a certain ordered part or which machine to use for a certain operation. This definition of case is related to the constraint satisfaction problem view of scheduling (e.g. Fox and Sadeh, 1990) and makes many connections between cases in the case base necessary. These connections represent the dependences of scheduling decisions on each other.

Second, cases can be memory packages that contain all the information involved in scheduling a certain order, i.e. a case contains a log of all relevant activities in the factory from the time of arrival of an order until the ordered product leaves the factory. Since the scheduling of incoming orders is influenced by the schedules of earlier and later orders, cases are once again strongly interconnected.

We could also try to define cases from a more *resource* centered point of view rather than from the order based view above. However, no matter how one defines cases, strong interactions between them are inevitable. This is a consequence of the strong dependence of scheduling decisions on each other, on context, and on problem constraints, and is to be seen as an intrinsic characteristic of job-shop scheduling problems. Thus, it seems that the goal of defining tightly coupled units capturing global scheduling information (cases) which are loosely interconnected (in the case base) is infeasible in this context. Therefore cases are taken to be sets of related pieces of information having to do with the scheduling of a certain order and connected with pointers. These sets have fuzzy (i.e. unsharp) and floating (i.e. changing with time) boundaries.

In the following subsections components of cases in CBS-1 are described.

Problem descriptions

The problem description in a case consists of the following components:

* goals,
* constraints on goals and
* problem environment.

The main *goal* is the generation of a schedule for a new order. Orders may specify vague values for certain fields, such as very fast for speed. These can be interpreted as *soft constraints* which can be relaxed to a certain extent to obtain a feasible schedule.

Constraints describe restrictions on the kinds of solutions to be generated, e.g. cost or quality requirements. The different types of constraints which can be specified here are much like in the ISIS system. However, the language used in expressing constraints must be a restricted language since retrieval and adaptation must be able to check equality and subsumption relations between constraints which would be infeasible if, for example, unrestricted first order predicate calculus expressions were allowed. Table 4-1 shows a sample order.

Constraints can be external or internal. External constraints can be found in the order form, e.g. speed. Internal constraints are introduced by the production company, e.g.

maximal production cost, earliest / latest start date, earliest / latest finish date, and priority of an order. There are predefined internal constraints reflecting company philosophy and internal constraints which are derived by a pre-processor from the order and the current state of the factory. Table 4-2 shows a possible constraint list for the order of table 4-1. For the following demonstrations simple feature lists are used.

Table 4-1: Sample order

Case No: 7845	
Order number:	3412
Customer name:	Mr. Henry
Customer importance:	very important
Part:	Ferrari Testarossa
Amount:	5
Order date:	13.6.1992 8:00
Due date:	13.8.1992 12:00 ± 5 h
Colour:	red
Speed:	very fast
Wheels:	standard
Remote control range:	short
…	…

Table 4-2: Internal constraints

Case No: 7845 cont.	
max. prod. costs	AS 1000,00 / piece
priority	high (for an important customer)
Customer importance	very important
earliest finish	12.8.1992 12:00
…	…

Table 4-3: Schedule for a sample machine

Schedule for machine 12	**Hueller Hille**
…	…
13.6.1992 10:00-12:00	Order 3407; Plan 2; Op. 3
13.6.1992 12:00-16:00	Order 3314; Plan 1; Op. 1
13.6.1992 16:00-18:00	Maintenance
13.6.1992 18:00-22:00	Order 3408; Plan 1; Op. 6
…	…

An internal model of the factory and its current status makes up the problem environment. This model is kept as part of the case base and updated when necessary, e.g. when events like machine breakdown occur. Thus, it does not have to be specified explicitly in every problem description. The information managed in this context is the same information that a Gantt-Diagram conveys. Table 4-3 shows the status information for a machine.

Solutions

The solution consists of an assignment of resources to operations over time. This represents a prediction of the development of the activities in the factory. The output of the system is an event-driven schedule and a set of commands to machines and personnel ensuring the execution of the schedule. The system also produces a prediction of the temporal development of the production process. A line of the form "13.6.1992 12:00-16:00: Order 3314; Plan 1; Op. 1" in table 4-3 represents a part of such a prediction. The event-driven schedule consists of rules of the form "if 1 x part1 and 1 x part2 and 2 x part3 are available then assemble them to part21."

Methods

A case further contains a pointer to the pool of *methods* available to the system. This pointer is used to identify the method used in scheduling the order contained in the case. Such a method could be "shift an interfering order such an amount of time, that the new order can be scheduled." Table 4-4 shows a situation in which this method could be used. In table 4-4, scheduling operation Op_1 of plan 1 for order no. 1243 on machine 15 at time 16.6.1992 9:00-15:00 made scheduling operation Op_2 of plan 2 for order no. 1423 on machine 15 on 16.6.1992 impossible. Shifting Op_1 to start an hour later would make it possible to schedule Op_2 between 00:00 and 10:00. The pointer to the method contained in cases makes it possible to retrieve methods and use them to solve similar problems.

Table 4-4: A conflict situation

Schedule for machine 15	Collet Minor
...	...
16.6.1992 00:00-09:00	idle
16.6.1992 09:00-15:00	Order 1243; Plan 1; Op_1
16.6.1992 15:00-24:00	idle
...	...
Op_1 needs machine 15 for 6 hours	Op_1 is indivisible
Op_2 needs machine 15 for 10 hours	Op_2 is indivisible

Given below are some methods which could be placed in the methods pool:

- Schedule the new order as late as possible. The advantages and disadvantages of this method were mentioned before.

- Schedule the new order as early as possible. This offers high security but may lead to increased storage costs.
- Schedule the new order so that critical machines retain as large blocks of idle time as possible. This avoids fragmentation and the problem depicted in table 4-4 for future orders.
- Schedule the new order so that the production costs are minimal. The production costs can be assessed by accumulating the costs of using the resources needed. This information is stored in the case base.
- Postpone or reschedule an old order to make resources free for a new, more important order. This is an example for a destructive scheduling method.

These are just a few examples to give the reader a feeling for the methods in the methods pool of the system. A typical methods pool will contain in the order of a hundred methods, designed for dealing with different kinds of orders, constraints and current patterns of availability of resources.

RETRIEVAL

When a new order arrives the *retrieval* component searches the case base for a previous order that is most similar to the current one. The methods for assessing similarity have already been mentioned. In case-based reasoning we try not to retrieve cases that cannot be adapted. Thus similarity is judged by the ease of adapting an old solution to become a solution to the new problem. This means that the definition of similarity - and hence retrieval - depends crucially on the capabilities of the adaptation component.

The most similar old order is not found by comparing all old orders to the new one but by exploiting the semantic net to get from one similar case (case sharing one or more constraints or other features with the new order) to another.

For example, given a new order we can easily retrieve all previous orders for the same product. This is possible since all cases have pointers to the descriptions of the products produced as well as to the plans used. The associated cases are similar to the new order in the sense that they deal with the same product. Using further constraints on quality or quantity we can further differentiate between these cases. Following other links we can get to further cases which may be of use. For example, having decided to use a certain method we can take a look at previous usages of that method and the problems that were encountered then. Further, using some deeper features such as constraint looseness may help in retrieving more useful cases. Finally, the adaptation component is not bound to use one case in generating a new schedule. It can as well use several cases, one in solving each specific scheduling decision problem. In the following, adaptation from a single case is assumed.

An example shall demonstrate the retrieval procedure. Suppose that the order shown in table 4-5 is received. Suppose further that to satisfy the order only one machine and one operation is needed, namely machine 32. Table 4-5 also shows the schedule for machine 32 representing the current status of the factory. This configuration (availability of resources, order characteristics, infeasibility of the scheduling task due to a side-effect of a previous scheduling decision) could then lead to a reminding of the case related to table

4-4. Thus the system could try to use the same method of moving the hindering operation slightly to get a larger block of idle time to schedule the new order.

The system could have other remindings too, such as that of a case in which the same problem was solved by splitting up the order in two parts, scheduling one part before the hindering operation and the other after it. This solution is probably worse than the previous one, because the duration of the operation will increase due to the doubled machine preparation time. Nevertheless, this approach could lead to a feasible schedule, too. At the present time no notion of optimality is supported in our system. The point is that remindings of earlier orders and methods used in scheduling helped a lot in solving the current scheduling problem.

After the most similar old order is selected, adaptation is performed. The result of the adaptation is a new case including a solution to the new problem. Next it is checked whether the new solution satisfies all constraints. If it does, we are done. Else either the next similar old order is tried or a soft constraint is relaxed. If after several adaptation tries no solution is found, then the system is unable to deal with the given problem and the user must be consulted. For example, the adapted unsuccessful solutions may be presented to the user or he may be requested to relax some hard constraints.

Table 4-5: A new order and current machine status

Case No: 8743	
Order number	3442
Customer name	Mr. Mayer
Customer importance	important
Part	base-plate
Amount	100
Order date	16.6.1992 8:00
Due date	16.6.1992 18:00
...	...

Assumptions: For this order machine 32 is needed for 8 hours executing plan 1, operation 1.

Schedule for machine 32	**EMCO**
...	...
6.6.1992 08:00-09:00	idle
16.6.1992 09:00-11:00	Order 3489; Plan 1; Op. 2
16.6.1992 11:00-18:00	idle
...	...

ADAPTATION

Adaptation is performed by applying the method associated with the most similar past case found by the retrieval component to the current order. Before applying the method some applicability checks, which are usually incomplete, are made. For the example in table 4-5, the adaptation component would check the applicability of the method "shift an interfering order such an amount of time, that the new order can be scheduled." An example for an applicability check is the verification of the validity of the proposition "the sum of the idle times of the required machine in the relevant time interval is greater than the total duration of the new operation." If the method is applicable, then a suitable rate for shifting the hindering operation must be calculated, the hindering operation must be rescheduled, and the new order must be scheduled. If the method is not applicable then another similar old case is searched. If such a case is found, the adaptation tries to apply the method associated with it to the current order. Otherwise either the problem is infeasible or lies beyond the capabilities of the system.

DISCUSSION

In this section several aspects of the system which have not been dealt with above are discussed.

The human interface

One major component of the overall architecture, which has not been discussed above, is the *human interface*. Experience shows that the human interface plays a crucial role in the acceptance of any system and specially of a scheduling system. The following human interface aspects are of utmost importance for the future implementation of the architecture in a real-world environment:

- The human scheduler has to have full control over the scheduling task. The system is to be more of an assistant making intelligent suggestion than a fully automated system. Ideally, the system would be integrated into a commercially available interactive scheduling tool which allows schedules to be evaluated and manipulated graphically.
- The main source of scheduling know-how is the human scheduler. Thus the interaction of the system with him is of crucial importance to knowledge acquisition. Knowledge acquisition is done continuously through explicit or implicit interaction with the user for learning new cases and scheduling methods.

Matters of human interface will not be discussed in any further detail in this chapter.

Knowledge acquisition

The architecture presented above offers the opportunity of using several *knowledge acquisition* and *machine learning* techniques which makes it suitable as the kernel of a flexible scheduling system.

- Just saving scheduling cases as they become available improves the knowledge of the system about the applicability of methods. This also brings an improvement of system problem solving behaviour.
- The case base is a very good starting point for several induction techniques and for data exploration efforts.
- New methods can be learned either directly or indirectly. The direct version is done by a user-friendly interaction with the human scheduler in which he describes the new method. The indirect version involves logging user behaviour in changing a certain offered schedule and trying to conclude the method he used by generalising the logged behaviour description. Many techniques which could be used in this context are still research topics (abduction, explanation-based learning). The point here is that the architecture offers the flexibility needed to incorporate such methods as they become available.
- The same kind of approach as described in the last point and induction can be used in learning case similarity rules.

Strengths and weaknesses of CBS-1

The major strengths of CBS-1 are as follows:

- It allows the use of several knowledge acquisition and machine learning techniques. This gives it the flexibility which is so important for open-world applications.
- The use of a methods pool makes it possible to integrate different approaches to scheduling in one system.

Its main weaknesses are given below:

- Response times cannot be guaranteed. On the other hand, the scheduling application described in this chapter is not a hard real-time problem and the approach lends itself well to parallel implementation (specially matching cases and similarity assessment) which may result in a sufficiently rapid scheduling process.
- The schedules generated are not optimal in any sense. However, generating optimal schedules is often infeasible anyway, since (1) the goal function is not well defined or changing and (2) the search space is too large, so that efficiency problems emerge.
- The storage of earlier cases and schedules requires quite a large amount of memory. This disadvantage loses its impact when the increasing capacities of secondary storage devices and the dropping prices are considered.
- The case matching process can lead to efficiency problems when the number of available cases increases. This disadvantage, too, loses its impact when the improved performance of modern computer systems and the dropping prices are considered. Most importantly, as already mentioned, the approach lends itself well to parallel implementation. Such implementations are also supported by the improved availability of parallel hardware.

CONCLUSIONS

CBS-1 is not the first system to attack scheduling tasks with case-based reasoning methods. Hennessy and Hinkle (1991), Barletta and Hennessy (1989), and Mark (1989) report of a system called Clavier which performs autoclave management and which shall schedule several autoclave ovens in a real-world environment. However, Clavier does not operate in the domain of dynamic job-shop scheduling and deals only with a small and special set of machines. Miyashita and Sycara (1992) introduce work on the CABINS system which operates in a domain comparable to the one of CBS-1. However, CABINS is concerned with the interactive repair of schedules and not with automatic schedule generation. Inserting a system like CABINS between CBS-1 and production control could lead to a more powerful scheduler capable of dealing with a richer set of scheduling problems.

Future work on CBS-1 will include the evaluation of the system in real-world environment. A further goal is to use fuzzy set and number theory in assessing case similarity.

REFERENCES

Barletta, R., and Hennessy, D. (1989) Case Adaptation in Autoclave Layout Design, *Proceedings of the Case-Based Reasoning Workshop*, Morgan Kaufmann, pp. 203–207.

Bezirgan, A. 1993, *Case-Based Reasoning Systems*, Technical Report, Christian Doppler Laboratory for Expert Systems, Vienna (forthcoming).

Fox, M. S. and Sadeh, N., (1990) Why is Scheduling Difficult? A CSP Perspective, *Proceedings of the 9th European Conference on Artificial Intelligence*, Stockholm, pp. 754–767.

Hennessy, D. and Hinkle, D. (1991) Initial Results from Clavier: A Case-based Autoclave Loading Assistant, *Proceedings of the Case-Based Reasoning Workshop*, Morgan Kaufmann, pp. 225–232.

Kolodner J. and Riesbeck, C. (1989) *Case-Based Reasoning*, Tutorial MA2 at the 11th International Joint Conference on Artificial Intelligence.

Mark, W. (1989) Case-based Reasoning for Autoclave Management, *Proceedings of the Case-Based Reasoning Workshop*, Morgan Kaufmann, pp. 176–180.

Miyashita, K. and Sycara, K. (1992) CABINS: Case-based Interactive Scheduler, *Working Notes, AAAI Spring Symposium Series, Symposium: Practical Approaches to Scheduling and Planning*, pp. 47–51.

Riesbeck, C. K. and Schank, R. C. (1989) *Inside Case-Based Reasoning*, Lawrence Erlbaum.

5

Enhancing Genetic Search to Schedule a Production Unit[*]

Bogdan Filipic
Institut "Josef Stefan", Univerza v Ljubljani

INTRODUCTION

Genetic algorithms (GAs), proposed by Holland (1975), are adaptive search techniques imitating natural selection and genetics. The key idea of GAs is to maintain a set of candidate solutions, called *population*. Members of the population are usually represented as strings (*chromosomes*) and evaluated according to a *fitness function*. The population is initialized at random and evolves in cycles (*generations*). In each generation, the population is affected by genetic operators and selection mechanism. Genetic operators, such as crossover, inversion and mutation, provide information flow among individuals, while selection promotes survival of the fittest population members. By treating string chromosomes, GAs process vast amounts of similarity templates (*schemata*), corresponding to numerous individuals not actually present in the current population. Through recombination and selection, progressively better strings are constructed from the best building blocks from past generations. As a consequence, the evolution process converges to highly fit population members representing near-optimal solutions to the considered problem. Due to robustness, efficiency and low computational cost, GAs are applicable in search, optimization and machine learning (Goldberg, 1989).

Scheduling is among the hardest combinatorial optimization tasks. From the computational complexity theory, most scheduling problems are known to be NP-complete (Garey and Johnson, 1979). In real-world *production scheduling*, problems are usually subject to a number of interacting constraints which harden finding high-quality solutions. Never-

---

[*] The work was originally published in the *Proceedings of the 10th European Conference on Artificial Intelligence* ECAI-92, Vienna, Austria, edited by Bernd Neumann, © 1992 John Wiley & Sons, Ltd. Reprinted by permission of John Wiley & Sons, Ltd.

The research has been supported by Ministry of Science and Technology, Republic of Slovenia, under Grant No. P2-1266-106.

theless, great practical importance makes scheduling a permanently active research area. Among many works related to the field, a comprehensive survey of problem variations can be found in (Conway *et al.*, 1967) where algebraic, probabilistic and computer simulation solving techniques are discussed. Heuristic search and constraint satisfaction approaches to scheduling have been studied intensively by Fox and coworkers (Fox and Sadeh, 1990), (Fox *et al.*, 1989), (Sathi and Fox, 1989). Recently, stochastic optimization methods have been applied to scheduling as well (Kovacic, 1991), (Zhou *et al.*, 1991).

As a general purpose optimization method GAs have already been tested in scheduling. The first attempt was reported by Davis (1985), who considered a hypothetical job-shop problem. He introduced a complex coding based on time independent preference lists for assigning tasks to work stations. Candidate solutions were decoded and evaluated through the simulation of the job-shop operations. Subsequent works include job sequencing with GAs (Cleveland and Smith, 1989), (Whitley *et al.*, 1989), where representation and recombination operators suitable for TSP-like problems were applied to optimize the overall processing time on real production lines. Recently, problem-specific chromosome representation and recombination operators for job-shop scheduling have been devised to enhance the performance of the algorithm (Bagchi *et al.*, 1991). In (Nakano and Yamada, 1991), an original binary representation of schedules combined with unique approaches to evaluation and survival was shown to fasten the algorithm convergence and improve the solution quality. Finally, global search provided by a GA and local expert search were integrated in an optimizer for laboratory equipment scheduling (Syswerda and Palmucci, 1991).

This chapter presents the development, implementation and evaluation of a GA to solve a highly constrained real-world scheduling problem. The objective was to *optimize energy consumption* on a group of machines in a textile factory. To tackle the problem, the traditional GA scheme was adjusted in several ways. The two phases of the algorithm where the construction of candidate solutions takes place, i.e. population initialization and string recombination, were carefully designed to eliminate illegal solutions. A unique genetic operator has been devised, adhering features of both multiple-point crossover and mutation. In addition, the elitist model and local improvement of candidate solutions were incorporated into the algorithm and their effect on the solution quality explored. The subsequent sections present the problem, the design of the scheduler and its evaluation.

THE SCHEDULING PROBLEM

Overview

We have been concerned with optimizing energy consumption in a production unit of a textile factory. The production unit includes 15 machines of identical functionality. The machines, however, differ in performance and, as a consequence, the time needed to carry out a particular job varies from 5.5 to 10 hours, depending on the machine. The machines operate according to a daily production plan that prescribes the number of jobs to be performed on each machine. The daily plan is occasionally modified, but typically remains unchanged over a number of days. Table 5-1 shows the configuration of the unit, the performance of the machines, and an example of a daily plan, requiring 33 jobs altogether.

Table 5-1: Overview of the production unit

Machines	Execution time [hours]	Daily plan [jobs / machine]
1, 2, 3, 4, 5, 6	10.0	2
7,8	10.0	1
9,10	5.5	3
11	5.5	2
12, 13, 14	6.5	3
15	6.5	2

Each job requires a 30 minute initialization procedure to be performed by staff before start. Working days in the production unit last from 6 am to 10 pm. Consequently, the initialization of the first jobs cannot start before 6:00, and their execution not before 6:30 in the morning. Similarly, last initializations must be carried out no later than in the period between 9:30 and 10:00 in the evening. Jobs eventually prepared at 10 pm are left to execute overnight together with all running jobs not finished until the end of the working day. There is another strong constraint that must be considered during the production process: according to limitations in personnel, the initialization of only two jobs can take place simultaneously.

Given a daily plan, a schedule is to be constructed that assigns setup times to jobs. Obviously, besides accomplishing the daily plan and satisfying time and personnel constraints, a legal schedule must encounter interrelations among jobs executed on the same machine. For example, when a certain job is delayed, subsequent jobs on the same machine have to be delayed as well. Similarly, a job started on a slower machine towards the end of a working day may still be executing at the beginning of the next working day. This again delays the remaining jobs on the machine.

Optimization criterion

The schedules are to be optimized with respect to energy consumption. The effective power of each of the machines in the production unit is 30 kW and the energy is only being consumed when a machine is executing a job. In the remaining factory units, there are devices that are not subject to scheduling, but also contribute to the overall energy consumption. They are called background consumers and a daily diagram of their instantaneous power $P_b(t)$ is available, assuming constant demand over 15 minute intervals. For the entire factory, there is a prescribed maximum demand limit $P_{max}(t)$, also called target load. The target load should be exceeded as little as possible, since the excess is paid at extra cost. Therefore, the quality of a schedule can be expressed in terms of the target load excess caused by machines in the observed production unit. Formally, at any moment, the contribution of the production unit actual demand P_u, to the target load excess is the following:

$$\Delta P = \begin{cases} P_u, & P_b \geq P_{max}, \\ P_u + P_b - P_{max}, & P_b < P_{max} \ \& \ P_u + P_b > P_{max} \\ 0, & \text{otherwise} \end{cases}$$

Schedule cost, measured in kWh, can thus be obtained as the corresponding energy consumption, i.e. the integral of power demand ΔP, over the entire day. The optimization task is to find the minimum cost schedule of jobs for the production unit.

Problem space discretization

The initial step in resolving the problem was the selection of an appropriate time scale. Given the execution times of the jobs and the setup time, a 30 minute interval was chosen to be considered as a time unit in the optimization process. Accordingly, the working day was divided into 32 time intervals and each setup took one interval.

After discretization, schedule construction was treated as assigning setup time intervals to jobs. For the presented daily plan that requires 33 jobs, there are $32^{33} \approx 4.7 \cdot 10^{49}$ alternative assignments altogether, not considering the constraints. This figure can be reduced by taking into account interrelations among jobs to be performed on the same machine. Let t_{min} and t_{max} denote the beginning and the end of a working day, respectively, and suppose machine m has to execute N_m jobs, each taking $SetupTime$ to initialize and $ExecTime_m$ to execute. For j-th job on machine m, we can then calculate the earliest and the latest setup time allowed, ES_{mj} and LS_{mj}, as follows:

$$ES_{mj} \ = \ t_{min} + (j - 1) \, (SetupTime + ExecTime_m)$$

$$LS_{mj} \ = \ t_{max} - SetupTime - (N_m - j) \, (SetupTime + ExecTime_m)$$

For each job there are $LS_{mj} - ES_{mj} + 1$ possible setup times, resulting in approximately $2.9 \cdot 10^{31}$ alternative assignments for the above 33 job daily plan.

GENETIC SCHEDULER DESIGN

Chromosomal representation of schedules

GAs require candidate solutions to be encoded in a way that ensures useful building blocks to emerge through recombination and selection. Typically, string representation is used, where chromosomes have either binary or symbolic gene values. In our approach, schedules are represented as strings of length N, where N is the total number of jobs to be executed daily. The value at i-th string position denotes setup time of the i-th job and can only be selected from the interval between the earliest and the latest setup time for that job. Moreover, the constraints stemming from job interrelations and personnel limitations also have to be satisfied. In other words, the GA maintains only legal candidate solutions.

The chosen representation is straightforward in that chromosomes directly represent the subject of optimization. Moreover, dealing only with legal solutions makes defining the fitness of candidate solutions easier. No penalty method needs to be involved to assign additional cost to individuals violating the constraints. The difficulty with penalties is that it is hard to distinguish between legal low-quality solutions and illegal solutions violating only few constraints. On the other hand, the direct representation is not easy to utilize. As realized in (Tsang and Warwick, 1990), where constraint satisfaction optimization problems were also solved with GAs, processing only legal solutions requires restrictive population initialization and recombination operators.

Population initialization

A GA typically starts from a randomly generated population of candidate solutions. In our algorithm, schedules are initialized by randomly assigning setup times to jobs and simultaneously checking the constraints. This is done by upholding two data structures when creating a chromosome. For each job, a list of currently available setup time intervals is maintained, and for every interval from t_{min} to t_{max}, the number of machines being initialized is kept in another list. The setup time lists initially contain all values between the earliest and the latest setup time possible for each job. The jobs are scheduled by picking values from these lists uniformly at random. When time t is assigned to a job, the number of machines being initialized at time t is increased by 1, and, if reaching the limit of 2, time t is deleted from setup time lists of all jobs to prevent additional jobs from being scheduled at time t. Next, interactions among the jobs are considered. If a job is delayed with respect to its earliest setup time, corresponding delays are computed for the remaining jobs to be executed on the same machine and their setup time lists are reduced. The entire schedule is built iteratively by repeating the above steps for each job.

However, the described construction fails when no setup intervals are left free for a job after scheduling a certain number of jobs. In such case, no backtracking is applied, but instead a partially built chromosome is discarded and the creation of an individual restarts from scratch.

Fitness function

Schedule cost represents the objective function according to which candidate solutions are optimized. For the purpose of the GA approach, the objective function is mapped to a fitness function that serves to rank population members in the selection step. Fitness is usually scaled to avoid premature convergence of the population, caused by highly fit individuals randomly arising in an early stage of the evolution.

The genetic scheduler assigns fitness $f(x)$ to an individual x representing a schedule with cost $C(x)$ in the following way:

$$f(x) = \left(\frac{C_{max} - C(x)}{C_{max} - C_{min}} \right)^k$$

where C_{min} and C_{max} are schedule cost lower and upper bounds, and k is a fitness function parameter. Obtained empirically, schedule cost bounds serve to normalize fitness values. By tuning the parameter k, we actually prescribe how differences in the objective function among individuals are treated. Increasing k, while $k > 1$, causes a wider and wider range of high cost solutions to be assigned low fitness, and only the best solutions to receive distinguished high fitness values. Although bringing an additional parameter to genetic optimization, this mechanism helps in preserving diversity of a population.

Problem-specific crossover operator

Much of the power of a GA arises from recombination, provided mainly by the crossover operator. Traditional "blind" crossover implementations, such as simple, multiple-point or uniform crossover, cannot be applied directly to the considered problem as they do not respect constraints posed on schedules. To serve our needs, a unique recombinaton operator was devised. The new operator can be viewed as an adjusted version of the multiple-point crossover, performing the role of both crossover and mutation.

Traditional multiple-point crossover generates two offspring from two parents by first randomly selecting a given number of crossing sites and then exchanging alternate pairs of equally positioned sections between the strings.

In contrast, our crossover produces one offspring from two parent strings. It operates in the following manner. First, the crossing sites are selected in the same way as with the multiple-point crossover, and one of the parents is selected randomly to play a dominant role in mating. Next, alternate sections of genes are copied directly from the dominant parent to the offspring. Finally, the genes that are to be contributed by the nondominant parent are checked in turn for consistency. If a gene value keeps the partially built schedule legal, it is passed on to the offspring, otherwise a value is chosen randomly from the setup times still available for the related job. The random selection of certain gene values adds the mutation component to the operator functionality.

Like schedule initialization, generating new schedules by crossover is utilized by updating lists of available setup times for jobs and the number of machines being initialized at each time interval. As well, when crossover fails to produce a legal schedule, new attempts are repeated until recombination succeeds.

Elitism and local improvement

Elitism is aimed to preserve the best individuals in a population. In function optimization, elitism was applied with varied success (de Jong, 1975). In our algorithm, this principle is implemented in a very pragmatic fashion. If the fittest member of a newly created population is worse than the best individual found so far, the worst individual in the current population is replaced with the best-so-far individual.

Integration of genetic search and local improvement of candidate solutions has already been studied on the traveling salesman problem, e.g. (Jog et al., 1989), (Mühlenbein et al., 1988). In addition, a GA including local improvement of individuals was shown to outperform a blind GA on a hypothetical problem of scheduling independent tasks (Filipic, 1991). Since similar effect was expected in the production unit scheduling, a local improvement procedure was designed and applied to individuals created at the recombination step in every generation. Using the hill-climbing principle, the improvement procedure upgrades a schedule iteratively. An iteration step consists of finding the job whose setup time change most improves the schedule, and implementing this change in the schedule. Setup times checked for improvement are those remaining in setup time lists of jobs after schedule construction. Iteration steps are repeated until no further improvement is possible.

The order of operations carried out in each generation is the following. First, selection and recombination take place as in traditional GAs. Then local improvement of individuals is performed, and finally, the elitism is utilized.

EXPERIMENTAL EVALUATION

The genetic scheduler has been thoroughly evaluated. Experiments were designed to investigate the effect of the algorithm extensions. For that purpose, four versions of the scheduler were tested: the pure GA with no extensions, the elitist GA, the GA with local improvement, and the GA including both elitism and local improvement. To compare the results, the problem space has been also searched randomly using the schedule initialization and local improvement procedures from the GA approach. Finally, the obtained schedules were compared to manually constructed schedules currently in use in the production unit.

The random search experiments consisted of finding and evaluating 10,000 legal schedules, while GAs were tested in 50 runs each. The following GA parameter values were adopted after some initial experiments:

- function evaluations, i.e. generations × population size: 30 × 30 in GAs without local improvement, and 20 × 20 in GAs including local improvement,
- crossover probability: 0.6,
- crossing sites: 2,
- fitness function parameter k: 5.

The best individual from the final population was adopted as a result of each GA run. Table 5-2 gives the final overview of results for the 33 jobs from the *production plan* in Table 5-1.

Table 5-2: Results of schedule optimization

OPTIMIZATION METHOD	SCHEDULE COST [kWh]			
	minimum	average	maximum	st.dev.
Random search	1004.00	1301.46	1666.25	103.25
Random search with local impr.	970.75	1045.25	1148.75	25.35
Pure GA	996.50	1027.42	1071.50	16.64
Elitist GA	948.00	1012.67	1047.00	19.53
GA with local improvement	959.00	984.58	1000.50	7.89
Elitist GA with local impr.	951.50	976.82	994.75	10.19

As expected, the results improve by adding new features to the algorithm and the best performance is achieved with the scheduler including both extensions. The cost of manually constructed schedules is about 1300 kWh, and is thus comparable with the average cost of randomly created schedules in our experiments. Evidently, the obtained results represent substantial improvement in energy consumption control of the unit.

During the experiments, the efficiency of the schedule initialization procedure and the performance of the crossover operator were also evaluated. Schedule initialization required 27.9 attempts on average to create a legal schedule (statistics over 10,000 obtained legal schedules), what indicates a low ratio of legal states in the problem space. The crossover performance was measured in terms of trials needed to successfully combine two string chromosomes and the ratio of randomly selected gene values. The average for the above GA experiments is 1.7 attempts per successful recombination and 5.9 % gene values set at random. The first outcome shows that not much time was spent on unsuccessful recombination attempts, while the second matches the usual probability of using mutation as a separate operator.

The algorithms were programmed in Pascal and the experiments run on a 80486/33 MHz personal computer, taking roughly 10 minutes per run for GAs without local improvement, and about 20 minutes for GAs including the improvement.

CONCLUSION

We have presented the development and evaluation of a GA designed to schedule jobs in a textile production unit. The traditional GA approach was adjusted to handle the optimization of schedules with respect to energy consumption. A direct representation of schedules was used in the algorithm, strictly preserving legal candidate solutions. The population initialization was specially designed and a new recombination operator was introduced, acting similarly to the multiple-point crossover and performing the role of mutation at the same time. Elitism and local improvement were added to the basic algorithm to improve the results.

Experiments confirm the relevance of the approach. The scheduler generates high-quality results and the required computational costs are tolerable for the particular production environment. The gained experience will be used in designing GA-based resource optimization systems for complex environments where integration with other techniques is desired.

REFERENCES

Bagchi, S., Uckun, S. Miyabe, Y. and Kawamura, K. (1991) Exploring Problem Specific Recombination Operators for Job Shop Scheduling, *Proceedings of the 4th International Conference on Genetic Algorithms*, Morgan Kaufmann, pp. 10–17.

Cleveland, G. A. and Smith, S. F. (1989) Using Genetic Algorithms to Schedule Flow Shop Releases, *Proceedings of the 3rd International Conference on Genetic Algorithms*, Morgan Kaufmann, pp. 61–69.

Conway, R. W., Maxwell, W. L. and Miller, L. W. (1967) *Theory of Scheduling*, Addison-Wesley.

Davis, L. (1985) Job Shop Scheduling with Genetic Algorithms, *Proceedings of the International Conference on Genetic Algorithms and Their Applications*, Lawrence Erlbaum, pp. 136–140.

De Jong, K. A. (1975) *An Analysis of the Behavior of a Class of Genetic Adaptive Systems*, Ph. D. thesis, University of Michigan.

Filipic, B. (1991) Scheduling with Genetic Algorithms, *Proceedings of the 13th International Conference on Information Technology Interfaces*, Cavtat, Croatia, pp. 161–166.

Fox, M.S. and Sadeh, N. (1990) Why is Scheduling Difficult? A CSP Perspective. *Proceedings of the 9th European Conference on Artificial Intelligence* (ECAI-90) Stockholm, pp. 754–767.

Fox, M.S., Sadeh, N. and C. Baykan (1989) Constrained Heuristic Search, *Proceedings of the 11th International Joint Conference on Artificial Intelligence* (IJCAI-89), Detroit, pp. 309–315.

Garey, M. R. and Johnson, D. S. (1979) *Computers and Intractability. A Guide to the Theory of NP-Completeness*, New York: Freeman.

Goldberg, D. E. (1989) *Genetic Algorithms in Search, Optimization and Machine Learning*, Addison-Wesley.

Holland, J. H. (1975) *Adaptation in Natural and Artificial Systems*, Ann Arbor: University of Michigan Press.

Jog, P., Suh, J. Y. and van Gucht, D. (1989) The Effects of Population Size, Heuristic Crossover and Local Improvement on a Genetic Algorithm for the Traveling Salesman Problem, *Proceedings of the 3rd International Conference on Genetic Algorithms*, Morgan Kaufmann, pp. 110–114.

Kovacic, M. (1991) Markovian Neural Networks, *Biological Cybernetics* **64** pp. 337–342.

Mühlenbein, H., Gorges-Schleuter, M. and Krämer, O. (1988) Evolution Algorithms in Combinatorial Optimization, *Parallel Computing* **7**, pp. 65–85.

Nakano, R. and Yamada, T. (1991) Conventional Genetic Algorithm for Job Shop Problems, *Proceedings of the 4th International Conference on Genetic Algorithms*, Morgan Kaufmann, pp. 474–477.

Sathi, A. and Fox, M.S. (1989) *Constraint-directed Negotiation of Resource Reallocation*, Technical Report CMU-RI-TR-89-12, The Robotics Institute, Carnegie Mellon University, Pittsburgh, PA.

Syswerda, G. and Palmucci, J. (1991) The Application of Genetic Algorithms to Resource Scheduling, *Proceedings of the 4th International Conference on Genetic Algorithms*, Morgan Kaufmann, pp. 502–508.

Tsang, E. P. K. and Warwick, T. (1990) Applying Genetic Algorithms to Constraint Satisfaction Optimization Problems, *Proceedings of the 9th European Conference on Artificial Intelligence*, Stockholm, pp. 649–654.

Whitley, D., Starkweather, T. and Fuquay, D. (1989) Scheduling Problems and Traveling Salesmen: The genetic Edge Recombination Operator, *Proceedings of the 3rd International Conference on Genetic Algorithms*, Morgan Kaufmann, pp. 61–69.

Zhou, D. N. Cherkassky, V. Baldwin, T. R. and Olson, D. E. (1991) A Neural Network Approach to Job-shop Scheduling, *IEEE Transactions on Neural Networks* **2** (1), pp. 175–179.

6

Distributed Genetic Algorithms for Resource Allocation

Claude Muller, Evan H. Magill, Patrick Prosser and D. Geoffrey Smith
University of Strathclyde

INTRODUCTION

A large number of *telecommunications* applications can be regarded as problems of *resource allocation* (i.e scheduling): design (Rowles *et al.*, 1991), work force management (Azarmi, 1991) and traffic management (Lusher, 1990). These applications are subject to severe constraints. For instance, mobile phone systems have to cope with a limited bandwidth and the allocation of the different frequencies has to be managed efficiently in order to serve a maximum number of customers. Also, telecommunications applications evolve in a highly dynamic environment and the search space is altered frequently. The third main problem faced by telecommunications applications is that the size of the search space can be very large. Therefore, efficient problem-solving techniques are required to address the severe demands of a telecommunications application.

Resource allocation can be viewed as the task of deciding what happens where and when (Parunak and van Dyke, 1987) and can be represented as a *constraint satisfaction problem* (CSP). A simple CSP consists of a set of variables and a set of constraints (e.g temporal, spatial) acting between the variables. Each variable has a domain containing values that may be assigned to the variable. The objective is to assign a value to each variable from its domain such that all constraints are satisfied. Usually, CSPs are employed to represent problems where the solutions depend upon a large number of constraints, e.g design, planning and scheduling.

There are a number of techniques which can be used to solve CSPs. Conventional techniques such as tree-searches and consistency algorithms can be guaranteed to find a solution if one exists. However, the *resource allocation problem* is known to be NP-complete (Garey and Johnson, 1979). This means that in the worst case, exponential time is required to find a solution. Hence, tree-searches and consistency algorithms may fail to provide a solution in reasonable time, even with the support of advanced features such as pre-processing techniques (e.g arc or path consistencies) or heuristics (e.g variables and values orderings). Therefore, different approaches must be considered for large scheduling problems. Neural networks (Minton *et al.*, 1990) and genetic algorithms (GAs) (Davis, 1990), (Tsang and Warwick, 1990) are currently under investigation. This chapter is concerned with the second approach (i.e. genetic algorithms) and the following section discusses such algorithms.

GENETIC ALGORITHMS

Genetic algorithms can be viewed as a class of optimisation methods based on natural principles (i.e. evolution and selection) (Davis, 1990). GAs exhibit a form of composite intelligence; they can perform a complex optimisation task simply by manipulating a population of bit-strings. Each bit-string represents a point of the search space.

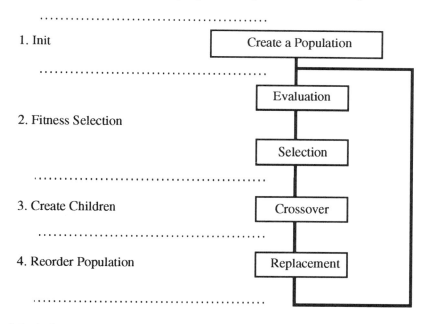

Figure 6-1: A simple genetic algorithm

As illustrated in figure 6-1, the process of a GA consists of the following steps. A population of bit-strings is created randomly. The different bit-strings are evaluated with a fitness function. Two bit-strings are selected with a probability depending on their *evaluation*; the bit-strings with the highest evaluation being more likely to be selected. The two bit-strings are then manipulated with different genetic-like operators (i.e. crossover, mutation and inversion) in order to create two children which then replace two strings of the previous generation. The cycle "evaluation, selection, crossover and replacement" is repeated until an optimal solution has been found or the algorithm reaches its time limit.

While classical techniques move from point to point in the search space, genetic algorithms work with a population of candidate solutions. This characteristic, associated with their stochastic nature, may help genetic algorithms to deal with large search spaces. The principal limitation of genetic algorithms is the incompleteness of the algorithm. Due to its stochastic nature, a genetic algorithm is not guaranteed to find the optimal solution, i.e. it is not guaranteed to visit every single state of the search space. Also, the reasoning of a genetic algorithm cannot be traced, the algorithm cannot provide explanations or ways to relax the problem.

A SIMPLE PROTOTYPE

As a first stage, a simple prototype is presented. The genetic algorithm is represented by an instance of the class genetic-agent. See the appendix for a detailed presentation of the object representations. A process is associated with this object. The different functions of the process are defined by the object. The user has complete control over the process, which can be initialised, started, suspended, resumed or terminated.

This prototype has been tested with the following scheduling problem (see the Appendix for Gantt charts representing the problem and one of its solutions). The principal task of the genetic operator is to manipulate a population of bit-strings (i.e. chromosomes), representing candidate solutions to the above scheduling problem and to find a schedule which maximises (or minimises) a given function. For this problem, the objective is to reduce the total tardiness of the job set. The following table details the operations which make up the job set. The domain of an operation represents the set of possible values for the start-time of the operation.

Table 6-1: Operations of job set

operations	A	B	C	D	E	F	G	H	I	J
duration	10	10	10	10	40	20	10	40	25	25
domain	20-50	20-40	30-40	20-99	50-200	80-200	100-200	0-200	0-150	0-150

These different operations form a job set which has to be performed on a single resource which can only handle one operation at a time.

The representation employed for the chromosome is as follows:

$$o_1\ s_1,\ o_2\ s_2,\ \dots,\ o_N\ s_N$$

This is a simple order-based representation. o_i refers to the ith operation to be instantiated and s_i is the start-time allocated to the operation.

Each chromosome of the initial population is created randomly and represents a possible ordering of the job set.

The *fitness function* maps the chromosome into a schedule. The following procedure is repeated for each operation present in the chromosome: the algorithm assigns the earliest possible start time. If a start time cannot be found in the domain of the operation, the algorithm relaxes the problem and allocates a late start time.

The different chromosomes are ranked with respect to the total tardiness of their schedule. The probability of a chromosome being selected as a parent is directly proportional to its rank in the population.

Once the two parents have been selected, an order-based crossover is used to produce two offsprings. For reasons of simplicity, there is no mutation and no inversion.

Finally, the two chromosomes with the worst fitness are deleted from the population and the two offsprings are included in the population. This cycle is repeated until either an optimal solution (i.e. no tardiness) has been found or the maximum number of generations has been reached.

The following table presents one optimal solution (i.e. no tardiness) found by the genetic algorithm (with a population of 20 chromosomes).

Table 6-2: Optimal solution

operations	A	B	C	D	E	F	G	H	I	J
start-time	50	40	30	60	175	80	165	100	0	140

DISTRIBUTED GAS FOR RESOURCE ALLOCATION

This section proposes a scheduling system based on a distributed architecture. It consists of a shared memory and a set of agents In the initial system, each agent is a genetic algorithm. Each agent receives the entire problem and cooperates with other agents to solve the problem in hand.

This system is related to the work in (Clearwater *et al.*, 1991) which claims that a set of cooperating agents solving constraint satisfaction problems can achieve remarkable results in terms of computational effort. More precisely, it claims that a superlinear speedup with respect to the number of agents can be achieved. The principal goals of this distributed scheduling system are as follows:

- To gain a computational advantage with the cooperation of several agents solving the same problem.
- To permit the solution of a problem from different point of view. This appears to be essential in solving problems with conflicting objectives such as scheduling problems.
- To permit the solution of a problem at different levels of reasoning.

Different perspectives and levels of reasoning among the agents are achieved through the fitness functions. Each agent can have a different fitness function. The main tasks of the fitness function are (1) find a schedule, i.e. translate the chromosome into a schedule and (2) evaluate the schedule.

Each agent can employ different "translation" techniques to map the chromosome into a schedule. One agent may attempt to schedule the operations with an *operation-based* perspective, similar to the strategy adopted by ISIS (Fox and Smith, 1984) whereas a second agent may employ a *resource-based* strategy, similar to the one employed by OPIS (Smith *et al.*, 1989).

Moreover, the different sets of rules employed to schedule the operations can also vary in terms of granularity. Some agents (i.e. *shallow* agents) may attempt to provide fast non-optimal schedules whereas other agents (i.e. *deep* agents) may involve more processing but deliver schedules of better quality. The reason behind these multiple levels of reasoning is to provide an answer at any time. If interrupted, the global system is able to provide an answer. The quality of this answer (i.e. schedule) increases with time as deep agents transmit their best element to the shared memory.

The second task of the fitness function is to evaluate the chromosomes and to rank them with respect to a certain objective function. The different agents could use a common objective function or each agent could use a specific objective function. Further investigation is required to define the benefits and drawbacks of each solution.

The shared memory is a means of communication between the different agents. All the agents employ a common representation and they cooperate by exchanging their fittest chromosomes. The shared memory holds the fittest chromosomes of each agent. Every agent can have access to this pool of "super-individuals" and incorporate them in its local population. Thus, the shallow agents have access to chromosomes built at a deeper level and can focus their search. Additionally, agents have access to schedules built with a different perspective.

EXTENSIONS

One of the limitations of genetic algorithms is the incompleteness of the algorithm. Due to its stochastic nature, a genetic algorithm is not guaranteed to find a solution. Clearly, the genetic algorithm does not perform a systematic exploration of the search space Observe that this is also the main advantage of the genetic algorithm. Therefore, a natural extension to this distributed system would be to integrate agents based on deterministic techniques. The ideal would be to develop and integrate an agent based upon an algorithm capable of exploiting and improving the schedules achieved by different genetic algorithms. The repair algorithm developed by Minton could be a good candidate (Minton *et al.*, 1990).

A second limitation of this initial system is that it does not respond to changes in the environment. Different events may occur within a dynamic environment, such as modification or deletion of an operation, addition of a resource or creation of a *temporal constraint* between two operations. A scheduling system must address these different situations. Hence, a genetic algorithm using a dynamic length representation is being developed to answer the dynamic aspect of scheduling problems.

CONCLUSION

This chapter has presented a scheduling system which consists of a collection of genetic algorithms cooperating and exchanging information via a shared memory. It is claimed that a distributed system is an appropriate solution for resource allocation problems. Computational advantage, multiple perspectives and multiple levels of reasoning are the main advantages expected from the system.

REFERENCES

Azarmi, N. (1991) A Knowledge Based Resource Scheduler for Network Maintenance, *British Telecom Technology Journal* **9** (3).

Clearwater, S.C., Huberman, B.A. and Hogg, T. (1991) Cooperative Solution of Constraint Satisfaction Problems, *Science* **254**, pp. 1181–1183.

Davis, *Handbook of Genetic Algorithms*, New York: Van Nostrand Reinhold.

Fox, M.S. and Smith, S.F. (1984) ISIS, a Knowledge-based System for Factory Scheduling, *Expert Systems* **1**, part 1, pp. 25–49.

Garey, M.R. and Johnson, D.S. (1979) *Computers and Intractability. A Guide to the Theory of NP-Completeness*, New York: Freeman.

Lusher, E.P. (1990) AI and Communications Network Design, *AI Expert*, August.

Minton, S., Johnston, M.D., Philips, A.B. and Laird, P. (1990) Solving Large-scale Constraint Satisfaction and Scheduling Problems Using a Heuristic Repair Method, *Proceedings of the 8th National Conference on Artificial Intelligence* (AAAI-90), pp. 17–24.

Parunak, H. and Van Dyke (1987) Why Scheduling is Hard (and how to Do it Anyway)?, *Proceedings of the 1987 material handling focus*, Georgia Institute of Technology.

Rowles, C., Leckie, C., Liu, H. and Wen, W. (1991) Automating the Design of Telecommunication Distribution Networks, *Proceedings of the 1st International Conference on Artificial Intelligence in Design*, Edinburgh, Scotland, UK.

Smith, S.F., Ow, P.S. and Potvin, J.Y. (1990) OPIS: an Opportunistic Factory Scheduling System, *Proceedings of the 3rd International Conference on Industrial and Engineering Applications of Artificial Intelligence and Expert systems* (IEA/AIE-90), Charleston, SC.

Tsang, E.P.K. and Warwick, T. (1990) Applying Genetic Algorithms to Constraint Satisfaction Optimization Problems, *Proceedings of the 9th European Conference on Artificial Intelligence* ECAI-90, Stockholm, Sweden, pp. 649–654.

APPENDIX

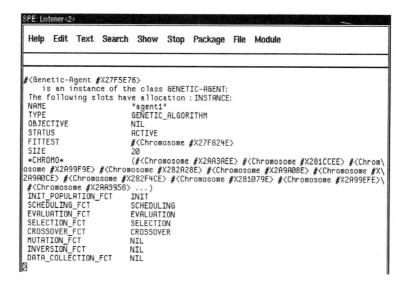

Figure 6-2: Object representation of a genetic agent

Each instance of the class genetic-agent (see figure 6-2) has the following slots:

name: A unique name given by the user, when the agent is created, for manipulation purposes.

type: The type of the agent (e.g genetic algorithm, repair algorithm).

objective: A documentation string describing the objective of the agent (e.g "reduce the total tardiness").

status: The status of the process associated with the object (i.e init, active, inactive or terminated).

fittest: The fittest element of the population.

size: The size of the population, i.e. number of chromosomes in the local population.

chromo: The list of chromosomes present in the local population.

init_population_fct: The name of the function called by the process to create the population.

scheduling_fct: The name of the function called by the process to "translate" (i.e. map) the order-based chromosome into a schedule.

evaluation_fct: The name of the function called by the process to evaluate the schedules.

selection_fct: The name of the function called by the process to select two parents from the population.

crossover_fct: The name of the function called by the process to perform the crossover operation.

mutation_fct: The name of the function called by the process to perform the mutation operation.

inversion_fct: The name of the function called by the process to the inversion operation.

data_collection_fct: The name of the function called by the process to collect data during the seach.

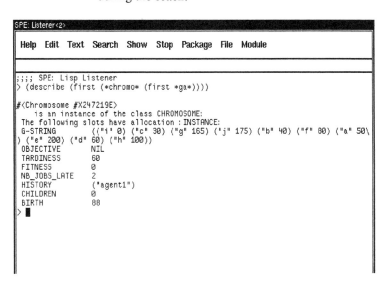

```
SPE: Listerer<2>

 Help  Edit  Text  Search  Show  Stop  Package  File  Module


;;;; SPE: Lisp Listener
> (describe (first (*chromo* (first *ga*))))

#<Chromosome #X247219E>
     is an instance of the class CHROMOSOME:
  The following slots have allocation : INSTANCE:
  G-STRING        (("i" 0) ("c" 30) ("g" 165) ("j" 175) ("b" 40) ("f" 80) ("a" 50\
) ("e" 200) ("d" 60) ("h" 100))
  OBJECTIVE       NIL
  TARDINESS       60
  FITNESS         0
  NB_JOBS_LATE    2
  HISTORY         ("agent1")
  CHILDREN        0
  BIRTH           88
> ▊
```

Figure 6-3: Object representation of a chromosome

Each instance of the class chromosome (see figure 6-3) has the following slots:

g-string: An order-based representation of the problem. Each couple of this string represents an operation and its allocated start-time.

objective: The objective of the agent dealing with the chromosome.

tardiness: The total tardiness of the jobs set.

fitness: The fitness of the chromosome.

nb_jobs_late: The number of operations that the scheduling function has not scheduled properly, i.e. number of operations with a late start time.

history: A list that traces the path followed by the chromosome. When the chromosome is entering the population of an agent, the name of this agent is pushed into this list.

children: The number of children of the chromosome.

birth: The date of the birth of the chromosome, i.e. number of cycles between the creation of the population (i.e. date 0) and the birth of the chromosome.

The two Gantt charts displayed below represent the problem employed to test the prototype detailed in Section 3 and one of its optimal solutions. The current domains (i.e. domains of possible start-times) of the different operations are represented by a set of large
horizontal white boxes. Within the first large white box, a smaller box represents the
duration of the operation. When the operation is allocated a start-time, a solid black bar
shows the scheduling decision, the length of the bar corresponds to the duration of the
operation, its position represents the start-time of the operation.

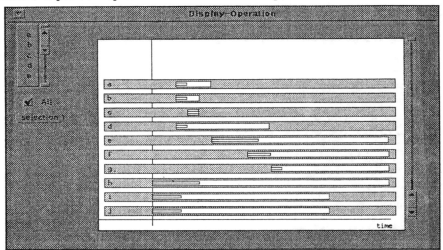

Figure 6-4: Current domains and durations of the operations

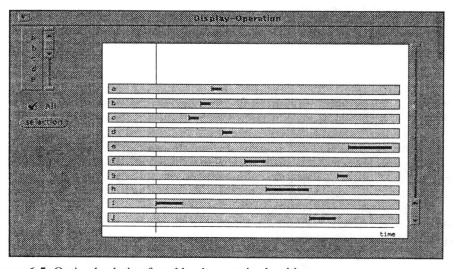

Figure 6-5: Optimal solution found by the genetic algorithm

7

A Multi-agent Model for the Resource Allocation Problem: a Reactive Approach*

Khaled Ghédira and Gérard Verfaillie
ONERA - CERT, Toulouse

CONTEXT AND MOTIVATIONS

The aim of our research is to show the advantage of distributed problem-solving based on an optimization process like *simulated annealing*. This advantage is exhibited through the example of conflicts between tasks to be allocated to shared resources with a limited capacity (*allocation problem*), for which a model composed of simple and reactive agents was developed. The good experimental results encouraged us to deepen the approach and to extend it to the revision problem using the reactive characteristic of the agents. This chapter: presents briefly that model, and introduces an efficient way to deal with the revision problem, which is a real headache for the centralized approaches.

Our problem, which is to assign tasks to shared resources, can be stated in the following manner:

- let $(r_1, ..., r_j, ..., r_{nr})$ be nr shared resources, each of them having a limited capacity;
- let $(t_1, ..., t_i, ..., t_{nt})$ be nt tasks;
- each task t_i can choose one of the p_i resources $(r_{i1}, ..., r_{ij}, ..., r_{ip_i})$;
- it needs one and only one;
- if a task t_i is allocated to a resource r_j, it consumes a quantity q_{ij} of this resource.

This problem is a sub-problem of the general planning problem and more precisely of the scheduling problem. It is known to be highly combinatorial (NP-Complete in the case of shared resources). Therefore this problem is an excellent experimental benchmark.

---

* The work was originally published in the *Proceedings of the 10th European Conference on Artificial Intelligence* ECAI-92, Vienna, Austria, edited by Bernd Neumann, © 1992 John Wiley & Sons, Ltd. Reprinted by permission of John Wiley & Sons, Ltd.

Our aim is to allocate a maximum number of tasks and so to satisfy as many tasks as possible. The number of satisfied tasks is called satisfaction.

The idea is to tackle this problem, which has always been discussed in terms of tree search structures, by a multi-agent approach (Bond and Gasser, 1988), (Durfee *et al.*, 1987). This approach is associated to a stochastic process, the simulated annealing algorithm (Aarts and van Laarhoven, 1987), (Aarts and Korst, 1989), (Kirkpatrick *et al.*, 1983), (Weisbuch, 1989), in order to avoid the trap of satisfaction local maxima (the satisfaction is the equivalent to the opposite of the energy in the classic simulated annealing algorithm).

Thus, we developed a multi-agent model (Ghédira and Verfaillie, 1991a), (Ghédira and Verfaillie, 1991b) and resumed the experimental and theoretical results which were established in the connectionnist models framework (Aarts and Korst, 1989), (Feller, 1950), so as to formulate the model in terms of Markov chains, to prove its asymptotic convergence towards an optimal solution and finally to speed up the simulated annealing algorithm by:

- a totally distributed implementation,
- a rapid cooling scheme,
- heuristics and
- a forced termination mechanism.

The implementation was developed with ACTALK (Briot, 1989), an Object-Based Concurrent Programming language in the SMALLTALK-80 environment. The good experimental results encouraged us to deepen this approach and to extend it to the revision problem.

THE MULTI-AGENT MODEL

The model involves Task and Resource agents in interactions, each of them seeking its maximal satisfaction (following the Eco-Problem solving concepts (Ferber, 1990): an approach based on interactions between agents, each of them seeking its own satisfaction). However, that is not sufficient: an Interface is necessary between the society of agents and the user essentially to detect that the problem is solved by the society. Consequently, a third and last class called Machine was created, which contains only one individual.

In order to simplify, we have defined the agent's general behaviour independently of its class: if agent is satisfied then satisfaction behavior, else unsatisfaction behaviour.

Each unsatisfied Task agent chooses one of the possible Resource agents, requires to be allocated to it and waits for the answer.

Each Resource agent tries to maximize its local satisfaction within the limits of its capacity. Its behaviour is based on its own simulated annealing algorithm: when the process starts, there is a high tolerance (the equivalent to the temperature in the classic simulated anealing) to local deteriorations of satisfaction and this tolerance progressively decreases until it reaches a zero-level. Consequently, Task agents may be refused, accepted or ejected. The probability to accept a state i (once it has been generated from a state j, as a result of an allocation requirement) is equal to $\exp((S(j) - S(i)) / T(k, r))$, where $S(i)$ is the satisfaction of the state i and $T(k, r)$ is the tolerance of the requested Resource agent r at the time k. When tolerance zero-level is reached, a Resource agent applies a forced termination mechanism: it only accepts the Task agents leading to an increase of the local satisfaction and becomes forbidden for the others. Thus, if all its possible Resource agents are forbidden, a Task agent is locked and does not seek to be satisfied any more.

If all the Task agents are either satisfied or locked, there are no more interactions and the Machine agent becomes satisfied. Then, it informs the user of the results.

REACTIVITY

The revision problem

The allocation problem, and more generally the scheduling and planning problems, are often subject to external perturbations which can arise during and/or at the end of the reasoning process. Such problems are called perturbated or dynamical problems. The aim of revision is to take into account these perturbations as quickly as possible and to modify the previous state (solution) as little as possible.

As far as our problem is concerned, the modifications may be related to Task agents to be added, Resource agents available with a smaller capacity.

Revision mechanisms

The revision problem is very difficult and is still the object of many researches in the frame of the centralized approaches. The revision mechanism falls (Rao, 1989) into two fields, coherence theory and foundational theory (TMS (Doyle, 1979), ATMS (de Kleer, 1986)). Both theories lead to a heavy manipulation of a large amount of data which is expensive in memory and run-time.

On the contrary, our approach naturally deals with this problem. Because there is no tree search but rather a motion in the space of states (in order to search for an optimal state), the system goes on with its reasoning starting from the current state (previous solution). Furthermore, because the behaviour of each agent is simple and its reasoning is local, the perturbations are dealt with locally and quickly. So, the new solution that is found is close to the previous one.

Let us consider the case of adding Task agents, keeping the same number of Resource agents. This implies both a change in the problem itself (states space) and in the sub-set of optimal solutions (figure 7-1).

Our goal is to have the same likelihood as before (i.e. before the modifications) to reach a global maximum. Therefore, it is necessary to reinitialize (increase) the tolerances and remove the forbiddings, as low tolerances reduce the probability to accept a new state and forbiddings could cut the way leading to an optimal solution. For this purpose, two mechanisms are proposed: the first one involves a systematic reactivation of all the agents, whereas the second one performs a selective reactivation (which is called reactivation propagation).

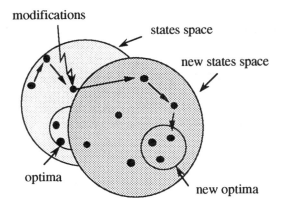

Figure 7-1: Change of optimal solutions

The systematic reactivation mechanism

The process is restarted from the current solution with reinitializing all the Resource agents: their tolerance is reinitialized and their forbiddings are removed.

The reactivation propagation mechanism

In this case, the current solution is also the starting point. Obviously, the new Task agents are unsatisfied. Therefore, they have to seek their satisfaction. Let us consider a Resource agent that is required:

> **if** it is satisfied (required quantity ≤ capacity)
>> **then** its behavior is satisfaction behavior (acceptance)
>> **else**
>>> • it reinitializes its Tolerance,
>>> • it removes its forbiddings (it is no more forbidden for any Task agents) and
>>> • it executes its unsatisfaction behavior (simulated annealing).

The Task agents which have just been ejected (if it is the case) ask their possible Resource agents that were forbidden for them to authorize them again. Those Task agents and the unlocked Task agents (if it is the case) try in turn to be satisfied and so on.

So the reactivation is performed gradually and only the agents that are requested are reactivated. The others are not concerned either directly or indirectly by these modifications and do not change their states. In this way, we keep the same likelihood to reach an optimal solution, and the modifications of the previous solution are minor, except perhaps for very constrained problems.

The experimentations

The systematic reactivation (SR) and reactivation propagation (RP) mechanisms were tested together with a non-revision mechanism (NR: all is restarted from scratch and the current solution is forgotten) taken as a reference. The experimentations were performed on allocation problem samples which were randomly generated. A characteristic parameter was defined: for each sample, it indicates the degree of difficulty of a problem. This parameter is the ratio between the average quantity required by the Task agents and the average quantity offered by the Resource agents.

The performance of the model is assessed through various curves representing the parameters: the global satisfaction, the number of refusals and ejections of the Task agents' and finally the difference between the new and the previous solution (number of different final allocations) versus the degree of difficulty of the problem.

The following figures show that RP gives the most faithful behaviour with regard to the previous solution (i.e the lowest difference: see figure 7-2).

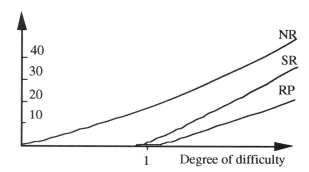

Figure 7-2: Difference new solution / previous solution

Moreover, it produces the best satisfaction (figure 7-3). The number of refusals and ejections is roughly the same especially for very difficult problems (figure 7-3).

For each degree of difficulty, the satisfactions corresponding to three mechanisms are showed (only if they are different).

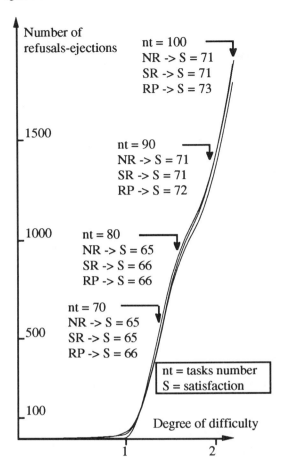

Figure 7-3: Refusal and ejections

CONCLUSION AND PERSPECTIVES

In addition to the original characteristics of the local implementation (i.e at the agent level) of the simulated annealing, the model has the advantage of a natural treatment of the revision. Indeed, external perturbations are considered as problem data and a reactivation propagation mechanism allows the modifications in the agent world to be dealt with quickly, locally and with a minimum of changes in comparison with the previous solution.

Our further studies will generalize the approach to constraint satisfaction and/or criteria optimization problems, using the CSP (Constraint Satisfaction Problem) (Haralick and Shapiro, 1979), (Haralick and Shapiro, 1980), (van Hentenryck, 1989) formalism whose main advantages are simplicity and generality.

REFERENCES

Aarts, E.H.L. and van Laarhoven, P.J.M. (1987) *Simulated Annealing: Theory and Applications*, D.Reidel.

Aarts, E.H.L. Korst, J. (1989) *Simulated Annealing and Boltzmann Machines: A Stochastic Approach to Combinatorial Optimization and Neural Computing*, Wiley.

Bond, A.H. and Gasser, L. (ed.) (1988) *An Analysis of Problems and Research in DAI, Readings in Distributed Artificial Intelligence.*

Briot, J.P. (1989) ACTALK: a Testbed for Classifying and Designing Actors Languages in the SMALLTALK Environment, *Proceedings of the European Conference on Object-Oriented Programming.*

de Kleer, J. (1986) An Assumption-based TMS, *Artificial Intelligence* **28**, pp. 127–162.

Doyle, J. (1979) A Truth Maintenance System, *Artificial Intelligence* **12**, pp. 231–272.

Durfee, E.H., Lesser, V.R. and Corkill, D.D. (1987) Cooperation through Communication in a Distributed Problem Solving Network, *Distributed Artificial Intelligence*, Michael N.Huhns (ed.), Los Altos: Morgan Kaufmann.

Feller, W. (1950) *An Introduction to Probability: Theory and Its Applications*, Volume1, Wiley.

Ferber, J. (1990) The Framework of Eco Problem Solving, *Proceedings of the 2nd European Workshop MAAMAW*, Saint Quentin en Yvelines.

Ghédira, K. and Verfaillie, G. (1991a) Approche Multi-agent pour le Problème d'Affectation, *Expert systems & their applications: Eleventh international workshop*, Avignon.

Ghédira, K. and Verfaillie, G. (1991b) *Approche Multi-agent d'un Problème de Satisfaction de Contraintes: le Problème d'Affectation*, Rapport interne N°1/3412-00/DERI/CERT, Toulouse, France.

Haralick, R. and Shapiro, L. (1979) The Consistent Labelling Problem: Part1, *IEEE Transactions on Pattern Analysis and Machine Intelligence* **1**.

Haralick, R. and Shapiro, L. (1980) The Consistent Labelling Problem: Part2, *IEEE Transactions on Pattern Analysis and Machine Intelligence* **2**.

Kirkpatrick, S., Gelatt, C.D. and Vecchi, Jr.M.P. (1983) Optimisation by Simulated Annealing, *Science* **220**.

Rao, A.S. (1989) *Dynamics of Belief Systems: A Philosophical, Logical and AI Perspective*, Technical Note 2, Australian Artificial Intelligence Institute.

van Hentenryck, P. (1989) *Constraint Satisfaction in Logic Programming*, The MIT Press.

Weisbuch, G. (1989) *Dynamique des Systèmes Complexes: Une Introduction aux Réseaux d'Automates*, InterEditions/Editions du CNRS.

8

A Method for Flow-shop Scheduling Problems with Due Dates[*]

Sandford Bessler
Kapsch AG, Wien

INTRODUCTION

In treating practical *production scheduling problems*, a gap between optimizing approaches (Lawler *et al.*, 1982) and constraint satisfaction solution methods (Minton *et al.*, 1990), (Keng *et al.*, 1988) can be observed in the recent literature.

The so-called *heuristics* in the constraint satisfaction literature are applied to find the next variable to be instantiated, in order to minimize the number of backtracks.

On the other hand, the heuristics for combinatorial optimization encounter difficulties with complex, dynamic problems, such as flow-shops with overlapping operations instead of precedence relationships, time windows or partial resource availabilities. Besides the queueing approach, mostly used in simulations, another approach has been used successfully for planning and scheduling problems: it uses a temporal constraint network for the representation of production requirements and scheduling decisions

The solutions found through constraint propagation are feasible, but they are usually far from being good. In this chapter we will illustrate how to combine constraint satisfaction and optimization heuristics, taking as example the sequencing of jobs in a permutation flow-shop with release and due dates. When trying to follow this approach in other applications, two questions have first to be answered:

- Is the model used in the heuristic not too simplistic? If this is the case the heuristic solutions may be completely different from a good solution of the accurate model.
- Can the search space of the heuristic be controlled? In case of the tabu search sequencing heuristic, the initialization part has to be modified to accept predefined

---

[*] This research was made under the EUREKA Program, under contract EU-358, project FORCAST (sponsored in part by the Austrian research funding organization FFF)

partial sequences. Otherwise the same solution would be produced for the same job input data.

THE PROBLEM

Simplified model for the optimization heuristic

The *flow-shop sequencing problem* is a static scheduling problem in which n jobs must be processed on m different workstations. Thus, each job is divided into operations, and is processed on the workstations in the same order, i.e. m_1, m_2, ... etc. The processing time of job i on the workstation j (operation o_{ij}) is p_{ij} and may be zero if the respective workstation is skipped. The objective of the classical flow-shop problem is to find a job sequence which minimizes the maximum flow time (*makespan*). For flow-shops (Baker, 1974) states that with respect to makespan, it is sufficient to consider only schedules in which the same job sequence occurs on the last two machines. In order to reduce the computation effort, we consider permutation schedules, which restrict even more the number of possible solutions.

The main assumptions for this simple model are:

* workstation availabilities are neglected (see the section on model extensions)
* the set-up times for the operations are included in the processing times
* parallel machines are not considered at the first stage (see the section on model extensions)

Alone the above flow-shop problem is NP-complete, i.e. intractable with exact mathematical programming methods. Additionally, the jobs have to be scheduled before their due dates. For this purpose, the earliest start time r_i and the due date d_i of each job are given.

The satisfaction of release and due date constraints will be checked by the constraint system, not by the heuristic.

A heuristic method

The idea to use an analogy between the job sequencing problem and the *traveling salesman problem* (TSP), in which the towns to be visited are the jobs, is not new (Baker, 1974) p. 166. The sequencing problem can be seen as an open TSP problem (without returning to the origin), if the distance between two jobs can be formulated.

Indeed, introducing a job C between two jobs A and B may increase the makespan by $d_{AC} + d_{CB}$ where the distance between two jobs proposed in (Widmer and Herz, 1988) reflects a possible overlapping between the $(j-1)$-th operation of job B and the j-th operation of job A:

$$d_{AB} = p_{A1} + \sum_{j=2}^{m} |p_{Aj} - p_{Bj-1}| + p_{Bm}$$

A problem arises in applications in which only a small set of the machines are used by each job. This can lead to the extreme where a job does not have machines in common with the preceding job. In order to take into account the skipped machines, a different distance calculation is proposed: for two jobs j_1 and j_2, the distance calculation implies building the schedule in which j_1 preceeds j_2 and returning the difference between the completion times of the two jobs.

An example: j_1 has two operations with durations $p_{j1,1} = 30$ and $p_{j1,3} = 10$ and j_2 has two operations with $p_{j2,2} = 30$ and $p_{j2,3} = 50$. The calculated distance $d_{j1,j2}$ is 50.

The traveling salesman problem can be approximatively solved with a *tabu search* heuristic (de Werra and Herz, 1989), (Glover,1989), (Glover, 1990). The tabu search is a method used in combinatorial optimization problems to guide local search and overcome local optimality. A move from a solution s to a neighbouring solution $s1$ may be forbidden, i.e. is "tabu" if the same move was made recently and would lead to a cycle. The tabu moves are maintained in a cyclic tabu list of length L, and are therefore "forgotten" after L iterations.

In the permutation flow-shop, each solution represents a sequence of all the jobs. The *neighbourhood $N(s)$* of s is defined as the set of solutions which can be obtained by exchanging the positions of two jobs $x(i)$ and $y(j)$ to j and i respectively. From this set, the permutation which corresponds to the lowest makespan and which is not "tabu" is selected.

This procedure stops if a predefined number of iterations is reached without makespan improvement. Note that the selected neighbouring solution may be worse than the current solution. More sophisticated use of the tabu search method is described in (Glover, 1990).

Controlling the heuristic

In order to solve more complex flow-shop scheduling problems with due dates, we need to inform the heuristic about those "good" job locations in a sequence, which have been found in previous heuristic runs, and which would eventually satisfy the due date constraints. This partial ordering of jobs remains valid in the full sequence found by the heuristic.

With a partial job sequence as input, the heuristic builds a starting full sequence and checks before performing a job sequence permutation, whether the ordering above still holds.

Temporal constraint network model

We will use the terminology from (Dechter et al, 1991). The temporal variables $X_1, X_2, ..., X_n$ represent start and end time points of activities (operations in our case). The domain of each variable is in our case a closed interval of positive integers (to represent a discrete time axis). The situation we deal with is referred to as simple *temporal constraint* satisfaction since a variable domain consists of only one interval.

The temporal variables represent the nodes of a constraint directed graph, whereas the constraints represent the arcs. For example, an operation with the (minimum) duration p_{ij} is represented by the constraint:

$$X_b^{ij} + p_{ij} \leq X_e^{ij}$$

where the two variables are the beginning and end of the operation.

Unary constraints, such as release and due dates, can be easily represented, as well as more complex quantitative constraints to express overlapping between two operations.

In addition to that, all Allen's temporal logic operators (Allen, 1983), (Meng and Raja, 1991) can be expressed, with the exception of the relation "not overlapping". In this way an accurate temporal model of production processes is built.

Let us define the simple precedence relation $P(o_{i1,j1}, o_{i2,j2})$ between the operations j_1 and j_2 of two jobs i_1 and i_2 by using the relation,

$$X_b^{i_2,j_2} \leq X_e^{i_1,j_1}$$

the order of the operations of a job $(i_1 = i_2)$ and the order of the operations on a certain workstation $(j_1 = j_2)$ can be specified.

The constraint network propagates the changes in the variables domains whenever a constraint is imposed or retracted. A schedule can be built by gradually imposing constraints corresponding to the sequencing decisions. This is a search process which would end successfully in our application, if all operations are sequenced. If imposing a constraint fails, the search algorithm will eventually retract some decisions and impose new ones, etc.

In order to illustrate the search procedure, let us consider a simple flow-shop example of seven jobs and three workstations.

Table 8-1: A simple flow-shop example of seven jobs and three workstations

Job no.	p_{i1}	p_{i2}	p_{i3}	r_i	d_i
1	50	20	100	0	400
2	110	05	50	0	500
3	70	45	130	0	800
4	150	60	20	0	450
5	100		150	0	900
6	60	15	200	0	1300
7		75	50	100	1500

The precedence relations for each job are generated, such that the domains for the first job will be for example:

$$X_b^{11} = [0, 230] \qquad X_b^{12} = [50, 280] \qquad X_b^{13} = [70, 300]$$

$$X_e^{11} = [50, 280] \qquad X_e^{12} = [70, 300] \qquad X_e^{13} = [170, 400]$$

It has to be noted that the domains are maximum domains, so that the instantiation of more than one variable at a time may be inconsistent.

The sequence is built by inserting the jobs one by one, the order being determined by some criticality function (Keng *et al.*, 1988), such as total processing time divided by the time window of the job. In our example the criticalities for each job are: for job-1: 170 / 400 = .425, for job-2: 165 / 500 = .33, etc.

The decreasing priority order of jobs is therefore: 4-1-2-3-5-6-7.

Putting the things together

The architecture of the system is illustrated in figure 8-1. The search is controlled by a supervisor which calls the constraint satisfaction (CS) and the heuristic module alternately, similar to the way the OPAL system (Bel *et al.*, 1988) does. The supervisor uses a backtracking algorithm to move from one job sequence to the other. At each decision node, the sequence proposed by the heuristic is constructed by imposing constraints to the constraint system. In case of failure, the supervisor decides when and if to let the heuristic generate a new sequence. The heuristic search process is restrained by giving to the heuristic module a partial sequence, corresponding to the constraints at the current decision node.

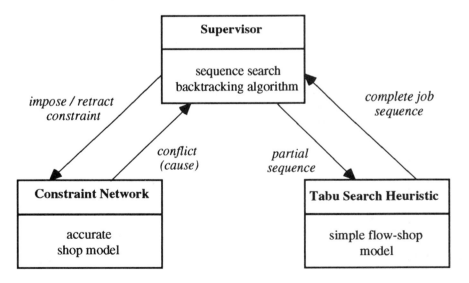

Figure 8-1: Architecture for job-sequencing

When the insertion of a new job in the sequence proposed by the heuristic fails, then the remaining positions for insertion are enumerated and checked (by imposing constraints), in order to improve efficiency.

In case of tight due dates, the benefit of the tabu search is small and the search relies mostly on constraint satisfaction.

The search tree for the seven job example is illustrated in figure 8-2.

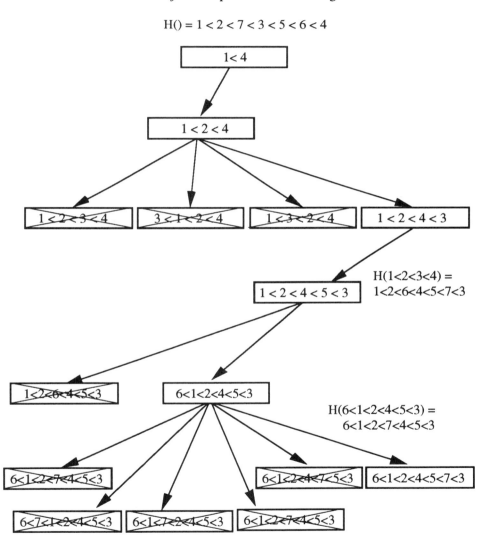

Figure 8-2: Decision tree for 7 job example

Model extensions

One important requirement in almost every factory is to deal with *parallel machines*, a feature which is not present in the flow-shop model. The machines in the flow-shop model are in fact machine groups. The introduction of this feature has to be performed both in the constraint model and in the simplified model. If we assume a machine group m has k identical machines, then in the constraint system an operation o_{jm} will start after a duration of p_{jm} / k measured from the start of the preceding operation. For k large enough, this approximation leads to a completion time of all the operations of $1 / k \sum_j p_{jm}$. The same approximation has to be made in the heuristic, when the distance between two jobs is calculated. Another important feature for practical use of this system is to provide the heuristic and the constraint system for the initial workload (started jobs and operations) in the factory. The durations of already scheduled operations are put into a dummy job, which remains the starting job throughout the procedure.

Computational results and final remarks

The runtime of the search procedure depends on parameters such as the number of tabu search iterations without improvement, nbiter, the tightness of the due dates, and, of course of the number of jobs. The number of operations in a job do not have an impact on the runtime of the heuristic, but affect the time of imposing and retracting sequencing decisions.

A few preliminary results for the test runs on a SUN 4 SPARC workstation are given below:

Table 8-2: Test runs

Example	CPU	Remarks
7 jobs, 3 machines	3 sec.	nbiter = 250
10 job, 10 machines	35 sec.	moderately tight due dates
20 jobs with about 10 operations/job	25 sec.	70 machines flow-shop

It is believed that sequencing for makespan minimization has an effect on the load balancing between different workstations. Other measures besides makespan could be optimized by changing the objective function. It should be noted, however, that a sequence is meaningful, only for environments which can be modelled approximatively as flow-shops.

A further research direction would be to consider job-shops optimization heuristics (van Laarhoven *et al.*, 1988), and redefine the neighbourhood functions to be used by the tabu search scheme.

REFERENCES

Baker, K.R. (1974) *Introduction to Sequencing and Scheduling*, Wiley.

Bel, G., Bensana, E. and Dubois, D. (1988) OPAL: A Multi-knowledge System for Industrial Job-shop Scheduling, *International Journal of Production Research* **26** (5), pp. 795–819.

de Werra, D. and Hertz, A. (1989) Tabu Search Techniques, A Tutorial and an Application to Neural Networks, *OR Spektrum*, pp. 131–141.

Dechter, R., Meiri, I. and Pearl, J. (1991) Temporal Constraint Networks, *Artificial Intelligence* **49**, pp. 61–95.

Elleby, P., Fargher, H.E. and Addis, T.R. (1988) Reactive Constraint-based Job-shop Scheduling, in *Expert systems and Intelligent Manufacturing* M.D. Oliff (ed.), Amsterdam: Elsevier Science, pp. 1–10.

Glover, F. (1989) Tabu Search Part I, *ORSA Journal of Computing* **1** (3), pp. 190–206.

Glover, F. (1990) Tabu Search Part II, *ORSA Journal of Computing* **2** (1), pp. 4–32.

Keng, N.P., Yun, D. and Rossi, M. (1988) Interaction-sensisitive Planning System for Job-shop Scheduling, in *Expert systems and Intelligent Manufacturing* M.D. Oliff (ed.), Amsterdam: Elsevier Science, pp. 57–69.

Lawler, E.L., Lenstra, J.K. and Rinnooy Kan, A.H.G. (1982) *Recent Developments in Deterministic Sequencing and Scheduling: A Survey in Deterministic and Stochastic Scheduling*, Reidel.

Meng, A. and Raja, B.A. (1991) Logos-TCS, An Expert System Language for Operations Management Based on Temporal Constraint Satisfaction, *Proceedings of the 9th National Conference on Artificial Intelligence* (AAAI-91), pp. 215–221.

Minton, S., Johnston, M.D., Philips A.B. and Laird, P. (1990) Solving Large-scale Constraint Satisfaction and Scheduling Problems Using a Heuristic-Repair Method, *Proceedings of the 8th National Conference on Artificial Intelligence* (AAAI-90), pp. 17–24.

van Laarhoven, P.L.M. , Aarts, E.H.L. and Lenstra, L.K. (1988) *Job Shop Scheduling by Simulated Annealing*, Report OS-R8809, Centre for Mathematics and Computer Science Amsterdam.

Widmer, M. and Hertz, A. (1989) A New Heuristic Method for the Flow Shop Sequencing Problem, *European Journal on Operations Research* **41**.

9

Using a Local Improvement Algorithm to Solve a Constraint Satisfaction Problem in Rostering

Barbara M. Smith
Division of Artificial Intelligence, School of Computer Studies, University of Leeds

THE ROSTERING PROBLEM

The ROSA system has been developed to produce weekly rotas for the junior anaesthetists at a large hospital. The department consists of consultant anaesthetists, who work the same pattern of operating lists every week, and the anaesthetists in the junior grades (Senior Registrar (SR), Registrar and Senior House Officer (SHO)), which are primarily training grades. Part of the junior anaesthetists' training is to work alongside a consultant anaesthetist. Apart from this they can, depending on seniority, do some operating lists on their own, or cover a consultant operating list if the consultant is absent. Because of changes from week to week, a rota is required for the juniors, showing what each will be doing in each of ten sessions (Monday to Friday, a.m. and p.m.). The requirements for the rota are described in more detail in (Smith and Bennett, 1992).

The rota is compiled by one of the SRs (the Admin SR), who spends half a day a week compiling the rota for the following week. Since each SR spends a maximum of six months as Admin SR, he or she is only becoming expert at compiling the rota by the time that the next person takes over. The job therefore takes much more time than it would if the same person did it all the time; it is also difficult to ensure consistency. The Admin SR is also responsible for making any adjustments to the rota after it has been compiled, for instance if someone is ill, and needs to be able to judge whether a particular operating list will be relatively straightforward, or requires someone with considerable experience in the specialty. Hence it is not appropriate to entrust the compilation of the rota to a clerk, but it was felt that a system which could produce the initial rota automatically, under the control of the Admin SR, would be of great benefit. We are not attempting, however, to provide a system which can assist in modifying the rota whilst it is in operation; it was felt that it would be too difficult to capture the knowledge required.

If the opportunities for training are included, it is not possible to compile a weekly rota which covers all the work, and the Admin SR tries to strike a balance between covering as many operating lists as possible and allowing adequate training. The first priority, however, is to cover those lists where the consultant is absent; other operating lists can, if necessary, be left uncovered, in which case the list is cancelled, and it is not essential that juniors should be assigned to all the training opportunities available.

COMPILING THE ROTA

The first step in compiling the rota for a given week (whether manually or by computer) is to record the planned absences of each junior anaesthetist and any predetermined assignments. This gives a partly completed rota, the gaps showing where the juniors are still available to do the remaining work. The Admin SR then needs to compile a set of tasks to be done in each session of the week, together with a set of people available to do them. In addition, some anaesthetists must be assigned a half day off during the week, and a half day for the Admin SR to compile the next rota must be set aside.

Compiling the rota then consists of assigning an anaesthetist to each task, taking into account the requirements of the different tasks, e.g. some operating lists require a particular grade of anaesthetist, some training lists are only appropriate for an anaesthetist training in that speciality, and so on. At the same time, the additional afternoons off must be assigned. The rota must be optimized, in the sense that the number of tasks left unassigned must be minimized, while a satisfactory balance is kept between training and covering the department's workload.

The number of tasks to be done varies from week to week, but is normally about 90-100, and the number of anaesthetists who can do each task averages about 5.5. The number of anaesthetists who need to be given a half day off is about 4 or 5. The size of the problem can be reduced if we recognize that some of the training lists, i.e. the general training lists which are principally for SHOs, are of much lower priority than other tasks. Acceptable rotas can be compiled by assigning the other tasks first, and then fitting the general training lists into the remaining gaps. This reduces rota compilation to two separate problems, the second of which is trivial. The first problem then has about 75 tasks to be assigned.

A MATHEMATICAL PROGRAMMING APPROACH

The first approach to compiling the rota automatically was to try an *integer linear programming* formulation. A possible approach to doing this is to introduce variables x_{ijk} and y_{ik}, where:

$$x_{ijk} = \begin{cases} 1 & \text{if anaesthetist } i \text{ is assigned to operating list } j \text{ in session } k \\ 0 & \text{otherwise} \end{cases}$$

$$y_{ik} = \begin{cases} 1 & \text{if anaesthetist } i \text{ is assigned an afternoon off in session } k \\ 0 & \text{otherwise} \end{cases}$$

The constraints are that no anaesthetist can be assigned to two things at once; that at most one anaesthetist can be assigned to each task, but that a task which involves covering for an absent consultant must be assigned exactly one anaesthetist; and that the anaesthetists who are supposed to get a half day off during the week must be assigned one. All these can be expressed as linear inequalities or equations in the x_{ijk} and y_{ik} variables. The objective is then to maximize the number of assignments:

$$\text{maximize} \ \sum_{ijk} x_{ijk}$$

Many of the x_{ijk} variables need to be set to 0 to express, for instance, the fact that some operating lists can only be done by some of the anaesthetists. Having done this, the number of x_{ijk} variables remaining is the number of tasks to be assigned in the given week, multiplied by the average number of anaesthetists who can do (and are available to do) each list. For the size of problem described in section 2, omitting the lowest-priority tasks, there are about 335 x_{jk} variables. There are also about 20 y_{ik} variables, so that altogether, the formulation has about 355 variables and about 170 constraints.

The mathematical programming approach was rejected, partly because it seemed unlikely that a problem of this size could be solved quickly. Furthermore, there are pre-ferred anaesthetists, or preferred grades of anaesthetist, for most operating lists, and to deal with this in an integer programming formulation, one would have to incorporate a cost for each anaesthetist / operating list combination in the objective function. This would make the formulation much more cumbersome, and require the invention of precise costs to reflect what is in reality only an ordering of the available anaesthetists. No attempt was made to solve the mathematical programming problem, and instead a constraint satisfaction approach was explored.

CONSTRAINT SATISFACTION PROBLEMS

The *constraint satisfaction problem* has been discussed extensively in the Artificial Intel-ligence literature (see references). It has applications in computer vision (e.g. scene la-belling), graph colouring, packing problems and some types of puzzle such as cryptarith-metic, and can be used as a formulation of many problems arising in Operational Re-search. In a constraint satisfaction problem there are a number of variables, each of which has a discrete set of possible values (its domain). There are also a number of constraint relations, specifying which values are mutually compatible for various subsets of the variables: for instance, the assignment of an anaesthetist to a task is incompatible with the assignment of the same anaesthetist to another task in the same session. A solution to the constraint satisfaction problem is an assignment of values to the variables which satisfies the constraints.

Although the definition of the CSP does not distinguish between solutions, so that all assignments which satisfy the constraints are equally acceptable, it is possible to represent optimization problems as CSPs. The objective is represented as an additional constraint, which changes each time a new solution is found. For instance, in a minimization problem, the constraint is that the value of the objective must be less that its value in the best solution found so far (or, initially, less than some very large number). This ensures that each solution is better than the previous one, and when all the solutions to the CSP have been found, the last one will be optimal. A similar scheme for representing discrete optimization problems as CSPs is described by van Hentenryck (1989).

In general, constraint satisfaction problems are NP-complete, so that although several algorithms exist for solving them (Haralick and Elliott, 1980), (Nadel, 1989), they are not guaranteed to find a solution in a reasonable time unless the problem is small or has special structure (Dechter and Pearl, 1988). However, in many cases there is a good chance of finding a feasible assignment quite quickly. Optimization problems, on the other hand, will almost certainly suffer from the exponential worst-case performance, since the search cannot be terminated when the first feasible solution is found. Despite this difficulty, it may still be possible to solve optimization problems using a constraint satisfaction formulation as a basis, as section 6 demonstrates.

Nadel (1989) surveys the available algorithms for the CSP, and compares their performance on some standard problems. One of the best algorithms in these experiments is the *forward checking algorithm* , described by Haralick and Elliott (1980). This algorithm is used by the ROSA system. Nadel describes forward checking as a hybrid algorithm, combining a backtracking tree-search algorithm with some consistency checking at each node. Essentially, it does additional checks as each choice of value is made, in order to identify infeasible choices as early as possible and hence reduce the number of choices which have to be made, and in the right conditions this will result in an overall timesaving.

THE ROTA COMPILATION PROBLEM AS A CSP

As mentioned earlier, the first stage in compiling the rota is to record the predetermined assignments and the planned absences for the week, and we are only concerned with the problem of assigning the remaining tasks to those anaesthetists who are still available after this first stage.

The variables of the CSP are used to represent the tasks to be assigned in the given week, and the domain of each variable is the set of anaesthetists who can do that task. In addition, there is a small number of variables which represent a half day off for an individual anaesthetist. The domain of such a variable is the list of sessions in which the anaesthetist could take a half day off.

The domain of each task variable is arranged in priority order, with the best choice of junior anaesthetist for the task appearing first. The forward checking algorithm selects values from the domain in the order in which they appear, and hence the anaesthetist appearing first in the list is the one most likely to be assigned, if available. Although ordering the domains is not guaranteed to give the overall best allocation of anaesthetists to tasks, it does in practice give acceptable results. It is, of course, essential that the forward checking algorithm should maintain the original ordering of the domains.

In order to express the relative priorities of the different types of task, they are divided into three categories: essential, preference and optional. The essential tasks are those arising from consultant absences: an anaesthetist must be assigned to each of these in order to achieve a *feasible solution*. (It is extremely unlikely that a situation could arise in practice where consultant absences could not be covered.)

The optional tasks are the training lists for the SHOs, in which they accompany a consultant. SHOs can be assigned to these tasks if there is nothing of higher priority which they could do instead; to reflect this, the optional tasks are assigned only after a satisfactory assignment of the essential and preference tasks has been found. The current state of the rota is then fixed and the optional tasks are assigned to those junior anaesthetists who have not so far been allocated to do anything in that session.

Any task which is neither essential nor optional is classed as a preference. To allow the algorithm to leave the preference and optional tasks uncovered if necessary, an extra value, NONE, is added as the final element in the domain of each of the corresponding variables. When this variable is considered by the algorithm, this value can be selected, if all the anaesthetists who could do this task have been assigned to something else.

It has been found that a good balance between covering the department workload and satisfying the juniors' training needs can be achieved by covering as many of the preference tasks as possible, i.e. the number of preference tasks assigned the value NONE should be minimized. This can be done by using an additional constraint to represent this objective, as described in section 3.

The constraints of the CSP firstly arise from the fact that an anaesthetist cannot do two things at once. In the forward checking algorithm, checking of constraints is done just after a trial assignment of a value to a variable has been made, and two cases need to be checked:

1. if the variable is a task variable and the value is not NONE, (i.e. it is an anaesthetist) then this anaesthetist cannot do any other task in the same session and cannot have a half day off in this session.
2. if the variable is a half-day variable, then the value is a session and the corresponding anaesthetist cannot also do a task in the same session.

These constraints may be thought of as general rostering constraints; similar constraints expressing the fact that no-one can be assigned to two tasks at the same time will occur in any rostering problem.

The anaesthetists' system also has a constraint representing the objective, as already described. This can be expressed as:

3. if the variable is a task variable and the value is NONE, and the number of tasks assigned the value NONE in the current partial solution, including this one, is already one less than the number of unassigned task variables in the best complete solution found so far (i.e. is already the maximum allowed), then no future task variable can be assigned the value NONE.

In addition, there are other constraints reflecting particular rostering rules used in the anaesthetics department, which have in fact changed several times during the course of the project. Currently, for instance, there is a rule that Registrars who are on a training block can be taken off training, and assigned to do an operating list on their own instead, at most once during the week. Constraints of this kind are likely to vary from hospital to hospital and, as experience has shown, to change over time. The system has therefore been designed in such a way that constraints are easy to express and do not require any change to the solution method.

IMPROVING A FEASIBLE SOLUTION

Having set up the variables and their domains, the forward checking algorithm is used to find an assignment of the essential and preference tasks and the half-day variables. The algorithm finds a first feasible solution very quickly (almost instantaneously as far as the user is aware). However, it is not entirely trivial to find a feasible solution: the order in which variables are considered is crucial, and for some variable orderings, the algorithm can take a very long time to find a solution. The variables with smallest domains cannot be assigned first, as is commonly advised (Nudel, 1983), because in this context they do not represent tasks which are hard to assign, but training lists which can only be assigned to a particular anaesthetist and so should not be given higher priority than other tasks. An ordering which has been found to be successful is to consider next a variable which was affected by the last assignment, and failing that one of the essential tasks. This ensures that the essential tasks are considered early, but at the same time the half-day variables are not left until the end, by which time they cannot be assigned.

Once a feasible solution has been found, the objective constraint operational and the algorithm tries to reduce the number of unassigned tasks. However, because of the size of the problem, finding the optimum solution would take a very long time. Often, finding any improvement to the first solution takes far longer than would be acceptable.

It is conceivable that improvements in the way that the forward checking algorithm is used might achieve a sufficient increase in speed to allow an optimal solution to be found; for instance, it might be possible to develop better variable ordering rules based on problem knowledge. However, rather than pursuing this possibility, we have used the forward checking algorithm only to produce a feasible solution, and looked for ways of improving such a solution. This approach produces good results very quickly, and it seems unlikely that an improved forward checking algorithm would be able to do any better.

In order to improve on the best solution that the forward checking algorithm can find quickly, an algorithm has been devised that considers each uncovered task in turn and looks for reassignments of related tasks which will allow it to be covered. This *local improvement* algorithm was developed through examining feasible but non-optimal rotas, and looking for reassignments that would improve them.

Suppose that there is an uncovered task that we want to try to find an assignment for. This is a variable which has been assigned the value NONE. All the anaesthetists in the variable's original domain must have been assigned to do something else in this session (otherwise the assignment of NONE would not have been made) but it may be possible to free one of these anaesthetists by reassigning the task that they are currently assigned to (a *swap*), or by moving a half day off from this session to another session (a *move*).

The following example (adapted from an actual rota) shows the kind of swaps within a session that can be made in order to improve the solution.

Table 9-1: Swaps within a session

Variable	Original Domain	Assigned
ORTHO-TRAUMA-THU-AM	(R-4 R-6 R-5 SHO-1 SHO-2 NONE)	R-4
CW-II-THU-AM	(R-4 R-6 R-5 SHO-1 SHO-2 NONE)	R-6
OBS-THU-AM	(R-5 R-4 R-6 NONE)	R-5
GARDNER-THU-AM	(R-5 NONE)	NONE
PSU-I/A-THU-AM	(R-4 R-6 R-5 NONE)	NONE

The variables are shown in the order in which the forward checking algorithm considers them, so that the value assigned is the first remaining value in the domain. (Values assigned to other variables representing tasks in this session have been omitted.) The two uncovered operating lists in this Thursday morning session (GARDNER and PSU-I/A) can be covered by making use of SHO-1 and SHO-2 who are so far unassigned in this session. The simpler swap is to assign the ORTHO-TRAUMA list to SHO-1, thus allowing R-4 to do the PSU-I/A list. Covering the GARDNER list entails a chain of two exchanges: SHO-2 takes the CW-II list, R-6 takes the OBS list, and R-5 can then do the GARDNER list.

A simple example of a move is to move an anaesthetist's half day off, from a session where there is an uncovered task that this anaesthetist could do, to another session where they have not been assigned to do anything. More complicated changes involve a swap, of the kind illustrated above, combined with a move. This is done if moving a half day off would allow an uncovered task to be done by the anaesthetist concerned, and the swap has to be done to free the anaesthetist in the session that the half day off is being moved to.

The local improvement algorithm considers each uncovered task in turn in the current solution, and for each anaesthetist in the original domain of the corresponding variable, each of the above changes is tried, starting with the simpler changes, until a move which will allow the task to be covered is found, or the variable's domain is exhausted. This procedure ensures that the first value in the domain which can be assigned to the task is found, thus observing the preference ordering of the values.

In all cases, potential changes to the current solution are checked against the constraints, so that even when new constraints are introduced, the algorithm still produces a feasible solution.

The local improvement algorithm works through the list of uncovered tasks once, and then presents the resulting solution as the best that it can achieve. The combination of swaps and moves seems to be adequate to produce an optimal rota; so far, we have not been able to see any further scope for reducing the number of uncovered tasks in the rotas produced, except by relaxing the constraints, although recent experiments with the CHIP system, reported below, suggest that very occasionally ROSA may produce a sub-optimal solution.

At this point, the rota will have several gaps, where an anaesthetist has not been assigned to do anything. The final stage in constructing the rota is to assign the optional lists to fill these gaps. The resulting rota is then printed out, with a note of any remaining uncovered operating lists.

RESULTS AND CONCLUSIONS

The ROSA system has been developed in Common LISP on a Sun 3/160; it is now also running on a PC. It can produce a weekly rota within 30 minutes, including entering the required data, compared with the half day allocated to compiling the rota manually. The system has been producing good quality rotas for over a year, and has coped with changes in the rota compilation rules. We have recently improved the user interface so that the system can be used by hospital staff.

ROSA combines a general-purpose constraint satisfaction algorithm (the forward checking algorithm) with a domain-dependent local improvement algorithm to achieve good results. However, although the methods used in ROSA appear to be very problem-specific, recent work (Smith, 1992) has shown that they can be seen as special cases of a general method applicable to other CSPs. Generating a consistent but not optimal initial solution, as in ROSA, is not appropriate for most CSPs, where consistency rather than optimality is the aim. Instead, a consistent but not complete initial solution is found, using a greedy algorithm which chooses a value for each variable consistent with previous assignments, breaking ties randomly; if no consistent value exists, the variable is not assigned. Leaving a variable unassigned corresponds to assigning the value NONE in ROSA. In order to complete the initial solution, a reassignment heuristic is used, similar to the ROSA local improvement algorithms: for each value in the domain of an unassigned variable, the heuristic attempts to reassign the variables whose current assignments prevent the value from being used. If the reassignments can be done without causing new conflicts to arise, the value can be assigned to the unassigned variable. Otherwise, another value is tried. In (Smith, 1992), experiments using a very simple reassignment heuristic of this kind on the n-queens problem are reported: the heuristic performs very well for large n.

The SPIKE system (Minton *et al.*, 1990) used for long-term scheduling of the Hubble Space Telescope, uses a similar basic approach, i.e. constructing an initial schedule and then improving it. In that case, the initial schedule is infeasible, but optimal in the sense that all the work is scheduled, and the improvement stage attempts to move towards feasibility, using a repair heuristic, the min-conflicts heuristic, which can potentially be applied to many different combinatorial optimization problems. However, although the repair heuristic is to some degree general-purpose, it has been found in SPIKE that the quality of the initial schedule is crucial to the quality of the final result, so that production of the initial schedule needs to be tailored to the domain.

Other recent work has investigated the application of the CHIP system (van Hentenryck, 1989) to the rostering problem. This work showed that a straightforward formulation of the problem in CHIP took an unacceptably long time to solve. The problem was simplified by taking advantage of the fact that the rota is almost decomposable into ten separate rotas, and it could then be solved optimally. The results confirmed that ROSA almost always produces optimal rotas. Even with the simplified problem, however, CHIP takes much longer to produce a solution than ROSA, and because of the assumptions made in simplifying the problem, it would be much less able to cope with changes to the problem than ROSA.

The experiences with CHIP and ROSA have shown that the rostering problem, although small compared with many other scheduling problems, is too big to be solved without resorting to heuristic methods of some kind. The SPIKE system demonstrates that repair heuristics can give good results in scheduling problems: the fact that reassignment heuristics, which are also a form of repair heuristic, have been applied successfully both in ROSA and to the n-queens problem suggests that a domain-independent reassignment heuristic might give good results in other scheduling problems.

REFERENCES

Dechter, R. and Pearl, J. (1988) Network-Based Heuristics for Constraint-Satisfaction Problems, *Artificial Intelligence* **34**, pp. 1–38.

Haralick, R.M. and Elliott, G.L. (1980) Increasing Tree Search Efficiency for Constraint Satisfaction Problems, *Artificial Intelligence* **14**, pp. 263–313.

Minton, S., Johnston, M.D., Philips, A.B. and Laird, P. (1990) Solving Large-scale Constraint Satisfaction and Scheduling Problems Using a Heuristic Repair Method, *Proceedings of 8th National Conference on Artificial Intelligence* (AAAI-90,) pp. 17–24.

Nadel, B.A. (1989) Constraint Satisfaction Algorithms, *Computational Intelligence* **5**, pp. 188–224.

Nudel, B.A. (1983) Consistent Labeling Problems and their Algorithms: Expected Complexities and Theory-based Heuristics, *Artificial Intelligence* **21**, pp. 135–178.

Smith, B.M. (1992) *Filling the Gaps: Reassignment Heuristics for Constraint Satisfaction Problems*, University of Leeds, School of Computer Studies Research Report 92.29.

Smith, B.M. and Bennett, S. (1992) Combining Constraint Satisfaction and Local Improvement Algorithms to Construct Anaesthetists' Rotas, *Proceedings of the 8th IEEE Conference on Artificial Intelligence Applications* (CAIA-92), pp. 106–112.

van Hentenryck, P. (1989) *Constraint Satisfaction in Logic Programming*, MIT Press.

10

Advanced Job-shop Scheduling in Aeronautical Manufacturing

Eric Bensana
ONERA-CERT/DERA, Toulouse

THE SCHEDULING CONTEXT

The scheduling context is typically manufacturing *job-shops* in the aeronautical industry (aircraft, missile production). This kind of industry, which is not mass-production, is an example of manufacturing where due-dates constraints are important. Because of the added-value of items produced, there is no storage, and delay on delivering final products may be very costly. So it is necessary, if possible, to meet due-dates.

We have mainly worked on two job-shops, one for missile components production, and one for production of parts needed to assemble the engine support for commercial aircraft. They have in common that the tasks performed are essentially machining, with long duration (up to several days), that MRP systems compute production plans on a horizon varying between two weeks and a few months. An order specifies the product type, the batch size, the processing sequence, the release and due dates.

Notations In the following, we will use:

- est_i: earliest starting time for task i,
- lst_i: latest starting time for task i,
- eft_i: earliest finishing time for task i,
- lft_i: latest finishing time for task i
- d_i: duration of task i,
- $\oplus$: precedence operator,
- $c_j = (A, B)$: conflict between tasks A and B,
- CS: conflict set.

Other notations will be introduced when needed.

THE OPAL SYSTEM

OPAL is a short-term job-shop scheduling system (Bel *et al.*, 1988), (Bel *et al.*, 1989), (Bensana, 1990), aimed at solving the *task sequencing problem* with respect to *technological* (processing sequence, resource use etc.) and *temporal constraints* (release and due dates). It builds admissible and preferred schedules. It has three components: a Constraint Based Analyser (CBA), an Expert Advisor (EA) and a Supervisor. The supervisor manages the cooperation between the CBA and EA, which share a common graph-based problem representation. The schedule is gradually built by making task sequencing decisions. Before running OPAL, the user selects from sets of predefined criteria and rules, a criterion and a set of rules which will be used by the EA to guide the search. The system accepts also some basic notions used in production systems like batch, batch overlapping and sequence dependent set-up, which will not be addressed in this chapter.

The Constraint Based Analyser

This module implements an algorithm which computes necessary sequencing decisions, with respect to precedence and temporal constraints (Erschler 1976), (Erschler *et al.* 1989). It is a scheduling dedicated constraint propagation mechanism, based on the notion of *task conflict*, to express *disjunctive constraints* coming from resource management constraints. It provides a way to link disjunctive constraints and temporal constraints.

A conflict is a pair of operation competing for the use of the same resource. If there are n tasks assigned to a resource, there are at most $n (n - 1) / 2$ conflicts. The real number depends on the temporal location of the tasks (two tasks with disjoint temporal windows cannot form a conflict).

The iterative procedure consists in applying basic sequencing rules to solve conflicts by enforcing necessary precedence relations, and propagation rules, when a new relation is added, to update the time limits of the temporal windows associated with tasks. It is a basic forward chaining mechanism, which terminates on:

- **failure:** detected by sequencing or propagation rules,
- **saturation:** when $CS = \emptyset$ or when rules cannot deduce new precedence relations.

Sequencing rules

Sequencing rules simply use starting time, ending time and duration of tasks in conflict. Suppose we have a conflict $c = (A, B)$, such that $est_A \leq est_B$, we compute $L_{A,B} = lft_B - est_A$, $L_{B,A} = lft_A - est_B$ and $D_{A,B} = d_A + d_B$, then we have the following four rules:

R1:   if $(D_{A,B} > L_{A,B}) \wedge (D_{A,B} > L_{B,A})$ then **failure**

R2:   if $(D_{A,B} \leq L_{A,B}) \wedge (D_{A,B} \leq L_{B,A})$ then **nothing**

R3:   if $(D_{A,B} \leq L_{A,B}) \wedge (D_{A,B} > L_{B,A})$ then **impose** $A \oplus B$

R4:   if $(D_{A,B} > L_{A,B}) \wedge (D_{A,B} \leq L_{B,A})$ then **impose** $B \oplus A$

The rules R3 and R4 allow to solution of *conflicts* (disjunctive constraints).

Propagation rules

They are triggered when a new precedence is added. It means that some time limits are updated, and then these modifications are propagated to neighbouring tasks, along precedence constraints: forward for modification of starting time, and backward for finishing time. These *propagation rules* are similar to those used in constraint programming language, known as *forward checking*. For example:

TR: if $X \oplus Y$ then **update** est_Y to $\max(est_Y, eft_X)$, and **update** lft_X to $\min(lft_X, lst_Y)$

FR: if $lft_X - est_X < d_X$ then **failure**, fired each time est_X or lft_X is modified

The Expert Advisor

When the CBA stops because it cannot make any more decisions, at least one choice for pending conflicts has to be made, to go on building the schedule. To help, the supervisor selects a decision among all those possible at this point; the EA classes them with respect to its current heuristics base, which is composed of a criterion and a set of *decision rules*. The role of EA is to guide the search for an admissible schedule according to preferences modelized as criteria and rules.

The selection criteria

Selection criteria focus the search. They are used to select among the current set of conflicts those which are interesting to solve. A criterion evaluates a conflict by computing its interest rating; it is implemented as a function which takes as input a conflict and gives as result a number I ($0 \le I \le 1$), 0 meaning that the conflict is uninteresting to solve, 1 for very interesting. It is a strategic level.

For example, given the current set of criteria, we can focus the search on critical resource, critical orders, chronological selection, bottlenecks, increase search efficiency, etc. If no criterion is specified all conflicts will be equally rated to 1.

The fuzzy decision rules

Fuzzy decision rules are used to express a preference evaluation for the decisions which can be made to solve a conflict. The emphasis has been put on the way to express compromise between antagonistic points of view. It is a tactical level.

For a conflict $c = (A, B)$, we consider the three options $A \oplus B$, $B \oplus A$ or $A \parallel B$. ($\parallel$: no decision operator). The last option has been made explicit to deal with cases where rules can be applied but are not meaningful. To illustrate that point let us take the example of the SPT rule, well known in discrete event simulation; this rule express the point of view that it is better to put the task with shorter duration first, but if the tasks in competition have very close duration, that rule loses its meaning (close to abstention notion). Rules are characterized by their:

weight: π_k ($0 \le \pi_k \le 1$)

condition part: which tests if the rule is applicable to the conflict

preference part: which expresses a preference μ ($0 \le \mu \le 1$) for each option.

To express the preferences the rule will first compute $I_{A,B}$ related to $A \oplus B$ and $I_{B,A}$ related to $B \oplus A$. To compare them, $R = I_{A,B} / I_{A,B} + I_{B,A}$ is computed, $(0 \leq R \leq 1)$, and the preferences are stated by computing how much R belongs to the *fuzzy set* of *low*, *high* and *medium* fractions, as they are defined in figure 10-1. The preference for $A \parallel B$ is always given with respect to medium, but for the two other options, it depends on the rule (better when R is low like in SPT, better when R is hight if priority involved). To change it, it is sufficient to exchange $I_{A,B}$ and $I_{B,A}$ in the computation of R.

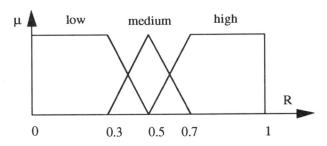

Figure 10-1: The fuzzy sets membership functions

For example if we go on with the SPT rule, comparison element is the task duration, $I_{A,B} = d_A$ and $I_{B,A} = d_B$, if $d_A = 10$ and $d_B = 90$, we get the 3-uple $(1, 0, 0)$, which express a strong preference for $A \oplus B$, if $d_A = 45$ and $d_B = 55$ we get $(0.25 , 0.75, 0)$, which express a weak preference for $A \oplus B$, but a rather strong preference for $A \parallel B$.

The comparison elements, $I_{X,Y}$, can be associated to tasks (like duration or margin) or to other objects related to task (such as batch, resource etc.), or may be attached to the sequence between the two tasks (like set-up for example).

Although that kind of preference evaluation is widely used in our rule base, we may have also rules using other types of evaluation. The only constraint is that the results should be given as a 3-uple of number between 0 and 1.

Currently we have fifteen basic rules, which can be divided into:

priority rules: like SPT (shortest-processing-time), EDD (earliest-due-date), FIFO (first-in-first-out), etc. coming from simulation practice,

margin rules: which try to select the sequencing which saves as much as possible of the margins. It should be noted that some of them inspired by the CBA rules, perform well, and give very flexible schedules,

specific rules: which are application dependent and defined if required.

The aggregation mechanism

We use the following notations:

- DS: decision set, RS: rule set, EV_i: elementary votes set for conflict c_i
- $\mu_{k,i,j}$: preference rate of rule k, conflict i, decision j
- $P_{i,j}$: combined preference of all rules, conflict i, decision j (fuzzy percentage),

For example if all the expertise is static, the sorting made by the EA, at the first time, is valid during all the search, and then there is no need to call EA again.

To allow us to control and tune the role of the EA during the search, we have implemented a trust indicator, which enables the supervisor to compute the number of steps S during which a sorting will remain valid: $S = max(1, \alpha * N_c)$, where N_c is the current number of conflicts and $\alpha (0 \leq \alpha \leq 1)$ is a parameter. We may have several behaviours depending on α:

- $\alpha = 0 \Rightarrow S = 1$, so we are in the basic behaviour, EA will be called at each step,
- $\alpha = 1 \Rightarrow S = N_c$, S has the maximal value and then EA will not be called again,
- else EA will be called again after S steps.

To compute α we take into account the type of criterion and rules used and the impact of the first call to CBA: $\beta = N_1 / N_0$ (with N_0 - N_1: number of conflicts solved during the first call to CBA). β can be seen as an evaluation of the performance of the first call to the CBA and then a measure of how constrained is the problem. So if rules and criterion are static then $\alpha = 1$ else $\alpha = \beta$.

Mastering the complexity

As scheduling problems remain combinatorial, nobody can guarantee a time boundary to get a solution. If the problem has no solution, we will, within the basic scheme, give a "no solution" answer to the user. These facts are unacceptable in a workshop.

To overcome these drawbacks, another mode of schedule generation is possible within the system. It is not an additional module, but it consists only in some modification of the general scheme. Propagation and failure rules are modified to avoid backtracking, the sequencing rule R1 is disabled and the failure rule in the propagation is replaced by a slightly different version: if $lft_X - est_X < d_X$ then $lft_X = eft_X$. It allows us to generate schedules where due dates constraints are no longer considered as hard constraints.

In addition, a final three-phases propagation step is needed. The first phase computes only earliest starting time. Then, in the second phase, we compute for each order O its final time limit FT_O, from its earliest completion time, ECT_O (earliest finishing time of the last task of the processing sequence of O), and its due date DD_O. If $ECT_O \leq DD_O$ then $FT_O = DD_O$ else $FT_O = ECT_O$ and O is late. FT_O is then used to compute the latest finishing time in the third phase. It should be noted that late orders have no margin and thus we are able to highlight critical paths, which can be used for schedule revision for example.

This mode can be triggered at the beginning of the search if the user wants to. In this case we have a kind of greedy algorithm, where the EA play the role of a heuristic. It can be also automatically switched on during the search, up to the end, when a condition expressed by the user is satisfied (elapsed time, number of backtrack made, percentage of conflicts solved etc.)

Presentation of results

OPAL gives as solution, the sequencing of tasks for resource and for each task i, the final est_i and lft_i. Results are displayed as Gantt charts.

In operation, the user can interactively modify locally the proposed schedule by changing the sequencing or assignement, or introducing urgent orders etc. In that case, the system does not guarantee any more that due-dates are met, because it relies on the three-phases propagation step, described in the previous section, to compute starting end ending time of tasks, for a given set of decisions characterizing a schedule. This allows the user to eventually take into account preferences which cannot be translated in rules or criterion, or overcome decision made by propagation.

EXTENSIONS AND GENERALIZATION

Modelization of fuzzy due-dates

The solving approach, used in OPAL, puts emphasis on meeting due-dates constraints. In real life applications, these informations are often computed by MRP systems, which make imprecise assumptions about lead times. Consequently, they should not be given so much importance. Moreover, even if they are computed with accurate data, they can be negotiated with customers. So they should be considered as *soft constraints*.

A model extension has been proposed (Mathe 1987), using *fuzzy set theory* to model the imprecision pervading release and due dates, and thus replacing temporal windows by *fuzzy temporal windows*. Instead of giving orders a release date and a due date, they are given two release $[r_{min}, r_{max}]$ and two due dates $[d_{min}, d_{max}]$, with the following interpretation: the manufacturing of an order cannot begin before r_{min} but should begin after r_{max}; it should end before d_{min} but cannot end after d_{max}.

Aggregation of preferences

To express compromise between several heuristics rules in the EA, OPAL uses a voting paradigm (rule = voter, decisions = candidates, aggregation = majority vote).

That approach has been generalized, with the help of social choice theory (Bel *et al.*, 1989), (Koning, 1990), and by using quantified expression of preferences (preference intensity) and fuzzy sets theory for aggregation. The properties defined in the social choice theory have been extended to deal with quantified preferences. Rules can be of imperative or advice type according to the kind of information they give, and the specific aggregation mode (dictatorship, veto, several types of democracy) can be associated to a sets of rules of the same type. A general architecture, named DEBORA, has been developped and can be instantiated to solve the scheduling problem as OPAL does, but may also be used for any kind of decision problem.

Generalization to CSP solving

Some of the ideas developped in the OPAL frame can be easily generalized to *constraint satisfaction problem*. We have no room here to define the CSP formulation and the way of solving it, see (Nadel, 1989), (Prosser, 1993) for a detailed presentation. We will only summarize by saying that because of the underlying combinatorics', CSP solving relies mainly upon the classical backtrack algorithm, by alternating some kind of partial consistency checking algorithm and labelling.

Guiding the labelling

It is then readily seen that the approach used for the Expert Advisor and generalized in the DEBORA architecture can be used also to guide the search when solving a CSP, and thus allows the implementation of domain-dependent heuristics.

Soft constraints

As we have softened the due dates constraints in scheduling, we may have in CSP two kinds of constraint: hard ones and soft ones. Actually the CSP framework cannot deal properly with these two kinds of constraint. We assumed that fuzzy sets is a good supporting theory to deal with, as it has been demonstrated in OPAL. In (Schiex 1992), a possibilistic CSP framework is proposed to handle soft constraints.

SYNTHESIS AND CONCLUSION

Synthesis

OPAL has been developped in COMMON-LISP on SUN workstations and is used now as a support for testing new developments such as problem decomposition, adaptative behaviour (changing expertise during search), new Constraint Based Analyser (to detect unfeasible problems) etc.

A commercial version of OPAL, called ORIGAN, which includes only some features presented here, but is extended to deal with other types of resource (multi-heads machines) has been developped and installed in a workshop. It generates schedules over a two-weeks horizon, for about a thousand conflicts between 2 and 15 mn on a SUN4.

Our main activities are now oriented to the CSP framework and improvements which can be made (soft constraints, incrementality etc.) and towards the reactive aspect of scheduling, schedule revision and maintenance (a system called REMORA is under development).

General conclusion

One of the most important challenge AI has to face today is to prove its capacity to handle real problems. Scheduling is a good testbed because problems are difficult to solve (even with classical techniques) and economically meaningful. Although knowledge-based scheduling systems are not yet actually widely spread in industry, mainly because of the quality of existing environments not ready to accept such powerfull tools, such systems, like OPAL, have proved that they can afford real life scheduling problems. The CSP framework and the recent development of constraint based programming languages, like CHIP, PROLOG III, CHARME, PECOS etc. should increase the trend. But AI has brought also a new approach to problem analysis and solving, by clearly identifying the kind of knowledge involved, including OR or simulation based, and the different ways of generating schedules.

REFERENCES

Bel, G., Bensana, E. and Dubois, D. (1988) OPAL: A Multi-knowledge Based System for Job-shop Scheduling, *International Journal of Production Research* **26** (5), pp. 795–819.

Bel, G., Bensana, E., Dubois, D. and Koning, J.L. (1989) Handling Fuzzy Priority Rules in a Job-shop Scheduling System, *Proceedings of the 3rd IFSA Conference*, Seattle, USA, August.

Bel, G., Bensana, E., Dubois, D., Erschler, J. and Esquirol, P. (1989) A Knowledge-based Approach to Industrial Job-shop Scheduling, in *Knowledge-based Systems in Manufacturing*, A. Kusiak (ed.), Taylor and Francis, pp. 207–246.

Bensana, E. (1990) Melting OR and AI techniques: Towards a Short Term Scheduling Environment, in *Manufacturing Systems and Environment: Looking towards the 21st Century*, pp. 431–436, Tokyo, Japan JSME.

Erschler, J. (1976) *Analyse sous Contraintes et Aide a la Decision pour Certains Problèmes d'Ordonnancement*, Thèse d'état, Université Paul Sabatier, Toulouse, November

Erschler, J., Lopez, P. and Thuriot, C., (1989) Scheduling under Time and Resource Constraints, *Workshop on Manufacturing Scheduling*, 11th Joint Conference on Artificial Intelligence, Detroit.

Koning, J.L. (1990) *Un Mécanisme de Gestion de Règles de Décision Antagonistes pour les Systèmes à Base de Connaissances*, Ph. D. thesis, Université Paul Sabatier, Toulouse.

Mathe, N. (1987) Prise En compte de l'Imprécision des Délais dans la Construction d'Ordonnancements Prévisionnels, DEA d'automatique, ENSAE, Toulouse, Juin.

Nadel, B.A. (1989) Constraint Satisfaction Algorithm, *Computational Intelligence* **5**, pp. 188–224.

Prosser, P. (1993) Scheduling as a Constraint Satisfaction Problem: Theory and Practice, in *Scheduling of Production Processes*, Chichester: Ellis Horwood.

Schiex, T. 1992, Possibilistic Constraint Satisfaction Problem or how to Handle Soft Constraints, *Proceedings of the 8th International Conference on Uncertainty in Artificial Intelligence*, San Francisco, CA, USA, July.

Stallman, R.M. and Sussman, G.J. (1977) Forward Reasoning and Dependency Directed Backtracking in a System for Computer-aided Circuit Analysis, *Artificial Intelligence* **9**, pp. 135–196.

11

The Temporal Model of CRONOS-III: A Knowledge-based System for Production Scheduling

Ulrico Canzi*, **Giovanni Guida****
* CEFRIEL, Milano, Dipartimento di Elettronica per l'Automazione, ** Università di Brescia, Brescia

INTRODUCTION

CRONOS-III is the most recent version of a knowledge-based tool for *production scheduling* which covers a wide class of application environments (Canzi *et al.*, 1989), (Canzi *et al.*, 1990), (Canzi *et al.*, 1992). It represents a major advance with respect to previous approaches (Fox and Smith, 1984), (Bruno *et al.*, 1986), (Smith *et al.*, 1986), (Kanet and Adelsberger, 1987), (Chiodini, 1989), (Lee *et al.*, 1991), (Sycara *et al.*, 1991). In fact:

- it can support a realistic world model, including hierarchical production cycles, technological alternatives, technological constraints between tasks, set-ups, periodic activities, sharable resources, resources with finite or continuous sets of states, and complex relationships between tasks and resources;
- it is based on an advanced temporal model, specifically oriented towards scheduling problems and including the possibility of representing soft constraints which can be respected or violated to a degree.
- it implements a complete search strategy, namely depth-first with non-chronological backtracking, encompassing an effective use of heuristics (both for guiding the search and for directing backtracking).

Unlike other scheduling systems CRONOS-III is devoted to finding a schedule that respects all stated constraints, but is not necessarily an optimum schedule. Clearly, the types of constraints allowed are rich enough to guarantee that the schedule produced is fully appropriate for the user exigences. For example, CRONOS-III allows the user to define a domain-specific quality function and to state an acceptable quality factor for the schedule to be constructed. The user can also specify through soft constraints that some due dates may be violated, stating however an upper bound to the allowed violations.

Scheduling is a special case of temporal reasoning and therefore it requires an appropriate temporal model for representing temporal knowledge about operations, due dates and constraints, and for reasoning about them. Several temporal models have been proposed in the literature in recent years - for a survey see (Maiocchi and Pernici, 1991), but none of them is explicitly devoted to the scheduling task. The present chapter describes TEMS, the temporal model of CRONOS-III, purposely designed for dealing with scheduling problems. TEMS supports a quantitative representation of time and is grounded on an interval-based ontology. It allows the user to define complex temporal constraints, necessary in scheduling problems but generally not allowed by other temporal models. TEMS also supports the representation of soft temporal constraints which can be respected or violated to a degree, thus constituting a substantial extension of ordinary constraints.

This chapter is organized as follows. The next section provides a general overview of CRONOS-III, focusing in particular on system architecture, problem representation, scheduling strategy, and performance. After that two sections are devoted to illustrate the basic concepts of TEMS and the ordinary temporal constraints and to introduce the concept of soft temporal constraint and discusses its main properties. The following section deals with temporal reasoning and shows the use of TEMS in scheduling. Finally, some concluding remarks and the main directions of future work ends the chapter.

CRONOS-III

Background

CRONOS-III is a knowledge-based tool devoted to deal with production scheduling problems in a variety of application environments. Before it can be used for a specific scheduling problem, it must be appropriately tailored to the application domain at hand. The knowledge engineer, using an interactive graphical interface, must represent the specific production environment, namely: products and production cycles, available resources (plants, machines, raw materials, personnel, etc.), set-up operations, periodic activities such as shifts, maintenance interventions, etc. The knowledge engineer can also add domain-specific heuristics and tailor the quality function. Later, when a scheduling session is started, the user specifies a set of production orders to be executed, their due dates, the acceptable quality factor for the schedule, and the actual resource availabilities. CRONOS-III is then executed producing either a complete schedule which can meet all the specified requirements, or, in the case where a schedule with the desired features does not exist, a failure.

The development of CRONOS-III required about 8 man-years. It is implemented in Lisp and KEE (IntelliCorp, Mountain View, CA) on an IBM RR/PC workstation (16 Mbyte core memory, 300 Mbyte disk memory, risc processor) under the AIX operating system.

The architecture of CRONOS-III

The architecture of CRONOS-III, shown in figure 11-1, is inspired by the *blackboard model* (Erman *et al.*, 1980), (Hayes-Roth, 1985), (Nii, 1986).

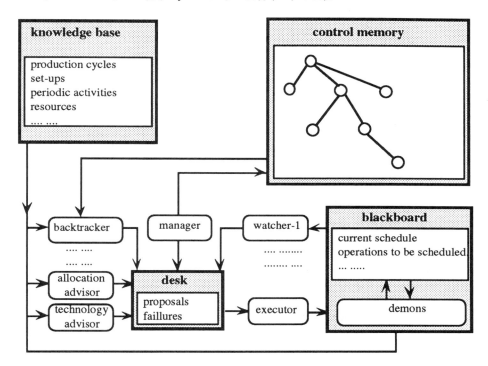

Figure 11-1: CRONOS-III architecture

Several specialists cooperate to solve a scheduling problem. They can read in a common knowledge base containing *domain knowledge* and can read and write in a common working memory, the blackboard, where the current state of the scheduling problem is stored (the partial schedule generated so far, the set of operations still to be scheduled, etc.). The blackboard is an active device which can preserve the consistency of the stored problem information through appropriate demons. When the content of the blackboard is modified, the relevant blackboard demons start a constraint propagation phase which either can keep the current problem description in a consistent state or signal a failure.

A shared control memory called desk is devoted to store the control messages exchanged among the specialists (and the demons), namely: proposal for actions to be undertaken or failures. At any new scheduling step, the current content of the desk is stored in a specific control memory, which contains a representation of the search tree explored so far, and the desk is then cleared. The activity of the specialists is directed by a dedicated specialist, called the manager.

In the present version, CRONOS-III includes five classes of specialists:

- The advisors are knowledge sources that can be specialized by the knowledge engineer with *domain heuristics*. At any step of the scheduling process they suggest the next sub-problem to be tackled and the way to solve it, and write their proposals on the desk. Each advisor is competent in one specific aspect of the scheduling problem. In the current version of CRONOS-III, there are two advisors: the technology advisor which is responsible for the technological choices and the allocation advisor which deals with the temporal allocation of the operations to be scheduled.

- The executor is devoted to execute the first solution proposal on the desk, thus changing the content of the blackboard.

- The watchers are knowledge sources that can be created or specialized by the knowledge engineer. During the scheduling process they watch the current state of the schedule being constructed and generate a failure if it exhibits unwanted characteristics. For instance, the work-load watcher checks that workers are not loaded beyond a given threshold: if this constraint is violated, the watcher immediately detects the problem and generates a failure. In the current version of CRONOS-III, there are five watchers.

- The backtracker is devoted to managing the backtracking strategy adopted in the search process: when a failure occurs, it identifies the most appropriate backtracking point (for example, the point where the last decision apparently responsible for the present failure was taken) and restores the correct problem-solving state (blackboard and desk). At present, the backtracker implements a *back-jumping* policy (Dechter, 1989).

- The manager is devoted to coordinating the activation of the other specialists.

Problem representation

In CRONOS-III a scheduling problem is represented by a set of production orders to be executed, their due dates, the acceptable quality factor for the schedule, and the actual resource availabilities.

Each production order can be satisfied by executing an appropriate production cycle. A *production cycle* is an *AND / OR-tree* which represents the operations necessary for manufacturing, constructing or building a given product. In a production cycle each non-elementary operation is decomposed into alternative sets (OR links) of conjunctive operations (AND link), which represent different *production technologies*. Therefore, each operation can be performed by executing all the operations of just one of the operation sets specified in its decomposition. A production cycle also specifies the constraints among operations, both temporal and technological, which must be respected during their execution. Each operation is bound to the set of alternative resources needed to execute it by an engagement request, which also defines the minimum and maximum durations of the time interval during which the resources must be engaged for the execution of the operation. Clearly, if several resources are needed for the execution of an operation, this will feature more than one engagement request. A time interval during which a resource is not engaged in the execution of an operation is called an *availability*. An engagement request becomes an *engagement* when one of its resources is actually assigned to the operation requesting it, during the needed time interval. Clearly, this implies that the involved resource has at least one availability in which a time interval of the duration defined by the engagement request can be allocated.

On the basis of the above definitions, a *scheduling problem* may be viewed as the problem of finding an appropriate allocation in the given resource availabilities of all engagement requests of the operations involved in the production cycles necessary to satisfy a given set of production orders, respecting all the specified temporal and technological constraints among operations, and in such a way as to meet the stated due dates and acceptable quality factor. A collection of engagements which satisfy all the above stated conditions for a subset of (respectively, all) the engagement requests relevant to a given set of production orders is called a partial schedule (respectively, a schedule). Initially, when a scheduling problem is faced, the partial schedule is empty: there are only availabilities and engagement requests, but no engagements at all. During the scheduling process, the construction of the partial schedule proceeds step-by-step. The elementary scheduling step is either a technological choice about alternative decompositions of an operation to be executed or an allocation of an engagement request into an availability. Each time a new engagement is defined the relevant resource availability receives a new constraint which is then propagated to all connected engagements or availabilities. Scheduling is therefore a combination of searching and temporal reasoning, namely temporal constraint propagation. Searching is guided by the strategies illustrated in the next section, while temporal constraint propagation will be discussed later.

Scheduling strategy

Each advisor is able to answer two specific questions about the problem-solving strategy to be adopted:

First question: "What is the next sub-problem to tackle?"

> For the allocation advisor, this question means *"What is the next engagement request to consider?"*, while for the technology advisor it means *"What is the next technological choice to consider?"* To answer this question the "most-constrained" heuristic (Keng and Yun, 1989) is adopted. Therefore, the allocation advisor proposes to consider the engagement request which can be allocated in the smallest set of existing availabilities, while the technology advisor proposes to consider the technological choice with the smallest set of alternatives.

Second question: "Which solutions do you suggest for the sub-problem considered?"

> For the allocation advisor, this question means *"How should the considered engagement request be allocated?"*, while for the technology advisor it means *"How should the considered technological choice be decided?"*. To answer this question the "least-impact" heuristic (Keng and Yun, 1989) is adopted. Therefore, the allocation advisor suggests the allocation of the engagement request considered either in the largest resource availability or in the resource availability suitable for allocation of the smallest set of other engagement requests, while the technology advisor suggests the selection of the decomposition which either requires the shortest execution time or ensures the best quality factor.

The operation of the manager during a scheduling session can be described as follows:

repeat
   if desk is empty **then**
      ask all advisors: "What is the next sub-problem to tackle?"
      {each advisor writes on the desk a sub-problem proposal}
      select one sub-problem proposal from the desk
      {the manager always selects the most constrained sub-problem}
      ask the proposer of the selected sub-problem: "Which solutions do you suggest for
        the sub-problem considered?"
      {the advisor writes on the desk a list of solution proposals for the sub-problem
        considered}
   end if
   activate executor
   {the executor executes the first solution proposal on the desk , thus changing the
     content of the blackboard}
   {the blackboard reacts to this change through its demons: constraint propagation is
   performed: either a consistent state is reached or a failure message is written on the
     desk}
   if there is no failure message on the desk **then**
      activate all watchers
      {if the schedule shows some unwanted characteristic, the relevant watcher detects it
      and writes a failure message on the desk}
   endif
   if there is no failure message on the desk **then**
      store current state of the desk in the control memory and clear the desk
      else {there is a failure message on the desk}
        activate backtracker
        {the backtracker finds the most appropriate backtracking point and resumes the
          correct problem-solving state}
   end if
   until a schedule is produced {success} **or** the backtracker cannot backtrack {failure}

Algorithm 11-1: Scheduling strategy

The control strategy illustrated above, and in particular the heuristics on which the operation of the advisors is based, implies that engagement requests are not allocated in any predictable sequence (for example, in the past-to-future direction), but are dealt with in an opportunistic way (Hayes-Roth and Hayes-Roth, 1979), (Keng and Yun, 1989).

Performance

As already mentioned above, the search strategy employed by CRONOS-III, namely depth-first with backtracking, ensures a complete exploration of the search space.

However, for a wide class of problems, the heuristics embodied in the advisors make the scheduling process almost backtrack-free.

The experimental activity carried out with CRONOS-III has concerned a variety of test cases, including, among others, a real plant for *production of computer modules*. The test cases considered range from 10 to 100 engagements; problems with more than 100 engagements can not be dealt with by the present implementation of CRONOS-III due to memory constraints. In average, CRONOS-III can solve a scheduling problem with 100 engagements in about 30 minutes (including some garbage collections), wasting only about 10% of the total computing time for backtracking. Figure 11-2 shows the correlation between the number of engagements and the time required to produce a schedule derived from 25 experiments.

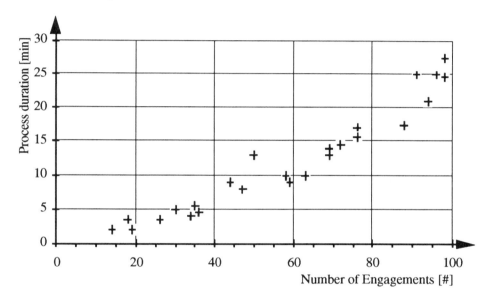

Figure 11-2: Performance of CRONOS-III

TEMS: BASIC CONCEPTS

In *temporal reasoning*, and particularly in scheduling problems, instants, intervals and durations may be either known or unknown. Unknown entities are represented by variables with appropriate domains. *Temporal constraints* are used to represent knowledge about unknown entities. In general any type of inequality (algebraic, non-algebraic, differential, etc.) involving unknown temporal entities (in addition to constants and other non-temporal entities) or any combination of inequalities through logical connectives (AND, OR, NOT) can be used to define a temporal constraint. When defining a temporal model, there are two possible policies: either allowing the temporal model to represent all possible kinds of temporal constraints mentioned above, or allowing it to represent just an appropriate subset of temporal constraints considered sufficient to deal with a specific domain of interest. Clearly, the latter choice is motivated by the aim of supporting of a more effective and compact representation of temporal entities and a more efficient temporal reasoning. Most of the temporal models proposed in the literature (Maiocchi and Pernici, 1991) adhere to this policy. For example, temporal logic (Allen, 1983), (Allen and Koomen, 1983), (Allen, 1984) considers 13 binary relations between lapses. These include all the necessary entities for representing a qualitative concept of time, but clearly they do not exhaust all possible relations between intervals when a metric is considered. For instance, a constraint like "The time interval between the finish of action A and the start of action B is at least of n seconds" can not be represented. Time Maps (Dean and McDermot, 1987) can deal with an absolute measure of time, but they can not represent constraints involving more than two instants. For instance, a constraint involving two durations like "Action A is longer than action B" can not be represented.

According to the above discussion, also the temporal model of CRONOS-III is not intended to be a fully general temporal model. It aims to be suitable for dealing with a wide class of scheduling problems, but, of course, it can be definitely inappropriate for other tasks. Accordingly, it is called TEMS: a TEmporal Model for Scheduling.

TEMS has an interval-based ontology. Its basic element is the lapse: a *time interval* characterized by a start instant and a finish instant. The start and finish instants of a lapse A are denoted by $s(A)$ and $f(A)$. Time instants are assumed to be isomorphic to the real axis extended by the symbolic values +inf and -inf; the continuous and infinite sequence of time instants is therefore called temporal axis. A lapse A may then be considered as a segment on the temporal axis: its length $f(A)$ - $s(A)$ is called duration and is denoted by $d(A)$. Note that in general positive, negative, and null durations are allowed.

The set of all possible lapses can be represented in a start / finish plane (Rit, 1986) as shown in figure 11-3. In the start / finish plane a point represents a lapse having start instant x and finish instant y. Positive lapses are all above the line $x = y$, negative lapses below it, and null lapses just on it.

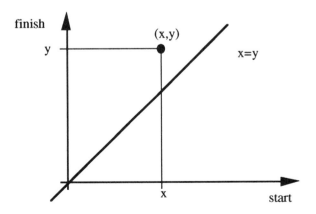

Figure 11-3: The start / finish plane

Since TEMS has an interval-based ontology, individual instants may neither be unknown nor be constrained; only lapses may be unknown or constrained. Of course, any constraint involving an unknown lapse must be defined in terms of its start instant, finish instant, and duration.

In TEMS constraints are classified regarding the number of involved lapses: in general, an n-ary constraint involves n unknown lapses.

In TEMS only one type of unary constraint is allowed. It is based on the concept of *set of possible occurrences* (sopo) proposed in (Rit, 1986). A sopo is a set of possible values for an unknown lapse. In general, it can be represented with an irregular area in the start/finish plane. Like (Rit, 1986), we only consider sopos with an hexagonal shape, like that shown in figure 11-4. A sopo constraint on the unknown lapse A can be defined through the predicate sopo defined as follows:

$$sopo(A, \textit{est}, \textit{lst}, \textit{eft}, \textit{lft}, \textit{mind}, \textit{maxd}) = \begin{cases} \textit{est} \leq s(A) \leq \textit{lst} \\ \textit{eft} \leq f(A) \leq \textit{lft} \\ \textit{mind} \leq d(A) \leq \textit{maxd} \end{cases}$$

where *est* and *lst* are the earliest start time and latest start time, *eft* and *lft* the earliest finish time and latest finish time, and *mind* and *maxd* are the minimum duration and maximum duration, respectively.

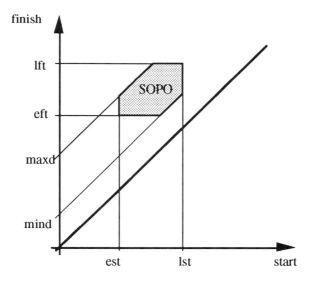

Figure 11-4: A sopo in the start / finish plane

Four types of binary constraints between two lapses *A* and *B* are allowed in TEMS. They are defined below:

$$\text{contains}(A, B) \quad = \quad \left\{ \begin{array}{l} s(A) \leq s(B) \\ f(A) \geq f(B) \end{array} \right.$$

$$\text{meets}(A, B) \quad = \quad \left\{ f(A) = s(B) \right.$$

$$\text{temp}(A, B, ib, eb) \quad = \quad \left\{ \begin{array}{l} s(B) - f(A) \geq ib \\ f(B) - s(A) \leq eb \end{array} \right.$$

$$\text{duration}(A, B, \alpha, \beta, lb, ub) \quad = \quad \left\{ \begin{array}{l} \alpha \cdot d(A) + \beta \cdot d(B) \leq ub \\ \alpha \cdot d(A) + \beta \cdot d(B) \geq lb \end{array} \right.$$

In the temp relation the value ib is called internal bound and represents the minimum time interval which must separate the two lapses, from the finish of lapse A to the start of lapse B. Note that ib may also have a negative value when lapse A overlaps lapse B. The value eb is called external bound and represents the maximum time interval which can elapse from the start of lapse A to the finish of lapse B. Clearly, eb must be at least equal to ib plus the sum of the minimum durations of the two lapses. A temp can allow modelling many useful binary constraint between lapses; for instance:

- $(ib = 0$ and $eb = +\inf)$ denotes the classic precedence relationship;
- $ib > 0$ implies a gap between the finish of first lapse and the start of the second; this gap can be upper-bounded by appropriately assigning the value of eb;
- $ib < 0$ means that the first lapse can overlap the second at most for the absolute value of ib.

In a duration constraint lb and ub denote lower bound and upper bound respectively, while a and b are two real coefficients. The duration constraint states therefore that the linear combination through the given coefficients a and b of the two unknown durations A and B can range between lb and ub.

There is a very great variety of conceivable n-ary constraints. They may be as intricate and poorly meaningful as "Start of lapse A minus finish of B is greater than finish of lapse C minus start of lapse D", or simple and useful like "Duration of lapse A is greater than the sum of durations of lapses B and C". In the present version, TEMS cannot deal with n-ary constraints.

In TEMS two constraints involving the same lapses can be combined into one new constraint using a suitable set of combination rules. Nine combination rules are defined in TEMS (& denotes the combination operation, and $\Rightarrow$ the result of the combination): one for unary constraints (CR0) and eight for a unary and a binary constraint (CR1 to CR8), namely two for each binary constraint. For the sake of brevity, we do not give the complete list of combination rules here; two examples are reported below:

CR0: sopo$(A, a_1, a_2, a_3, a_4, a_5, a_6)$ & sopo$(A, b_1, b_2, b_3, b_4, b_5, b_6) \Rightarrow$

sopo$(A, max(a_1, b_1), min(a_2, b_2), max(a_3, b_3), min(a_4, b_4), max(a_5\ b_5), min(a_6, b_6))$

CR3: sopo$(A, a_1, a_2, a_3, a_4, a_5, a_6)$ & temp$(A, B, ib, eb) \Rightarrow$

sopo$(B, (a_3 + ib), +\inf, -\inf, (a_2 + eb), -\inf, (eb - ib - a_5))$.

Combination rules are the basis of temporal reasoning, as it will be shown below.

A distinctive feature of TEMS is the concept of soft constraint which will be illustrated in the next section.

TEMS: SOFT TEMPORAL CONSTRAINTS

Ordinary temporal relations like those introduced in the previous section are not enough, in general, to adequately represent the variety of situations which may occur in scheduling problems. In fact, as has been already discussed by (Dubois and Prade, 1989), the effectiveness and efficiency of many scheduling systems is hardly challenged when the scheduling horizon (the distance between the start-date and the due-date) is very tight. In this case it may often occur that a schedule is considered unfeasible, even if some constraints are only slightly violated. This does not sound realistic: start-dates, due-dates and several other temporal constraints are often not precisely known and some of them are not rigid: a slight violation could be acceptable, possibly with some form of penalty. A better approach would therefore be to consider some temporal constraints only as preferences, with an explicit specification of the allowed violations together with the related penalties.

This reasoning brings to notice the issue of designing some sort of temporal relation which can support the representation of flexible time constraint of the type mentioned above. Several literature proposals (Dubois and Prade, 1989) argue that to this purpose appropriate techniques for representing uncertain information about time are needed, such as *fuzzy sets*, probability, possibility theory, etc. We claim that the problem of dealing with flexible constraints cannot be identified with that of representing imprecise uncertain or vague information about time. In fact, the kernel of the problem mentioned above is not that knowledge about time may be affected by uncertainty or vagueness: this is indeed an important but different issue, not dealt with in this chapter. The point about flexible constraints is that our knowledge of time is generally precise, but we need appropriate techniques to deal with temporal constraint which are not only fully respected or fully violated but can be respected or violated to a degree. In other words, we need a mechanism to represent preference degrees, in addition to yes / no requirements. Therefore, we do not need to extend the notion of time point or of temporal interval, but we need to expand the codomain of temporal constraints from the set {respected, violated} to a larger set of violation degrees. In order to deal with this issue we have introduced in TEMS the new concept of *soft temporal constraint*, that will be illustrated below.

The common concept of temporal constraint introduced in the previous section is called ordinary constraint. Ordinary constraints are expressed in TEMS through ordinary inequalities of the type

$$x \leq th \text{ (respectively, } x \geq th)$$

where x is an expression containing variables over the domain D_X and th is an assigned threshold value in D_X. An ordinary inequality may only be respected or violated.

A soft inequality is a pair (ineq, wgt), where:

- ineq is an ordinary inequality $[x \leq th]$ (respectively, $[x \geq th]$);

- wgt: $D_x \rightarrow R^+ \cup \{+inf\}$ is a weight function which, for any possible violation $\beta = x$ - th (respectively, $\beta = th - x$) of ineq, computes a corresponding weight, a factor in the set of positive real numbers extended by the special symbol +inf expressing the degree of gravity of the violation. It is assumed that for any $\beta \leq 0$, $wgt(\beta) = 0$.

Among several possibilities for defining the weight function wgt (for example, a step-wise constant function, a polynomial function, etc.), we adopt here a continuous, step-wise linear function which assumes the value +inf over a given finite value of violation. This form offers an adequate expressive power and allows an easy and coherent combination of soft inequalities. The weight function wgt can therefore be represented by a finite list of pairs (β_i, γ_i), called the soft-list, where:

- β_i is an acceptable violation of the threshold th;
- γ_i is the weight corresponding to the acceptable violation β_i.

For any possible value of β, the soft-list allows the corresponding weight γ to be computed as follows:

$$wgt(\beta) = \quad \textbf{if } \beta \leq 0 \textbf{ then } wgt(\beta) = 0$$
$$\textbf{if } 0 < \beta \leq \beta_1 \textbf{ then } wgt(\beta) = \beta \cdot \gamma_1/\beta_1$$
$$\textbf{if } \beta_i < \xi \leq \delta_{i+1} \textbf{ then } wgt(\beta) = \gamma_i + (\beta - \beta_i)(\gamma_{i+1} - \gamma_i)/(\beta_{i+1} - \beta_i)$$
$$\textbf{if } \beta > \beta_n \textbf{ then } wgt(\beta) = +inf$$

Clearly, wgt = 0 means respected, wgt = +inf means violated, and any value of wgt between 0 and +inf means violated to a degree. Two examples of penalty functions are shown in figure 11-5.

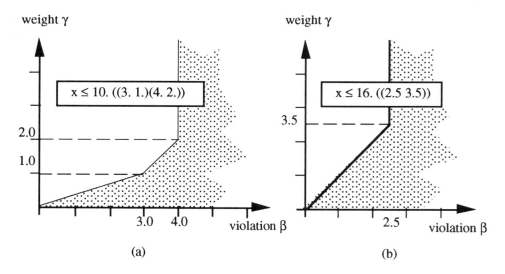

Figure 11-5: Examples of weight functions

Ordinary inequalities are of course a particular case of soft inequalities with an empty soft-list: any violation β of the stated threshold implies wgt(β) = +inf.

Soft constraints are constraints containing soft inequalities. In TEMS any constraint that contains explicitly stated bounds - i.e. sopo, temp, and duration constraints - may use soft inequalities instead of ordinary inequalities thus yielding a soft constraint.

The nine combination rules introduced in the previous section for ordinary constraints still apply to soft constraints, but in this case their form is more complex. For the sake of brevity, the detailed treatment of this subject is not presented here.

TEMPORAL REASONING

CRONOS-III uses searching and temporal reasoning to perform scheduling. As illustrated before, each time the content of the blackboard is changed by the executor, the blackboard reacts through an appropriate set of demons which perform constraint propagation: either a consistent state is reached or a failure is generated. Constraint propagation concerns technological constraints, set-ups, and also temporal constraints. The temporal reasoning mechanism adopted by CRONOS-III consists just in this constraint propagation phase which follows any change on the blackboard involving temporal entities.

The use of a distributed demon-based mechanism to implement temporal reasoning allows an easy and effective implementation of the nine combination rules (both for ordinary and soft constraints) into a small set of demons associated to the various object classes present in the blackboard and concerning temporal entities, namely: operations, availabilities, engagements, and temporal constraints (sopo, contains, meets, temp, duration). Thus, the demon-based approach allows a very complex problem such as the temporal propagation to be decomposed into a large number of simpler problems, relieving at the same time the designer from the task of explicitly dealing with control issues.

Figure 11-6 shows a simplified example of temporal constraint propagation. In the initial situation, the three lapses A, B, and C are each one constrained by their sopos shown in figure 11-6 (a). Moreover, A and B are mutually constrained by temp(A, B, 5, +inf), and B and C by duration(B, C, 1, 1, 15, +inf).

Suppose that, during the scheduling process, the executor modifies the sopo of A increasing the earliest start time (event 1) - see figure 11-6 (b). Note that, due to the particular shape of sopo of A, namely its minimum duration , also the earliest finish time of A is affected by this operation. The demon bound to the sopo of A performs this modification and propagates it to the lapse B through the constraint temp(A, B, 5, +inf). Since A can not finish as early as before and the time interval between the finish of A and the start of B is lower bounded (5 time units), also the earliest start time of B must be changed. This implies in turn a reduction of the maximum duration of B. The demon bound to the sopo of B performs this change and propagates it to the lapse C through the constraint duration(B, C, 1, 1, 15, +inf). Since the duration of B is now shorter than before, but the sum of the durations of B and C is lower bounded (15 time units), the minimum duration of C must be increased. The demon bound to the sopo of C performs this change and propagation stops.

In a following scheduling step, the executor modifies the sopo of C decreasing the maximum duration C(event 2) - see figure 11-6 (c). Since the sum of the durations of B

and C is lower bounded (15 time units), the minimal duration of B must be increased. The demon bound to the sopo of B performs this change and finally propagation stops.

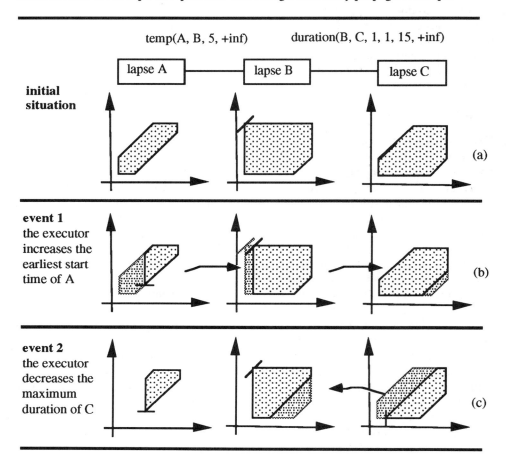

Figure 11-6: An example of temporal constraint propagation

Temporal propagation carried out through the demon mechanism shown above is reasonably efficient if the constraint network is loop-free or if some point-shaped sopos are present in the network. Otherwise, propagation becomes rather slow, thus affecting the efficiency of the whole scheduling process. Often, however, when the number of constraints increases and the constraint network becomes more and more complex, also the number of point-shaped sopos increases, thus partially balancing the greater dimension and complexity of the network.

CONCLUSIONS

Among several literature proposals concerning temporal models, two are especially worth comparing with TEMS, namely temporal logic (Allen, 1983), (Allen, 1984) and time maps (Dean and McDermott, 1987).

TEMS shares with temporal logic the interval-based ontology, but, differently from it, it focuses on a quantitative notion of time. Temporal logic does not allow unary constraints, being concerned only with relations among lapses. For what concerns binary constraints, the contains relation of TEMS differs from that of temporal logic due to the use of "≤" and "≥" instead of "<" and ">", while the meets relation of TEMS exactly mirrors that defined in temporal logic. All other binary constraints of TEMS can not be represented in temporal logic. TEMS can not deal with disjunctive temporal relations, while temporal logic can.

With respect to the Time Maps whose ontology is based on time points, the concept of time instant is substituted in TEMS by that of lapse. However, any time map can be represented in TEMS using lapses of null duration to represent time instants and temps to represent point-to-point constraints. On the other hand, time maps can not represent any constraint allowed in TEMS; in particular they can not represent the duration constraint like, for example, "The sum of durations of lapses A and B is greater (or lesser) than a given duration".

TEMS proved to be general and powerful enough to represent any reasonable temporal relation necessary in a scheduling task. A unique feature of TEMS is the concept of soft constraint. In the experimental activity carried out so far, this turned out to be useful and appropriate to deal with the major part of the practical situations encountered in real scheduling problems.

Future research activity on TEMS will focus on three main issues:

- the refinement of the formal basis of TEMS, and the improvement of its expressive power (explicit representation of disjunctions, representation of complex binary constraints such as, for example, "The duration of lapse A depends on the start of A", representation of n-ary constraints, etc.);
- the analysis of the efficiency of the temporal constraint propagation mechanism of TEMS (Tolba *et al.*, 1991), presently based on an object-oriented representation and on the extensive application of demons, and its possible improvement through a matrix representation of constraints similar to that proposed in (Dechter *et al.*, 1991), enhanced with the capability to deal with soft inequalities and n-ary constraints;
- the analysis of the appropriateness of the instant-based technique used for the implementation of the lapse-based ontology of TEMS and its possible improvement.

Acknowledgements

The authors would to thank all the researchers who have been working in the CRONOS project over the past years, namely: D. Dominoni, G. Maifredi, E. Paolucci, M. Poggio, W. Poloni, S. Pozzi, C. Sarasini, and A. Smiljanic.

REFERENCES

Allen, J.F. (1983) Maintaining Knowledge about Temporal Intervals, *Communications of the ACM* **26** (11), pp. 832–843.

Allen, J.F. (1984) Towards a General Theory of Action and Time, *Artificial Intelligence* **23**, pp. 123–154.

Allen, J.F. and Koomen, J.A. (1983) Planning Using a Temporal World Model, *Proceedings of the 8th International Joint Conference on Artificial Intelligence*, Karlsruhe, FRG, pp. 741–747.

Bruno, G., Elia, A. and Laface, P. (1986) A Rule-based System to Schedule Production, *IEEE Computer* (7), pp. 32–40.

Canzi, U., Guida, G., Poloni, W. and Pozzi, S. (1989) CRONOS-II: A Knowledge-based Scheduler for Complex Manufacturing Environments, *Proceedings 2nd International Conference on Data and Knowledge Systems for Manufacturing and Engineering*, Gaithesburg, MD, pp. 76–82.

Canzi, U., Guida, G., Maifredi, G. Paolucci, E. and Poggio, M. (1990) CRONOS-III: Requirements for a Knowledge-based Scheduling Tool Covering a Broad Class of Production Environments, *Proceedings International Workshop on Expert Systems in Engineering*, Lecture Notes in Artificial Intelligence 462, Springer-Verlag, Vienna, Austria, pp. 168–175.

Canzi, U., Guida, G., and Smiljanic, A. (1992) Knowledge-based Production Scheduling with CRONOS-III, *Proceedings of the 3rd International Conference on Data and Knowledge Systems for Manufacturing and Engineering*, Lyon, France, pp. 383–390.

Chiodini, V. (1989) SCORE: An Integrated System for Dynamic Scheduling and Control of High Volume Manufacturing, *Proceedings of the 5th IEEE Conference on Artificial Intelligence Applications* (CAIA-89) Miami, FL, pp. 272–278.

Dean, T.L. and McDermott, D.V. (1987) Temporal Data Base Management, *Artificial Intelligence* **32**, pp. 1–55.

Dechter, R. (1989) Enhancement Schemes for Constraint Processing: Backjumping, Learning, and Cutset Decomposition, *Artificial Intelligence* **41**, pp. 273–312.

Dechter, R. Meiri, I. and Pearl, J. (1991) Temporal Constraint Networks, *Artificial Intelligence* **49**, pp. 61–95.

Dubois, D. and Prade, H. (1989) Processing Fuzzy Temporal Knowledge, *IEEE Transaction on Systems, Man, and Cybernetics*, **SMC-19** (4), pp. 729–744.

Erman, L.D., Hayes-Roth, F., Lesser, V.R. and Reddy, D.R. (1980) The HEARSAY-II Speech-understanding System: Integrating Knowledge to Resolve Uncertainty, *ACM Computing Surveys* **12**, pp. 213-253.

Fox, M.S. and Smith, S. (1984) ISIS: A Knowledge-based System for Factory Scheduling, *Expert Systems* **1**(1), pp. 25–49.

Hayes-Roth, B. (1985) A Blackboard Architecture for Control, *Artificial Intelligence* **26**, pp. 251–321.

Hayes-Roth, B. and Hayes-Roth, F. (1979) A Cognitive Model of Planning, *Cognitive Science* **3**, pp. 275–310.

Kanet, J.J. and Adelsberger, H.H. (1987) Expert Systems in Production Scheduling, *European Journal of Operational Reasearch* **29**, pp. 51–59.

Keng N. and Yun, D.Y.Y. (1989) A Planning / Scheduling Methodology for the Constraints Resource Problem, *Proceddings of the 11th International Joint Conference on Artificial Intelligence* (IJCAI-89), Detroit, MI, pp. 998–1003.

Lee, I.B.H., Lim, B.S. and Nee, A.Y.C. (1991) IKOOPPS: An Intelligent Knowledge-based Object-oriented Process Planning System for the Manufacture of Progressive Dies, *Expert Systems* **8** (1), pp. 19–32.

Maiocchi, R. and Pernici, B. (1991) Temporal Data Management Systems: A Comparative View, *IEEE Transactions on System, Man, and Cybernetics,* **SMC-3** (4), pp. 504–524.

Nii, P.N. (1986) Blackboard Systems: The Blackboard Model of Problem Solving and the Evolution of Blackboard Architectures, *AI Magazine* **7** (2), pp. 38–53.

Rit, J.F. (1986) Propagating Temporal Constraints for Scheduling, *Proceedings of the 5th National Conference on Artificial Intelligence* (AAAI-85) Philadelphia, PA., pp. 383–388.

Smith, S., Fox, M.S. and Ow, P.S. (1986) Constructing and Mantaining Detailed Production Plans: Investigations into the Development of Knowledge-based Factory Scheduling Systems, *AI Magazine* **7** (4), pp. 45–61.

Sycara, K.P., Roth, S.F., Sadeh, N. and Fox, M.S. (1991) Resource Allocation in Distributed Factory Scheduling, *IEEE Expert* **6** (1), pp. 29–40.

Tolba, H. Charpillet, F. and Haton, J.P. (1991) Representing and Propagating Constraints in Temporal Reasoning, *AICOM* **4** (4), pp. 145–151.

12

INTESIMPRO – Simple Dynamic Scheduling for Discrete Manufacturing*

José Lazaro, José Maseda, Fernando Díaz, Helge Sturesson and Gonzalo Escalada
LABEIN, Vizcaya

INTRODUCTION

There is a current increase of concern in the area of manufacturing scheduling as can be seen in the number of papers and projects in recent years, e.g. (Fox, 1983), (Smith and Fox, 1987), (Le Gall and Roubellat, 1989), (de Swaan Arons and Riewe, 1989). That interest, motivated by increasing global competitiveness which necessinates to improvements in customer satisfaction and resource utilization, happens in parallel with the availability of new more powerful hardware and new basic techniques. The latter, although mainly based on Operations Research, have also been influenced by emerging fields such as *Artificial Intelligence* (AI). Among the topics where such an influence can be detected, we will mention issues such as knowledge representation, constraint management, object-oriented and rule-based programming, and search techniques.

The objective of the INTESIMPRO system is to solve scheduling problems for discrete manufacturing using some of those AI techniques. Two points with respect to that system should be mentioned:

- It is not completely general. A system can efficiently compute only certain classes of the great number of the existing production models (Newman, 1988).
- It is not optimal. Since the scheduling problem is NP-hard, finding a solution that satisfies all the constraints may take exponential time. Moreover, the dynamic manufacturing context may invalidate a solution in a very short time. Hence, a system designed to find the (optimal) solution verifying all the constraints cannot be used in most practical applications.

---

* This research was financially supported by the Basque Government, Gobierno Vasco - Eusko Jaurlaritza, as a part of the project INTESIMPRO.

Our contribution is structured as follows. The second section describes the type of factories we are dealing with. The third, shows their representation. After that, a simple and incremental search of a scheduling solution is outlined. The fifth section describes the first method used to solve dead ends. The sixth explains the use of constraint relaxation to find a solution when the previously described method fails. The seventh section describes the way unexpected events can be handled by the system. Finally, some conclusions are outlined.

MODEL OF THE PROBLEM

Our system is designed for a *job-shop* manufacturing facility with M_i machines (some of them are similar or even equivalent considering their functionalities) in which O_j orders, with due dates and release dates, probably based on the output of an MRP II, are to be manufactured.

The system assumes that some orders may have been scheduled previously and some of them may be in process at the time the scheduler is working. Those orders are not to be considered by the scheduler unless a disturbance comes up.

Each order produces a variable quantity of a type of product, and associated to each product there is a unique *process plan*. That is the normal case unless an assembly type of manufacturing is considered. However, the process plan may admit several routes, depending on the number of similar machines which are available. For the time being, we assume that only one resource is required to perform an operation.

In our model, set-up times and load and unload times are not included, assuming that they are either small with respect to the operation duration or they have a constant duration which can be incorporated into the operation duration. Preemptive scheduling is not considered either, unless there is a special problem such as a resource breakdown or a lack of raw materials.

During the definition of our domain, we have also had to deal with the problem mentioned in (Prosser, 1993): if processing time is fairly different among similar resources, there is a great uncertainty with respect to the time interval in which the operation can be performed until the resource assignment is finally performed. But, if the time interval is not known, it is difficult to evaluate the most suitable resource for the operation. We have tackled that problem by assuming that equivalent machines require the same amount of time to perform an identical operation for a given product.

REPRESENTATION

There are several ways to represent the manufacturing plant with all the activities, resources and concepts involved in scheduling. The system describes the model by means of frames and semantic networks as in (Fox, 1983), (Smith and Fox, 1987) because they match, very intuitively, the relationships among the real objects, they are flexible with respect to the type of plant and, moreover, that type of representation is powerful enough to include all of the relevant features of the factory which we have been able to identify as needed.

As an example, let us represent, more precisely, the type of relationship between activity and a generic operation:

{   activity   {   operation
    [start]   [is-a activity]
    [end]   [in-order]
    [duration]   [next-operation-order]
    [in-resource]   [previous-operation-order]
    [next-activity-resource]   [time-window-begin]
    [previous-activity-resource] }   [time-window-end]
                                               [load] }

Figure 12-1: Representation of the relationship between activity and operation

The semantic network associated to the taxonomy of activities takes the shape shown in figure 12-2. Analogously, there are also taxonomies associated to other manufacturing concepts such as, for instance:

Calendar: Working day, Holidays, Day off, etc.
Resource: Machines, buffers, tools, personnel, parts, etc.

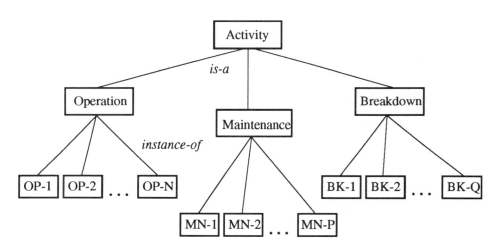

Figure 12-2: Semantic Network for the activity concept

INCREMENTAL SOLUTION

The manufacturing scheduling problem can be considered as a special case of one of the formulations of the *constraint satisfaction problem*, CSP, in which finding only one valid solution is enough. Therefore, some similarity between their problem solving techniques can be identified. All instances of the CSP consist, at least, of an incremental module and a backtracking mode, the latter being more or less sophisticated.

In our scheme, scheduling decisions are initially taken order by order. The system considers both the release date and the due date of every order and propagates them forwards and backwards in time to obtain the interval in which every operation of any order can be performed without interfering with those *temporal constraints*. That interval is usually called time bound or time window. Allocating operations inside those intervals guarantees that the order will be produced before its due date. After that, an order criticality function, selected from a pool of five simple *dispatching rules* which are already implemented, is calculated. As it is already known, those rules are based on order types and/or their available and required processing times, to schedule most critical orders first. At that point in the scheduling process, the user can manually modify the sequence produced by the system in order to allow for special characteristics not directly implemented in the automatic mode. Then, each operation, from the release date to the due date, is successively considered for scheduling taking into account the work load already scheduled. Part of those previous assignments are considered movable while others, closer in time, are considered fixed to encourage plan stability.

Although some other scheduling techniques have already been developed, such as resource-based scheduling, as in the OPIS system, probabilistic-oriented scheduling as in the CORTES system, and/or bottleneck scheduling, of which OPT is a good example, for the time being, no special attention has been paid to those incremental issues in the system described here, since it is more oriented to test and evaluate the backtracking and reactive aspects incorporated in the approach, which are described in the following sections.

As a different functionality, although related to the contents of this section, the system has the possibility to schedule maintenance activities, which may also belong to different classes, with different durations and characteristics. In that case, the resource to be maintained is selected by the user, and according to the type of maintenance, and the existing schedule, the most suitable time is assigned by the system. The temporal assignment is based on the load already committed to that resource in order to avoid interfering with the current schedule.

BACKTRACKING

The above described strategy may result in a dead end (bottlenecks) due to lack of resources or because the system is not, as a result of the heuristic character of the whole problem solving process, on the optimal path of the search. In the former case, there is not a proper solution and some kind of constraint relaxation is required. In the latter case, some form of reassignment may lead to a better situation than that currently under examination. If even that does not work, the system will have to relax some constraint.

We have considered three different types of reassignments, always based on values of operations and resources that interact with the problematic operation. In fact, that means to assume, implicitly, that our measure of previous assignments is not very far from the best one. With respect to the reassignments, we consider only local operations, either in time or in resource.

The modules used to reallocate operations are called sequentially, and they are quit as soon as a solution is found. Whenever such a solution is not found, although it must be pointed out that this does not imply that such a solution does not exist, the system activates the relaxation procedure. At this moment, and due to the complex, subtle and long propagating interactions existing in the problem, it has been preferred to increase efficiency in proposing a schedule, albeit relaxed, at the cost of losing some quality in the solution found, rather than to have to spend too much time searching for the optimal schedule, if that exists.

Let us describe all three available methods in some more detail:

- The first method simply tries to solve the problem by shifting operations. It will do so until there is success or no more equivalent resources can be tested, but it will not transfer operations from the resource they are assigned to, to another resource. It tries to take full advantage of idle times which arise due to intra-order and capacity constraints. The procedure stops successfully when some idle time appears that let us introduce the operation in the new position. Otherwise, the procedure stops as soon as a capacity constraint in the order does not allow more shifting.
- The second tries to exchange the problematic operation with another one which belongs to its time window and is performed on a similar machine. This operator is briefly outlined in the following pages. It is worth mentioning that only operations of some orders can be moved by the scheduler.
- The third operator tries to schedule, more precisely, the operations which seem to be in conflict. It defines a set which contains the current operation and those that interact with it, both with respect to its time interval and with respect to its resource type. For each of these operations O_i, with duration D_i, time bound duration T_i and number of equivalent resources M_i, the heuristic ratio defined as

$$C_i = \frac{D_i}{T_i * M_i}$$

is evaluated in order to successively assign each operation to the least critical resource available for that operation, so as to achieve some kind of balanced work load. If there is no solution under these purely heuristic procedures, *constraint relaxation* is proposed to the user.

procedure exchange (R, O_{ij})
let R   Resource
O_{ij}, $|O_{ij}|$ Operation and its duration
$O_{ij}-$, $O_{ij}+$ Earliest and latest starting time for O_{ij}
O_k Generic operation (overlapping [$O_{ij}-,O_{ij}+$])
$D(O_k, O_{ij})$ Duration of the interval of O_k included in
                                       [$O_{ij}-$, $O_{ij}+ + |Oi_j|$]
$|LB-1| + D(O_k, O_{ij}) + |LB+1|$ Duration $D(O_k, Oi_j)$ plus extra time due to adjacent
                                       free intervals overlapping [$O_{ij}-$, $O_{ij}+ + |Oi_j|$]
$D(LB', O_k)$ Duration of interval LB in [O_k-, $O_k+ + |Ok_l|$]

result := false
while (exists O_k overlapping $[O_{ij}-, O_{ij}+]$) **and** (O_{ij} is not assigned) **do**
  if ($|O_{ij}| < |LB-1| + D(O_k, O_{ij}) + |LB+1|$)
    then begin
      while (exists R' equivalent to R) **and** (O_{ij} is not assigned) **do**
        while (exists free time interval LB in R') **and** (O_{ij} is not assigned) **do**
          if ($|O_k| < D(LB', O_k)$)
            then begin
              assign O_{ij} in (LB-1, Ok, LB+1)
              (re)assign O_k in LB'
              result := true
            else next free interval LB in R'
          end if
        end while
      next equivalent resource R'
      end while
    end if
    next O_k
end while
return result (true or false depending on the success of the partial (re) assignment)
end procedure exchange

Algorithm 12-1: Exchanging operations

RELAXATION

The solution obtained through relaxation will just satisfy relaxed constraints. So, its quality can be measured as a function of the increments of the following parameters: delays in delivery, additional cost and loss of product quality.

Estimation of the quality of a solution

We can distinguish the following parameters, represented as vector:
- Internal Variables (I): Due date delay, overtime and quality loss due to routing.
- Relaxation Variables (R): Due date satisfaction, cost and product quality.

The values of the R vector are function of variables I. Thus, we can write,

$$R = H * I$$

where H is a matrix expressing the relaxation costs R obtained by modifying the internal variables I. Thus, H_{kj} indicates cost/influence per unit of the internal variable I_j. For instance, let us assume that R_k is the additional production cost and I_j the overtime required to complete the job. If any additional hour costs 50, then H_{kj} will be equal to 50.

Now, we can estimate the distance from a solution S_0 that verifies all the constraints, to that S obtained by relaxing them. For this purpose, we consider the relative influence of a particular variable R_k on the quality of a solution by means of a scaling factor. If W is a weight vector, where W_k measures the contribution of each cost R_k to $\| S_0 - S \|$ then we can write:

$$\| S_0 - S \| = W^T * R = W^T * H * I$$

Therefore, we can evaluate the quality of a solution S as a function of the internal variables defined with the vector I.

Relaxation tree

The algorithm searches for a solution by making progressively relaxation whenever intricate dead ends are met. This search is performed in a relaxation tree and is heuristically guided by the estimated penalty associated with relaxation states. The root is associated with the first dead end state where no relaxation has been considered yet. Each node of this tree has associated:

- A scheduling state, which represents the assignments of resources and time already decided;
- A value $(W^T * H * I) / N$, where N is the number of scheduled operations. It indicates the penalty for each scheduled operation of the associated scheduling state.

The successors of a node are defined as follows:

After carrying out the relaxation corresponding to a node, the processing of scheduling operations continues. When a new dead end is found then the set of possible relaxations (delaying due dates, increasing overtime, etc.) leads to the different successors. The system keeps as backtracking situations a number of nodes polynomial in the number of already scheduled operations. This allows us to keep a suitable trade-off between the computing requirements and quality of the obtained solution. For instance, a high polynomial degree would be advantageous when considerable computing means are available in comparison with the problem complexity dealt with.

DYNAMIC BEHAVIOUR

Due to the dynamic character of real manufacturing processes, schedules cannot be something fixed in practice. There is a frequent appearance of particular situations such as arrival of rush orders, resource breakdown, operation failure and lack of raw materials which originate disturbances that produce an unforeseeable alteration of the schedule. As a result of that, it seems convenient to build a system that not only allows the operator to include and/or modify data in the computed schedule, but also can react to the appearance of several kinds of incidents during the manufacturing process.

Manual modifications of the schedule are monitored automatically by the system to avoid inconsistencies such as improper route allocation or assignment to an unavailable resource. The criterion for re-scheduling in case of incidents is that such a process should affect only orders directly involved in the event. Although this criterion restrains the domain for rescheduling, it also reduces its complexity and computing time.

procedure resource breakdown rescheduling
let R   Resource that breaks down
  [a, b]   (Estimated) Breakdown interval
  $\{O_i\}$ Set of affected operations by resource breakdown
  $[O_{i-}, O_{i+}]$ Time window of operation i
  D_i Duration of operation i
  n   Number of affected operations

Determine set $\{O_i\}$, where each operation O_i is allocated on resource R
                                                            during interval [a, b]
shift O_n, last operation affected by resource breakdown
if shift O_n = success
    then delete O_n from set $\{O_i\}$
end if
order set $\{O_i\}$ by urgency criterion
i = 0
while $\{O_i\}$ not empty **do**
    select alternate resource for operation O_i, with free space >= D_i on
                                                            interval $[O_{i-}, O_{i+}]$.
    if alternate resource for O_i does not exist
        then unschedule O_i and next operations of its order
        else reallocate O_i on alternate resource
    end if
    delete operation O_i from set $\{O_i\}$
    i = i + 1
end while
compute new priorities for unschedule orders
re-schedule unscheduled orders by general method
end procedure resource breakdown rescheduling

Algorithm 12-2: Resource breakdown rescheduling

If a resource breaks down, all operations assigned to that machine during the time interval estimated as necessary for repairing it, must be unscheduled, and then classified by an urgency criterion. After that, the system tries to reallocate them on alternative resources following the urgency sequence. If an operation of the list cannot be reallocated, its order is temporarily unscheduled starting from that critical operation. After considering every operation in the list of affected activities, some orders may have been unscheduled. The re-scheduling process continues by reevaluating the priorities of those unscheduled orders, taking into account only time and dates from critical operations. Then, the system will schedule again those orders following the general method. A more detailed version of this procedure can be seen above in this chapter.

In case of lack of materials, and once the delay in the arrival of needed materials has already been estimated, the method consists of trying first a shift in the critical operation for each affected order. Such a shift can be propagated, if necessary, to the following operations of the same order. If the shift cannot be done, the system tries to reallocate the operation on an alternative resource, and if this is not possible either, it unschedules the affected order from its critical operation. After having followed that procedure with every order affected by lack of materials, new priorities of unscheduled orders are computed, as in the case above, and then the system will reschedule them, following the general method.

CONCLUSION

Main trade-offs of the proposed algorithm were decided in favour of its average complexity. Thus, the approach distinguishes between simple and complex dead ends. The first are solved by operators with fairly small overhead and the second by constraint relaxation. Hence, with a small devaluation of the quality of the solution, excessive search is avoided and practical applications can be considered. Such a quality loss can be reduced within suitable limits by adapting heuristics and parameters to the application environment. At this moment, some of the modules are already implemented using an expert system tool as well as a conventional language, while others have already been defined in detail and are still under development.

The authors wish to sincerely thank the other members of their department for their valuable comments on previous versions of this work.

REFERENCES

De Swaan Arons, H. and Riewe, D. (1989) Integration of Dynamic Expert Scheduling in Production Control, *Esprit'89 Conference Proceedings*, Kluwer Academic Publishers, pp. 674–687.

Fox, M.S. (1983) *Constraint-Directed Search: A Case Study of Job-Shop Scheduling*, Ph. D. Thesis, Carnegie Mellon University.

Guida, M. and Basaglia, G. (1990) Integrating Operational Research and Artificial Intelligence in a Distributed Approach to Dynamic Scheduling: The B.I.S. Project, *Esprit'90 Conference Proceedings*, Kluwer Academic Publishers, pp. 544-558.

Le Gall, A. and Roubellat, F. (1989) A Decision Support System for Real Time Production Scheduling, *3rd ORSA/TIMS Conference on FMS*, Cambridge, MA. USA.

Newman, P.A. (1988) Scheduling in CIM Systems, in *Artificial Implications for CIM*, A. Kusiak (ed.), Berlin: IFS (Publications) Ltd/Springer Verlag, pp. 361–402.

Prosser, P. (1993) Scheduling as a Constraint Satisfaction Problem: Theory and Practice, in *Scheduling of Production Processes*, Chichester: Ellis Horwood.

Smith, S.F. and Fox, M.S. (1987) *Constraint-Based Scheduling in an Intelligent Logistics Support System: An Artificial Intelligence Approach*, Final Report, Carnegie Mellon University.

13

Scheduling and Routing Heuristics in an Automated Jobshop Environment

Manfred Gronalt
Institut für Betriebswirtschaftslehre, Universität Wien

INTRODUCTION

The use of numerically controlled machining centres in manufacturing has brought up the need to develop new and tailored production control systems for automated manufacturing (Kusiak, 1990), (Stecke, 1989), (Tempelmeier, 1992). Additionally, up to now more than 800 *Flexible Manufacturing Systems* (FMSs) are in use (Ranta and Tchijov, 1990). This chapter deals with *production scheduling* in FMS and sets special emphasis on *routing* and scheduling problems in order to reach an optimal solution in a static environment.

The referenced FMS can be seen as a random FMS according to the classifications of Rachamadugu and Stecke (1989) and Hutchinson and Khumawala (1991). The schedules are generated offline, that is the complete schedule for a set of parts is manufactured according to this schedule. Considering a specific set of already released jobs for production and already loaded tools to machining centres the routing flexibility is used to balance different machine workloads. After determination of different routes a scheduling problem is solved using a single pass procedure. This solution is then improved by using a *job exchange heuristic* which is controlled by variations of the *tabu search* method. For details of the tabu search heuristic see e.g. (Glover, 1989). Generated problem cases were used to find a set of good variations of the search methods.

LITERATURE REVIEW

FMS planning functions

It is well known that the operational planning functions cannot be solved within one approach or one model. Therefore several authors identify slightly different planning functions in order to reduce the complexity of the problem and to achieve admissible results.

Stecke (Stecke, 1986), (Stecke, 1989) identified the following steps: part type selection, machine grouping, determination of the part mix ratio, *resource allocation* and loading. Kusiak (1986b) distinguishes between four different planning hierarchies: aggregate planning, resource grouping, disaggregate planning, machine scheduling and material handling systems scheduling.

Schmidt (1989) considers problems of system-setup and operational planning. The operational planning includes input sequencing, routing, machine scheduling and monitoring. Bastos (1988) defines four essential functions of operational planning. In his sense operational planning consists of batching, routing, dispatching and sequencing. Solot (1990) identifies the following problem sets: input sequencing, operation sequencing, work station selection, part sequencing, material handling carrier selection, traffic control and operator selection. Hintz (1987) (see also (Gupta *et al.*, 1991)) formulated a multi-criterion approach based on *fuzzy reasoning* consisting of four components: master scheduling, tool loading, part type release and machine scheduling.

Recently some works (Kuhn, 1990), (Chen and Chung, 1991) which deals with the impact of loading, order release and routing strategies to the performance of the manufacturing system were reported.

Operational planning

The fundamental problems of scheduling are tool loading, determination of routing mix and machine scheduling (Chen and Chung, 1991). Calabrese and Hausman (1991) study the simultaneous determination of lotsizes and routing under steady state conditions. While Chen and Chung investigate the effects of loading and routing decisions on the performance of FMS, this chapter deals with the interaction and effects of routing and machine scheduling decisions. The approach choosen is to solve these problems offline (Hutchinson and Khumawala, 1991).

The determination of the routing mix

Rachamadugu and Stecke (1989) state that the possibility to select one out of several machine sequences for a particular order or workpiece is a key principle of FMS (Gall and Roubellat, 1989), (Lin and Solberg, 1989), (Chen and Chung, 1991). The use of this flexibility through automation contributes to shortening of order lead times. The determination of the machine sequences (routes) can be done before machine scheduling (Gall and Roubellat, 1989), (Bastos, 1988). Many authors discuss a simultanous determination of machine sequences and machine scheduling (Lin and Solberg, 1989), (Kusiak, 1989), (Rachamadugu and Stecke, 1989), (Chandra and Talvage, 1991). Agnetis *et al.* (1990) consider the determination of part routing in a flexible assembly system in order to minimize the critical machine workload or to minimize the total number of part transfers. If the routes are calculated separately one main criterion is to minimize the completion time of an order. In order to achieve this goal balancing of workload is a common means (Bastos, 1988), (de Luca, 1984). Reducing the workload on the bottleneck machine by introduction of alternative routes is another goal (Avonts *et al.*, 1988).

Machine scheduling

Production scheduling has to determine a timely assignment of operations of all released orders to resources in order to best meet a predefined goal (Rodammer and White, 1988). For the variety of process strategies different solution procedures are disussed (Blazewicz *et al.*, 1993).

Priority rules are the most popular instrument for production scheduling. They can be classified according to their use as static and dynamic or local and global (Panwalkar and Iskander, 1977). Some popular priority rules are:

* SPT: shortest processing time
* LPT: longest processing time
* EDD: earliest due date
* SLACK: $\min_{i = 1, \ldots, n} (d_i - p_i - t)$ minimum slack time
* FIFO: first in first out
* minimum product of processing time and sum of all processing times
* minimum quotient of processing time and sum of all processing times
* smallest number of remaining operations

Priority rules in FMS

Depending on the type of FMS (dedicated oder non-dedicated) scheduling in FMS has different tasks (Rachamadugu and Stecke, 1989). In dedicated FMS priorities are used to determine an input sequence (Gunal *et al.*, 1991). In non-dedicated FMS *resource scheduling* is the most important issue (Kusiak, 1988), (Raman *et al.*, 1989), (Mukhopadhyay *et al.*, 1991), (Chandra and Talavage, 1991). Kusiak uses the following priority rules: maximum number of subsequent operations, minimum number of schedulable operations per part, maximum number of immediately subsequent operations, maximum number of remaining operations of a workpiece, shortest processing time (SPT) minimum slack (SLACK) and random.

Integration of routing and scheduling

As already mentioned the use of alternative routes is one of the key elements in scheduling of FMS. Through the integration of routing and scheduling the obtained results should be improved. Conway *et al.* (1967) have investigated priority rules and possible alternative routes. Lin and Solberg (1989) try to use the information of the operation list to generate additional routes (Bard, 1989), (Kusiak, 1988). Kusiak develops a procedure for resource scheduling which integrates routing and scheduling in a knowledge based approach. Erschler *et al.* (Erschler and Roubellat, 1989), (le Gall and Roubellat, 1989) describe a problem with several unrelated machines. They solve the routing and scheduling hierachically and iteratively with constraint based analysis. Hutchinson and Khumawala (1991) compare two offline procedures (MILP) to a number of prioritity rules used in real time. Mukhopadhyay *et al.* (1991) present a heuristic for solving resource scheduling including tool allocation problem, parts scheduling, pallets scheduling, machines scheduling and material handling scheduling in order to achieve maximum production rate.

A HIERARCHICAL CONCEPT OF ROUTING AND SCHEDULING

Integrated routing and scheduling

In this chapter an approach for integration of routing and scheduling is presented. For each job there are a certain number of different routes due to technological constraints (tool loading) available. The production lotsizes x_{ir} for each route are treated as job data for scheduling. So the use of optimization methods is possible in each of the planning steps. Additionally with this approach dynamic situation like machine breakdowns can also be considered.

Given is a set M of machines $M_1, ..., M_m$, which could be rather the same (tool loading). Further is

j: index for machines, $j = 1, ..., m$
h: index for the machine type, $h = 1, ... H$
A_h: number of machines of type h
h_j: type of machine j, $1 \leq h_j \leq H, j = 1, ..., m$

$$m = \sum_{h=1}^{H} A_h$$

The jobs $(J_1, ... J_n)$ to be processed are determined by the work order size x_i, the number of operations O_i and a precedence relation R_{il}, $l = 1, ..., O_i$ of these operations. Each job consists of several operations (i, l) and each operation can be processed on one or more machines. The matrix of resources R_{il} (see table 13-1) describes the machine types which are able to perform the operation (i, l). So the actual processing time $p_{il}(j)$ of an operation is generated by assigning an operation to a particular machine $M_j = \{M_v \mid h_v = R_{ij}\}$.

Table 13-1: Resource matrix

R_{il}		1			
		1	2	3	4
	1	2	1	3	4
i	2	1	2	3	
	3	3	1	2	

For each machine S_j denotes the available capacity during the planing horizon, P_j the planned workload and K_j the workload exceeded the available workload.

$$K_j = \max(0, P_j - S_j) \qquad j = 1, ..., m$$

By determination of the route the sum of the overloading capacites should be minimized:

$$K \qquad\qquad \rightarrow \quad \min \qquad\qquad (1)$$

$$\sum_{j=1}^{m} K_j \qquad = \quad K \qquad\qquad (2)$$

$$\max(0, P_j - S_j) \qquad = \quad K_j \qquad\qquad (3)$$

$$\sum_{i=1}^{n} \sum_{r=1}^{R_i} x_{ir}\, p(m_{ir}) = \quad P_j \qquad\qquad (4)$$

$$\sum_{r=1}^{R_i} x_{ir} \qquad\qquad = \quad x_i \qquad\qquad (5)$$

The machine sequences $\mathcal{M}_{ir}$ consist of an ordered set of machines $\{M_j \mid h_j = R_{il}\}$ and the corresponding processing time.

$$p(m_{ir}) = \sum_{l=1}^{O_i} p^j_{il}\, y^j_{il}$$

Let $r = 1, \ldots, R_i$ be the index of routes and R_i be the maximum number of routes for job i

$$R_i = \prod_{l=1}^{O_i} A_{R_{il}}$$

and

$$y^j_{il} = \begin{cases} 1: & M_j \in \{\mathcal{M}_{ir}\} \\ 0: & \text{else} \end{cases}$$

The production lotsize of route r will be denoted with x_{ir} and the new jobs are $J_{i_1}, J_{i_2}, \ldots, J_{i_{R_i}}$.

A heuristic procedure of determination the routing mix

To find a solution for the *routing* problem a heuristic which iteratively reduces the work-load on overloaded machines is developed. After finding an initial solution, the procedure tries to reduce overloading on each of the machines. So the bottleneck machine and the job which contributes mainly to the overload of the bottleneck machine are searched. After this the production lotsize for this job is changed in order to eliminate the overload on the bottleneck. When doing this one has to consider that changing one route not only has an impact on the workload of machines on this route and but also on the workload of machines to which the workload is transferred.

procedure routing

L_i: load of Job J_i

δL_i: change of load of Job J_i

Step 0: **input** m, n, A_h, h_j, J_i, R_{il}, p_{il}^j and S_j

Step 1: Determine for each of the routes an initial solution:

$$x_{ir} = \frac{x_i}{\sum_{l=1}^{R_i} p_{ir} \, / \, p_{il}}$$

$p_{ir} = p_{m_{ir}}$

Determine the value of the initial solution:

P_j, K_j and K

if $\forall$ h: $A_h = 1$ **then stop** (no routing flexibility)

   else Step 2

Step 2: **if** $K = 0$ **then stop**

   else store actual solution;

K' = K and determine the machine

$\{ M_j \mid K_j = \max_{v = 1, \dots, m} (K_v) \}$

if $M_j = \{\}$ **then stop**

   else Step 3

Step 3: select a job J_i to change x_{ir}:

$\{J_i \mid \Delta L_i = \min_{v=1, \dots, n} (\delta L_v) \}$

$\delta L_i = \sum_{r=1}^{R_i} L_{ir}$

a) Decrease of load: $\{J_{ir} \mid M_j \in \mathcal{M}_{ir} \}$

$$a_r = \begin{cases} x_{ir}: x_{ir} \, p_{ir} < K_j \\ [K_j / p_{ir}] \text{ else} \end{cases} \tag{6}$$

$$L_{ir}^1 = x_{ir} \, p_{ir} \tag{7}$$

$$L_{ir}^2 = K_j \tag{8}$$

b) increase of load: $\{J_{ir} \mid M_j \notin \mathcal{M}_{ir} \}$

$$L_{ir}^3 = \sum_{r=1}^{R_i} a_r \, p_{ir} \tag{9}$$

Step 4: **if** $\Delta L_i \geq 0$ **then stop**

   else $K = K' + \Delta L_i$;

   goto Step 2

Algorithm 13-1: Routing

A heuristic procedure for generating initial solutions to the machine scheduling problem

After ascertaining the routes M_{ir} each route is now considered as a job. The procedure of Giffler and Thompson (1963) is used to generate an active schedule. Applying this algorithm production control can be done online and can also be applied to dynamic situations. One key element of this algorithm is that priority rules of any form can be embedded.

The SSR procedure of O'Grady / Harrison

O'Grady and Harrison (1988) (see also (Haupt, 1989), (Hadavi *et al.*, 1990)) propose a formal concept for implementing *scheduling rules*. A priority value $Z_i(t)$ of a job is determined from a linear combination of a few attributes of this job. When applying this priority function to the schedulable jobs the job with the lowest value is chosen.

$Z_i(t)$:   value of the priority function of job i in time t
t: decision point to select a job
$0 \le \alpha, \beta \le 1$:   weighting parameter
c: coefficient vector $(1, 0, ..., 0)$ of remaining processing activities of a job
d: coefficient vector of remaining operations $(-1, -1, ..., -1)$
e: coefficient vector of remaining operations $(1, 1, ..., 1)$

For the generation of an initial solution the following priority function is applied.

$$Z_i(t) = \beta \, (\alpha \, c \, p_i + (1 - \alpha) \, d \, p_i) + (1- \beta) \, e \qquad (10)$$

Suppose $\beta = 1$ and $\alpha = 1$ the priority function selects the job according to the SPT rule.

Improvement procedure for the machine scheduling problem

Most heuristics consist of an initializing and an improving procedure. The described heuristic uses the *tabu search* method to control the improvements of already chosen solutions. The basic idea of this concept is to improve actual solutions by moving operations backward and forward in time (Yang, 1989). So at a first step, operations which should be moved have to be selected. For each of the selected operations an *exchange mechanism* must be applied. For all operations which are affected by this exchange a new starting time has to be calculated. After this rearrangements a new solution is obtained and can be evaluated. The following algorithm shows the exchange mechanism. Notations:

b_l: Starting time of operation l
s_{il}:   earliest possible starting time if all operations of job i can be processed without any delay
     $s_{i1} = r_i$
     $s_{i2} = r_i + p_{i1}$
     $s_{il} = s_{i(l-1)} + p_{i(l-1)}$

$V(l)$:   set of predecessors of operation l
$N(l)$:   set of successors of operation l
$OB = f_l = b_l + p_l$
$UB = \max_{k \in V(l)} f_k$
$C = \{ l \mid b_l - s_l > 0 \}$:   Set of operations which shall be moved
$B = \{ l \mid UB < b_l \le OB \}$
$E = \{ l \mid b_l > OB \}$

Start initial solution s: {ordered set of operations (l) }

Step 0:   Determine C (Neighbor solutions)

Step 1:   select $k \in C$ und calculate UB, OB

$$\overline{s} = s \setminus B \cup E$$

if $UB \ge b_k$ **then** $C = C \setminus k$

Step 2:   discard k from B: $B = B \setminus k$
if $B = \emptyset$ **then begin**
   $C = C \setminus k$,
   go to Step 1;
else: go to Step 3;
end if

Step 3:   **while** $B \ne \emptyset$ **do begin**
   move $l \in B$ sequential backward
   start with $\{ q \mid \max_{q \in B} f_q \}$
   $B = B \setminus q, E = E \cup q$
end;

Step 4:   schedule operation k earliest possible
$b_k = UB, B = B \cup k$;

Step 5:   **while** $E \ne \{\}$ **do begin**
   move operations $l \in E$ forward
   start with $\{ q \mid \min_{q \in E} b_q \}$
   $B = B \cup q, E = E \setminus q$
end;
   $s' = \overline{s} \cup B$
   $C = C \setminus k$
   if $C \ne \emptyset$ **then goto** Step 1
      else stop;

Algorithm 13-2: Exchange mechanism

NUMERICAL EVALUATION

In order to evaluate the exchange procedure and to detect good parameters of the tabu method a number of test cases are generated. The cases were solved to minimize the mean flowtime criterion. Those methods which provide good solutions in all test cases are selected by means of an LP model.

Experimental design

The experiment variables are: number of machines m [3, 5, 9], number of different machine types H [1, 5] and number of work orders n [3, 5, 8]. A factorial design (case A-O) is implemented and infeasible combinations are eliminated. The routings $\mathcal{M}_i$ of the jobs, the corresponding processing times $1 \le p_{ij} \le 15$ and the order size $1 \le x_i \le 40$ are generated from uniformly disributed random variables. For the determination of the initial solution the parameters α and β of the priority function are varied in the interval [0, 1]. During optimization different generated neighbour solutions, the number of tabu elements as well as different starting conditions of the tabu list are taken into account. The characteristic components of a solution are described by combination of order and machine number. The upper bound for the number of iterations generated is set to 2000. The different neighbour solutions come from a different procedure to ascertain set C in the exchange procedure:

a $C = \{l \mid b_l - s_l < 0\}$ $\mathcal{T} = \varnothing$
b $C = \{l \mid b_l - f_{l-1} > 0\}$ $\mathcal{T} = \varnothing$
c $C = \{l \mid \text{random}\}$, $\mathcal{T} = \varnothing$

The heuristics are implemented in C. For each of the generated test cases (A-O) 243 variants to determine an optimal solution are calculated. The number of variants evolves from combinations of (α, β) to build initial solutions (9) the differing neighbour solutions (3) and length of the tabu list $\mathcal{T}$ (3) [2, 7, 10] and the maximum number of solutions generated (3) [1, 7, 9] without improving an actual best found solution (maxiter).

Research results and analysis

It turned out that the value of a batch of three variations can not be improved by inclusion of additionally variations. Furhtermore it can be stated that solutions generated with neighbor solutions a and b are never in the chosen batch.

The best variant is determined if the initial solution is generated stochastically and the neighbour solutions are generated stochastically. The length of the tabu list $\mathcal{T} = 2$ and the number of repetitive iterations is set to 9.

Tables 13-2 and 13-3 show the selected variations.

Table 13-2: Selected batch of variations

number of included variations	Variation
1	225
2	225, 237
3	210, 225, 237
4	210, 225, 237, 243
5	210, 225, 237, 242, 243
6	210, 225, 237, 239, 240, 243

Table 13-3: Description of selected variations

variation	neighbor solution	parameter constellation for initial solution	maxiter	T
210	c	3	7	10
225	c	9	9	2
237	c	3	9	10
239	c	5	9	10
240	c	6	9	10
242	c	8	9	10
243	c	9	9	10

An additional grade which calculates a relation to the SPT priority rule is presented in table 13-4.

Table 13-4: Relation SPT to Best TABU

Case	SPT	Best TABU	SPT / Best TABU
G	1547.333	1354	1.143
H	1160	982.6	1.181
I	1034.125	848.375	1.219
M	116.15	105.05	1.106
N	275.455	217.544	1.266
O	236.087	166.304	1.266
Σ	4369.15	3673.873	1.1892

Summary

This chapter deals with problems arising during operation of an FMS and presents some models for solving the routing and scheduling problems.

The routing heuristic minimizes overload on bottleneck machines and tries to balance the workload in the system. The routes are determined before machine scheduling is solved. In order to solve the machine scheduling problem formal *priority rules* are applied to generate initial solutions. These initial solutions are improved by using an exchange heuristic and tabu search. The parameter combinations found can be used for future scheduling problems to get quick answers in the investigated or related problem classes.

REFERENCES

Agnetis, A., Arbib, C., Lucertini, M. and Nicoló, F. (1990) Part Routing in Flexible Assembly Systems, *IEEE Transactions on Robotics and Automation*, pp. 697–705.

Avonts, L.H., Gelders, L.F. and van Wassenhove, L.N. (1988) Allocation Work between an FMS and a Conventional Job-shop: A Case Study, *EJOR* **33**.

Bard, J.F. and Feo, T.A. (1989) Operations Sequencing in Discrete Parts Manufacturing, *Management Science* **35**.

Bastos, J.M. (1988) Batching and Routing: Two Functions in the Operational Planning of Flexible Manufacturing Systems, *European Journal on Operations Research* **33**.

Blazewicz, J., Ecker, K. Schmidt, G. and Weglarz, J. (1993) Scheduling of Computer and Manufacturing Systems, Berlin:Springer.

Calabrese, J.M. and Hausman, W.H. (1991) Simultaneous Determination of Lot Sizes and Routing Mix in Job-shops, *Management Science*, pp. 1043–1057.

Chandra, J. and Talvage, J. (1991) Intelligent Dispatching for Flexible Manufacturing, *International Journal on Production Research*, pp. 2259–2278.

Chen, I.J. and Chung, C. (1991) Effects of Loading and Routing Decisions on Performance of Flexible Manufacturing Systems, *International Journal on Production Research*, pp. 2209–2225.

Erschler, J. and Roubellat, F. (1989) An Approach to Solve Real Time Scheduling Problems, *Nato ASI Series*, F53.

Le Gall, A. and Roubellat, F. (1989) A Decision Support System for Real Time Production Scheduling, in *Flexible Manufacturing Systems. Operations Research Models and Applications*, K. Stecke and R. Suri (eds), Amsterdam: Elsevier Science.

Glover, F. (1989) Tabu Search Part I, *ORSA Journal of Computing*, pp. 169–190.

Gross, J.R. and Kumar, R. (1988) Intelligent Control Systems, in *Artificial Intelligence Implications for CIM*, A. Kusiak (ed.), Berlin: IFS Ltd/Springer Verlag.

Gunal, A., Smith, M. and Panwalkar, S. (1991) *The Performance of Scheduling Rules in Flexible Manufacturing Cells by Job Types*, Technical Report, Texas Tech University.

Gupta, Y., Evans, G.W. and Gupta, M. (1991) A Review of Multi-criterion Approaches to FMS Scheduling Problems, *IJPE* pp. 13–91.

Hadavi, K., Shahraray, M. and Voigt, K. (1990) ReDs – A Planning, Scheduling and Control Environment for Manufacturing, *Journal of Manufacturing* **9**.

Haupt, R. (1989) A Survey of Priority rule-based Scheduling, *OR Spektrum* **11**.

Hintz, G.-W. (1987) *Ein wissensbasiertes System zur Produktionsplanung und -Steuerung*, Düsseldorf: VDI Verlag.

Hutchinson, J. and Khumawala, B. (1991) Scheduling Random Flexible Manufacturing Systems with Dynamic Environments, *JOM*, pp. 335–352.

Kuhn, H. (1990) *Einlastungsplanung bei flexiblen Fertigungssystemen*, Heidelberg Berlin: Physica.

Kusiak, A. (1986) Application of Operational Research Models and Techniques in Flexible Manufacturing Systems, *European Journal on Operations Research* **24**.

Kusiak, A. (1988) *KBSS: A Knowledge-Based System for Scheduling in Automated Manufacturing*, working paper.

Kusiak, A. (1990) *Intelligent Manufacturing Systems*, Englewood Cliffs: Prentice Hall.

Lin, Y.-J. and Solberg, J.J. (1989) Flexible Routing Control and Scheduling, in *Flexible Manufacturing Systems. Operations Research Models and Applications*, K. Stecke and R. Suri, (eds), Amsterdam: Elsevier Science.

de Luca, A. (1984) Optimal Production Planning for FMS: An 'Optimum Batching' Algorithm, in *Proceedings of the 3rd International Conference on FMS-IFS*, Böblingen: IFS.

Mukhopadhyay, S.K., Bibekananda, M. and Sandip, G. (1991) Heuristic Solution to the Scheduling Problems in Flexible Manufacturing Systems, *International Journal Production Research*, pp. 2003–2024.

O'Grady, P.J., and Harrison, C. (1988) Search Based Job Scheduling and Sequencing with Setup Times, *OMEGA* **16**.

Panwalkar, S.S. and Iskander, W. (1977) A Survey of Scheduling Rules, *Operations Research* **25**.

Rachamadugu, R. and Stecke, K.E. (1989) *Classification and Review of FMS Scheduling Procedures*, working paper.

Raman, N. Rachamadugu, R.V. and Talbot, F.B. (1989) Real-time Scheduling of an Automated Manufacturing Center, *European Journal on Operations Research* **40**.

Ranta, J. and Tchijov, I. (1990) Economics and Success Factors of Flexible Manufacturing Systems: The Conventional Explanation Revisited, *International Journal on FMS*, pp. 169–190.

Rodammer, F.A. and White, K.P. (1988) A Recent Survey of Production Scheduling, *IEEE* **18**.

Schmidt, G. (1989) *CAM: Algorithmen und Decision Support für die Fertigungssteuerung*, Berlin: Springer.

Solot, P. (1990) A Concept for Planning and Scheduling in an FMS, *European Journal on Operations Research* **45**.

Stecke, K.E. and Kim, I. (1986) A Flexible Approach to Implementing the Short-Term FMS Planning Function, in *Flexible Manufacturing Systems. Operations Research Models and Applications*, Amsterdam: Elsevier Science.

Stecke, K.E. and Suri, R. (eds) (1989) *Flexible Manufacturing Systems. Operations Research Models and Applications*, Amsterdam: Elsevier Science.

Tempelmeier, H. and Kuhn, H. (1992) *Flexible Fertigungssysteme*, Berlin: Springer.

Yang, T., Ignizio, J.P. and Deal, D. (1989) *An Exchange Heuristic for Generalized Job Shop Scheduling*, working paper.

14

Meta-Scheduling using Dynamic Scheduling Knowledge

Jürgen Sauer
Universität Oldenburg

SCHEDULING

The goal of scheduling is the temporal assignment of orders (e.g. for manufacturing products) to resources (e.g. machines) where a number of conditions have to be regarded. Scheduling covers the creation of a schedule of the production process over a longer period (*predictive scheduling*) and the correction of an existing schedule (or plan) due to actual events in the planning/ scheduling environment (*reactive scheduling* or *rescheduling*).

Nearly the same information is needed for scheduling and rescheduling and the same conditions must hold for the result, e.g. concerning the goals to be fulfilled.

A scheduling problem can be described by the tuple (R, P, O, HC, SC) with:

- a set of resources $R = \{R_1, ..., R_r\}$ like machines
- a set of products $P = \{P_1, ..., P_p\}$ with information about variants, operations, machines
- a set of orders $O = \{O_1, ..., O_o\}$ to manufacture products
- a set of *hard constraints* $HC = \{H_1, ..., H_h\}$ (e.g. production requirements), that have to be fulfilled, and
- a set of *soft constraints* $SC = \{S_1, ..., S_s\}$ (e.g. meeting due dates), that should be fulfilled but may be relaxed.

The result of scheduling is a schedule (or plan) showing the temporal assignment of operations of orders to the machines that shall be used.

The problem space of scheduling can be represented as a heterogeneous *AND / OR-tree*. The nodes contain a statement about the contribution of the children nodes to the solution and a value of the type corresponding to the layer of the tree. Figure 14-1 shows a graphical representation of the scheduling problem - including alternative production variants and machines. By integrating parameters like alternative variants or machines a more general view of scheduling is realized including some of the tasks of process planning.

Finding a solution to the scheduling problem is equivalent to finding a solution of the AND / OR-tree where the constraints are met. In figure 14-1 a solution is indicated by dark nodes and solid lines.

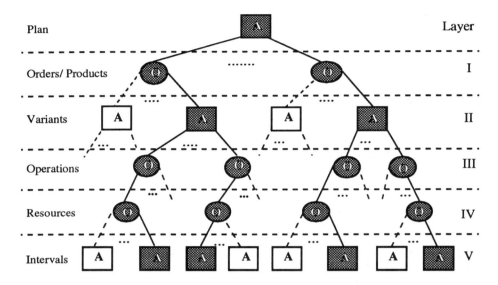

Figure 14-1: AND / OR-tree: problem space of scheduling

The determination of an optimal solution to a given scheduling problem requires, in the worst case, the generation of all possible solutions. This is not realistic because of the combinatoric size of this kind of problem. Optimal scheduling belongs to the class of NP-complete problems. Therefore, a crucial task of scheduling is the creation of "good" schedules without searching through the whole problem space. Knowledge-based approaches try to reduce the search space by using the experience and (heuristic) knowledge of a human production planner.

Because no general algorithmic approach that is sufficient for all scheduling and rescheduling problems is known yet, a scheduling system should offer multiple alternative algorithms applicable to varying circumstances in connection with a support in selecting the most appropriate approach for a given problem, e.g. specific rescheduling problems suggest an emphasis on either order- or resource-based algorithms (Ow *et al.*, 1988).

This chapter describes an appropriate representation of a huge variety of different scheduling approaches, their integration in one planning system and the representation and use of meta-scheduling knowledge to select the appropriate approach in a given situation.

DYNAMIC SCHEDULING KNOWLEDGE

Different kinds of knowledge are used in solving a scheduling problem. This knowledge can be divided into the areas of domain, situation, scheduling and meta-scheduling knowledge:

- The *domain knowledge* contains static information about the application environment, i.e. the structure of the scheduling problem (R, P, O) from (R, P, O, HC, SC), e.g. the set of orders, the possible products, their specifications, the available resources etc.
- The *situation knowledge* represents the current state of scheduling, e.g. the existing schedule, the remaining capacities of resources etc.
- The *scheduling knowledge* is divided into static and dynamic approaches for scheduling and rescheduling. Hard and soft constraints (HC, SC) belong to this knowledge.
  - The *static scheduling knowledge* contains complete algorithms, e.g. operations research algorithms but also knowledge based ones. These algorithms are firmly implemented and are not changeable.
  - The *dynamic scheduling knowledge* denotes chunks of heuristic planning knowledge, which can be used together or alternatively in finding solutions to scheduling problems. It provides the possibility for adequate description and integration of multiple algorithmic approaches in one system.
- The *meta-scheduling knowledge* contains the information necessary to determine the "best" algorithm due to the current scheduling problem, i.e. which algorithms are applicable for which tasks (goals) and which ones are appropriate for which events.

Most of the scheduling approaches developed so far are based on a divide-and-conquer technique and can be classified according to their perspective of the problem decomposition:

- *order-based*, i.e. one order is selected from all unscheduled orders and all operations of this order are completely scheduled before continuing with the next order, e.g. (Fox, 1987).
- *resource-based*, i.e. a resource is selected and then the appropriate operation is chosen out of the set of possible operations on this resource, e.g. (Liu, 1989).
- *operation-based*, i.e. one operation after another is selected and scheduled, e.g. (Keng *et al.*, 1988).

All algorithms work until all orders and their operations are scheduled.

Each of these approaches can be viewed as a scheduling strategy useful to create a solution to a scheduling problem. As the determination of such a solution is equivalent to finding a solution of the AND / OR-tree the ideas of using dynamic planning knowledge can be explained by means of the AND / OR-tree representation of the problem space. A planning strategy describes the traversing of the tree, where several heuristic rules are used to select the next node to be checked. At the different layers of the tree (orders, products etc.), different selection rules are possible, e.g. *priority rules* for the selection of orders. So the basic components of a scheduling algorithm are the underlying strategy (how to traverse the tree, e.g. select an order and then solve the problem for this order, then the next order etc.) and the heuristic rules used for the selection of the nodes at the different layers. The combination of different strategies and selection rules leads to a huge variety of possible scheduling algorithms. To exploit the power of this approach, an appropriate representation for strategies and rules is needed.

The basic idea for the representation of planning knowledge is the possibility of describing the strategies as skeletons, where special parts (selection of nodes in AND / OR-tree) can be refined with appropriate rules regarding the actual planning problem. The idea of using skeletons is adopted from (Friedland and Iwasaki, 1985), where skeletal plans are sequences of abstract operators describing plans for experiments and the refined skeletal plans are the desired result.

In the approach presented here a *planning skeleton* describes a strategy for searching in the AND / OR-tree (how to create a schedule step by step), but without any heuristic for the selection of the nodes of the tree. For example, a skeleton for an order-based strategy looks as shown in figure 14-2 (Roman numbers denote the layer of the AND / OR-tree on which the selection has to be done, rule gives an example of a rule that can be used).

```
while orders to plan
     select order (I)
          (rule: combination of bottleneck first, EDD, slack
             rule und user priority)
     select variant (II)
          (rule: 'stem variant' first, then alternatives)
     while operations to plan
          select operation (III)
          (rule: LIFO)
          select resource (IV)
             (rule: 'stem apparatus' first, then alternatives)
          select interval (V)
             (rule: forward from earliest start)
          plan operation or solve conflict
     end while
end while
```

Figure 14-2: Order-based planning skeleton with possible rules

Figure 14-2 shows the skeleton of the order-based approach implemented within the EUREKA-project PROTOS (PROLOG Tools for Building Expert Systems) (Appelrath, 1987), (Sauer, 1990), (Sauer, 1991) together with the used rules on the different layers. Figure 14-3 shows two other examples of representing planning strategies in terms of skeletons.

operation-based	resource-based
select variant for every order (II)	select variant for every order (II)
find operations of orders (I)	find operations of orders (I)
while operations to plan	**while** operations to plan
select operation (III)	**select** resource (IV)
select resource (IV)	**select** operation (III)
select interval (V)	**select** interval (V)
plan operation	plan operation
end while	**end while**

Figure 14-3: Planning skeletons for scheduling

Rules are used for the selection of nodes at each layer of the tree and thus guide the search for a good solution. For each layer of the AND / OR-tree there exists a set of alternative rules, some of which are listed in figure 14-4.

Layer
- I   selecting orders
  - combined and weighted rules
  - increasing start days (FIFO)
  - increasing number of alternatives (critical products first)
  - increasing planning intervals (critical products in time first)
  - increasing user priority (critical products of the user first)
- II   selecting variants
  - given order with stem first
  - inverse order
  - increasing production factor (critical variant first)
  - decreasing production factor (simple variant first)
- III   selecting operations
  - increasing operation number
  - decreasing operation number
  - increasing number of alternative resources (critical operation first)
  - decreasing number of alternative resources (simple operation first)
- IV   selecting resources
  - given order with stem first
  - increasing resource factor (simple resource first)
  - decreasing resource factor (critical resource first)
- V   selecting intervals
  - forward from given starting date
  - backward from end date to starting date, then forward from end date

Figure 14-4: Possible rules usable for selection in skeletons

With this kind of knowledge representation a large variety of scheduling and rescheduling algorithms can be created dynamically by combining planning skeletons and appropriate rules for selections, making a library of different scheduling and rescheduling approaches available.

A crucial problem, especially if a library of scheduling approaches is available, is the selection of the "best" approach in a given problem situation. Meta-knowledge can be used to support this task. One first approach was presented by the OPIS system (Smith *et al.*, 1990) where one algorithm out of four possible ones is selected due to the values of several parameters describing the actual scheduling situation. In our approach meta-knowledge is used more generally and can be used to select

- appropriate strategies for scheduling and rescheduling both as fixed algorithms or as skeletons,
- the rules within the skeletons, and
- conflict solution strategies useful within the skeletons for scheduling and re-scheduling.

Different sources of meta-knowledge may be exploited. The meta-knowledge covers the goals which shall be achieved, the events that have to be tackled, and other information specific to the situation in which an approach is appropriate.

A *goal* is a planning task that shall be met by the plan to be generated. Goals may be global ones like meeting due dates or local ones like machine utilization or reduction of set-up times. Events describe cases of external or internal errors which mainly affect the planning result; in most of the cases this is the existing plan. External events are e.g. cancellations of orders or new high priority orders. Internal events are e.g. breakdowns of machines or other resources.

REPRESENTATION OF SCHEDULING KNOWLEDGE BY HEURISTICS

A language called HERA (heuristics for representation of scheduling knowledge) has been developed for the representation of the scheduling and meta-scheduling knowledge. HERA is based on PROLOG providing all the features of declarative knowledge representation and the integration of PROLOG code as well as calls to other languages. The "classical" representation of heuristics as if-then rules is extended by an explicit representation of goals and events and by control constructions usable in the action part to describe planning strategies. Heuristics then look like

heuristic *name*		% name of the heuristic
if **situation**	*situation*	% description of the situation to use the heuristic
goal	*goal*	% description of the goals that can be achieved
event	*event*	% description of the events that can be solved
then *actions*		% description of the strategy (the heuristic)
end heuristic		

Figure 14-5: Heuristic

The if-part of the heuristic contains the meta-knowledge which is used to select the appropriate strategy. The description of the situation consists of a sequence of PROLOG calls (mainly retrieval operations) concatenated by AND. Goals and events are represented by definite PROLOG atoms.

goal <goalname>.   e.g. goal meet_due_dates.
event <eventname>.   e.g. event machine_breakdown.

The action part (then-part) of the heuristics is used to call fixed strategies or to describe the scheduling and rescheduling strategies completely or as planning skeletons. The syntax of the action part is:

<actions>	::=	<action>	<action> **and** <actions>
<action>	::=	**while** <w_condition> **do** <actions> **end while**	
		or [<action>, <act_list>]	<simple_action>
<act_list>	::=	<simple_action>	<simple_action>, <act_list>
<simple_action>	::=	**heuristic-call**(<heuristic_name>, <goals>, <events>)	
		<rulecall>	<operation>	<PROLOG_literal>.

Figure 14-6: Then-part of heuristic

If a fixed strategy has to be called, the action part only consists of a PROLOG call. If a strategy or a skeleton has to be described, control constructs are needed to represent the traversing through the AND / OR-tree:

*   **and**: actions are concatenated by AND
*   **while**: used for treating AND-nodes (all descendants have to be considered). While the <w_condition> holds the <actions> are executed.
*   **or**: used to support an intelligent search process. Several rules or heuristics, e.g. for checking different parts of the tree, may be listed and will be applied in the given order.

simple_actions are:

*   calls of PROLOG-procedures
*   calls of predefined rules or simple (update) operations
*   heuristic calls: this gives the possibility to call a heuristic explicitly by name (first argument) or to specify goals or events (second and third argument) for the automatic selection of appropriate strategies. Heuristic calls with specified goals and events are used as the abstract operations within planning skeletons.

Figure 14-7 shows an example of a heuristic calling a fixed algorithm (heuristic plan_PROTOS), with the meaning: "if a set of orders is given, the goal of scheduling is meeting the due dates, no event has occurred, and no actual plan exists then the PROTOS algorithm may be used", and the PROTOS strategy already mentioned (figure 14-2) represented as heuristic where all the control constructions are used.

```
heuristic plan_protos
  if situation        no_plan
     goal             [planning:meet_due_dates]
     event            []
  then call(protos_algorithm)
end heuristic.

heuristic plan_order_based_protos
  if situation        no_plan
     goal             [scheduling:[meet_due_dates]]
     event            []
  then
     create_orderlist
     and
     while orders_to_plan do
       select_order_fifo
       and
       select_interval_earliest_start
       and
       select_variant_stem_first
       and
       while steps_to_plan do
       select_step_fifo
       and
       select_app_stem_first
       and
       or[plan_step, heuristic-call(solve_overlap_basic,[],[])]
     end while
  end while
end heuristic.
```

Figure 14-7: Two examples of heuristics represented with HERA

The scheduling environment R, P, O (classes of objects), operations on objects like RETRIEVE or MODIFY, and the rules needed are represented in a similar manner, e.g. rules as:

> **rule** *name*
>   **if situation** *situation*
>   **then** *rule_actions*
> **end rule.**

name is the name of the rule, *situation* describes the situation in which the rule is to be used and *rule_actions* represents a list of simple actions consisting of basic PROLOG-procedures, rule-calls and update- or retrieval-operations.

META_PLAN: USING DYNAMIC SCHEDULING KNOWLEDGE

Scheduling and in particular rescheduling are such tough problems that no algorithmic approach will solve them in a satisfactory manner in the near future. Therefore, the objective of system approaches should not be the replacement of the human experts, but their support in order to extend their problem solving capabilities. Thus a computer-based scheduling system supporting the human production planner in a user-friendly interactive manner should combine a graphical user interface with multiple algorithmic scheduling methods.

The prototypical system META_PLAN realizes such an approach. The graphical user interface provides a comprehensive presentation of information as well as multiple tools for interaction, especially for manual scheduling and user-directed selection of scheduling and rescheduling algorithms. The algorithmic part consists of a great variety of knowledge for scheduling and rescheduling and a meta-scheduler for the selection of appropriate approaches. Figure 14-8 shows the architecture of META_PLAN consisting of eight components.

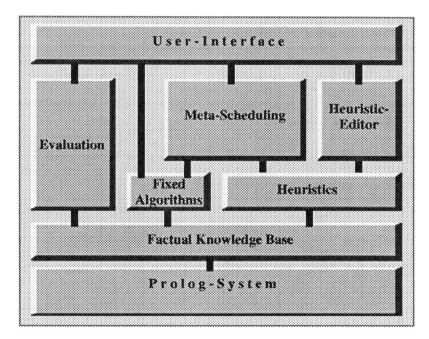

Figure 14-8: System architecture of META_PLAN

The "User-Interface" provides a user-friendly and problem adequate graphical presentation of the information currently in the knowledge base, e.g. a Gantt chart representation of the existing schedule, and multiple tools for interaction.

The "Evaluation" component offers several functions for evaluating schedules, e.g. sum of delays.

The "Meta-Scheduling" component realizes the selection and interpretation of the appropriate scheduling strategies. The new scheduling problem is analysed, the appropriate skeletons are identified and refined to solution algorithms, the alternative algorithms (static as well as dynamically created ones) are judged and the applicable approaches are ranked with respect to their appropriateness for the current problem.

To identify appropriate heuristics the actual goals and events are compared to the corresponding descriptions in the heuristics. Appropriate are those where the intersection of the goal description and the actual goals is not empty and where all actual events are tackled. The "best one" of these (where most of the actual goals are met) is applied first. If the interpretation of a heuristic succeeds, a new plan has been generated. If the interpretation of a heuristic fails, the next heuristic is chosen until a solution is found or no appropriate heuristic is available. In this case no solution is found.

The interpretation of a heuristic consists of the interpretation of the situation part and of the action part of the heuristic. As the situation part consists of a sequence of PROLOG calls concatenated by AND, the interpretation is done by the PROLOG interpreter itself. If the situation described in the situation-part is equivalent to the actual situation then the heuristic is used, i.e. the action part is interpreted. Figure 14-9 shows some of the rules used for the interpretation of actions.

A rule is interpreted like a heuristic. The main difference is that the rule_actions in the action-part of the rule are more simple. Rule calls are leading to an interpretation of the corresponding rules, basic procedures for sorting lists or retrieving information from the database are interpreted by the PROLOG system.

In a simulation part the chosen scheduling algorithm is applied to the new scheduling problem and the result is displayed graphically to the user. Additionally the user has the choice of scheduling order after order, eventually changing the algorithms at every order, or scheduling the whole set of orders with one selected approach. The expert can either confirm or reject the result of simulation. This component is a meta-scheduler since it builds schedulers, not schedules (Kempf, 1989).

---

if the next action is the empty-action **then** the interpretation succeeds.

if the next action is an OR-action **then** the OR-connected actions are interpreted in the given order. If one action succeeds, the OR-action succeeds. If no action succeeds, the OR-action fails.

if the next action is a WHILE-action **then** the actions in the body are repeatedly interpreted as long as the condition holds. If the condition fails at the beginning, no action of the body is executed.

if the next action is a rule-call or heuristic-call **then** the corresponding rules or heuristics are interpreted.

if the next action is a basic procedure **then** it is interpreted by the PROLOG-system.

Figure 14-9: Interpretation rules

The "Heuristic-Editor" component enables the acquisition of new and the alteration of current knowledge represented with HERA.

The knowledge base of META_PLAN is spread across three components. The "Fixed Algorithms" module contains several fixed scheduling algorithms which can be selected by the meta-scheduler. It also provides an interface for integrating fixed scheduling algorithms (e.g. from operational research) written in other languages together with the meta-knowledge necessary for their application giving META_PLAN features of a hybrid scheduling system. The "Heuristics" component contains the dynamic plannning knowledge consisting of strategies, skeletons and rules represented with HERA. The "Factual Knowledge Base" contains the static and dynamic facts of the scheduling area, e.g. production requirements, orders, and the schedule.

The system is implemented in PROLOG using features of the underlying "PROLOG System" like definite clause grammars and interfaces to user-interfaces (OpenWindows).

Scheduling using META_PLAN then looks as follows:

Starting with the input of some tasks (e.g. scheduling, rescheduling), goals (e.g. meeting due dates) and events (e.g. insertion of new orders, cancellation of already scheduled orders, machine breakdown) a new scheduling problem arises. The new problem is defined by the tasks, goals, events and the current situation, e.g. the existing schedule and the available capacities. The user has the possibility to solve the new problem partly or entirely by manual scheduling. Alternatively the system can analyse the new problem and select the most appropriate algorithm (static or dynamic) to solve it. The user may alter this proposal or confirm it. Now the execution of the chosen algorithm can be simulated and the result is presented graphically. The user can choose whether the result should be entered in the knowledge base as the new schedule or not, and he/she can make manual corrections at all times.

CONCLUSION

A method for the adequate representation and integration of a huge variety of different scheduling approaches together with the meta-knowledge needed to select appropriate ones has been introduced in this chapter. The basic concepts of scheduling algorithms are their underlying strategies and heuristic rules for selections. These strategies and heuristic rules are represented separately by means of planning skeletons and rules, respectively. A planning skeleton describes a strategy for searching in the AND / OR-tree, but without any heuristics for selections of nodes. Rules are used for the selection of nodes at each layer of the tree. Based on this representation of planning knowledge a scheduling algorithm is created dynamically by the substitution of the abstract operators within a skeleton with the rules. The various possibilities for combining skeletons and rules dynamically lead to a great variety of scheduling approaches. The meta-knowledge used covers the goals to be reached, the events or disruptions to be solved and specific information about situations.

This method provides high flexibility for scheduling and rescheduling (various different scheduling algorithms are available, each showing selective advantages for specific problems), the user (he/she is supported in selecting the "best" strategy and can create his/her "own" scheduling algorithm) and extensions (other skeletons and rules can be integrated easily).

In addition, META_PLAN, a hybrid scheduling system providing the flexible use of the dynamic planning knowledge as well as the meta-scheduling knowledge has been described. A prototype of this system has been realized in the context of the PROTOS project.

REFERENCES

Appelrath, H.-J. (1987) Das EUREKA-Projekt PROTOS, *Proceedings of the 2nd International GI-Conference '87 Knowledge-based Systems*, IFB 155, Springer.

Fox, M. (1987) *Constraint Directed Search: A Case Study of Job-Shop Scheduling*, London: Pitman.

Friedland, P.E. and Iwasaki, Y. (1985) The Concept and Implementation of Skeletal Plans, *Journal of Automated Reasoning* 1, pp. 161–208.

Kempf, K. (1989) Manufacturing Planning and Scheduling: Where We Are and Where We Need To Be, *Proceedings of the 5th Conference on Artificial Intelligence Applications* (CAIA-89), Miami, Fla, pp. 13–22.

Keng, N.P., Yun, D.Y., Rossi, M. (1988) Interaction Sensitive Planning System for Job-shop Scheduling, in *Expert Systems and Intelligent Manufacturing*, D. Oliff (ed.), Amsterdam: Elsevier Science, pp. 57–69.

Liu, B. (1989) *Knowledge-Based Production Scheduling: Resource Allocation and Constraint Satisfaction*, DAI Research Paper 436, University of Edinburgh.

Ow, P.S., Smith, S.I. and Thiriez, A. (1988) Reactive Plan Revision, *Proceedings of the National Conference on Artificial Intelligence* (AAAI-88), St. Paul, Minn. pp. 77–82.

Sauer, J. (1990) Design and Implementation of a Heuristic Planning Algorithm, in *The EUREKA-Project PROTOS*, Appelrath, H.-J., Cremers, A.B., Herzog, O. (eds), Zürich, April.

Sauer, J. (1991) Knowledge Based Scheduling in PROTOS, *Proceedings of the IMACS World Congress on Computation and Applied Mathematics*, Dublin, pp. 1749–1750.

Smith, S.F., Muscettola, N., Matthys, D.C., Ow, P.S. and Potvin, J.-Y. (1990) OPIS: An Opportunistic Factory Scheduling System, *Proceedings of 3rd International Conference on Industrial and Engineering Applications of Artificial Intelligence and Expert Systems*, IEA/AIE, Charleston, SC, pp. 268–274.

15

Task-oriented Design for Scheduling Applications

Jürgen Dorn
Christian Doppler Laboratory for Expert Systems, Technische Universität Wien

INTRODUCTION

In several projects it has been shown that knowledge-based technology in the form of expert systems is appropriate for complex scheduling problems. However, the knowledge-based approach competes with mathematical methods from *Operations Research*. It depends on the application, whether knowledge-based or mathematical models should be used. Often models from Operations Research are declined because the existing models do not represent exactly the actual problem and the costs for adopting the model would be very high.

There are mainly three advantages why knowledge-based systems are preferred in some applications. First, in knowledge-based systems it is easier to apply heuristics to reduce the inherent complexity in scheduling. Second, knowledge-based systems offer the possibility to reason with incomplete, uncertain or inexact knowledge. Finally, in knowledge-based systems the existing knowledge is described explicitly and should therefore be easier maintainable. The third reason supports also the first two points.

Although knowledge-based systems exist since the early seventies, there are still some problems with the professional construction of knowledge-based systems. A number of different knowledge-based techniques, methods and tools were developed in recent years for scheduling applications. However, a new application in a real production environment is usually developed from scratch since the reuse of them is too costly. Scheduling tools like ISIS (Fox, 1987), OPIS (Smith *et al.*, 1986), OPAL (Bensana, 1993), CORTES (Sadeh, 1991) and CRONOS-III (Canzi and Guida, 1993) were developed with the intention to reuse them in new applications. This intention failed because they are restricted to sub-areas of the scheduling problem. Most often a mixture of different techniques and existing tools would be appropriate. Furthermore, these tools and techniques must be able to be interfaced to other soft- and hardware systems.

Expert systems for a certain application are often developed in an ad hoc manner and rapid prototyping is used as an excuse for not formally specifying the design and documenting the implemented system. However, for many experienced knowledge engineers rapid prototyping is only a technique for analysing a problem instead of an overall technique for system development. As a consequence, for the development of large expert systems a design methodology as in traditional software engineering is looked for. This methodology should support the *structured design*, the *maintenance* of the developed software and the *reuse* of parts of the software.

In the late sixties the need for a methodological approach was recognized in traditional programming. The discipline Software Engineering was founded with the intention to cope with the so called software crisis and to stimulate the research for a better understanding of the software production process (Naur and Randell, 1968). Software life cycle models were created in order to formalize the development of software. Methodologies were defined for analysis, design specification, implementation, validation, verification, and maintaining of software. One ambitious goal was the reuse of software. An actual and promising approach to reuse software in traditional software engineering is the object-oriented paradigm (Rumbaugh *et al.*, 1991) and (Coad and Jourdan, 1991). In object-oriented systems a problem is structured into objects that have their own data structure and methods to manipulate these data. Single objects or classes of objects are the granularity of reuse.

For knowledge-based systems this paradigm appears not to be adequate since not objects are in the focus of the problem solving competence of knowledge-based systems. One of their strong points is the explicit representation of reasoning. In first knowledge-based systems the representation of reasoning through production rules was stressed. Today it is known that most reasoning processes are more complex than a simple combination of such rules. Nevertheless, also in the new generation of expert systems the reasoning capabilities are central for problem solving. It makes no difference for this argumentation whether this reasoning is done by means of constraint satisfaction and propagation techniques (Prosser, 1993), genetic algorithms (Filipic, 1993), neural networks (Adorf and Johnston, 1992), a case-based approach (Bezirgan, 1993) or with fuzzy logic (Dubois, 1989). This accentuation of the reasoning capability distinguishes them from data base systems.

Krueger (1992) gives a survey on the different approaches in software reuse. He states that for all approaches the abstraction process is the main criterion for software reuse. Since in knowledge-based systems we generate abstractions from the reasoning process, we should try to model reusable entities that describe the reasoning process. Consequently, many researchers demand a task-oriented model for *knowledge acquisition* (analysis), design, and maintenance of expert systems (Breuker and Wielinga, 1991), (Bylander and Chandrasekaran, 1988), (Clancey, 1985), (McDermott, 1989) and (Musen, 1989).

In the analysis phase a task model is developed that describes how the expert solves a problem. This model may contain several tasks. The design of the expert system may be different from the expert's view of the solution since the system cannot imitate the expert in all aspects. Nevertheless, the same tasks exist and this should be transparent to facilitate the maintenance. After deciding which tasks must be performed, we choose from different reasoning methods one or more to achieve a task. Besides the advantage of a professional construction, it is expected that tasks designed for one application may be reused easier in another one. If a new system is developed whose domain consists of other objects and other strategies, the tasks may be reused. This is achieved by describing tasks in such a generic way that the differences are not visible on the abstract reasoning level.

Another advantage of a *task-oriented design* could be the combination of techniques from different disciplines. Such a design can be the right level to describe the combination of techniques from *Artificial Intelligence, neural networks, genetic algorithms, case-based reasoning, fuzzy logic* and *Operations Research.*

The ambitious objective is, then, to achieve a library of different tasks that may be reused. Since the libraries developed in the cited projects are mainly for classification and diagnosis, I want to start here the discussion of a library of scheduling tasks. However, what do scheduling tasks look like?

In the scheduling literature a lot of different strategies exist to conquer the complexity of scheduling problems. The "traditional" knowledge-based strategy was described by Fox (1987): From a given set of orders one is chosen that is scheduled next. Often it is better to examine free machines or resources and to select one order that can be produced next (Ow and Smith, 1988). However, these strategies are often too simplistic to master the complexity in realistic scheduling problems.

A more sophisticated strategy is to look for bottleneck resources. In (Adams *et al.,* 1988) a mathematical framework was given in the operations research context. A similar approach was introduced with the "Min-conflicts-Strategy" in (Minton *et al.,* 1990). They first look for conflicts between constraints and then they try to solve these conflicts. A similar approach of Berry (1993) is based on probabilistic reasoning.

A further strategy is based on the idea to generate first a very simple schedule that is repaired afterwards. This idea was described first in (Minton *et al.,* 1990) and (Zweben *et al.,* 1990) and was also successfully applied in our expert system (Dorn and Shams, 1991). This strategy besides others seems also to be adequate for reactive scheduling.

However, the problem with most of these strategies is that they are described only in natural language without giving an exact algorithm. The "way" to the solution of a problem is often described only vaguely and not as formal as the knowledge representation. Therefore, it is difficult to reuse them.

In the next section I describe two applications from steelmaking plants. Although both are in the same domain and both are flow-shops the heuristics and strategies applied by the human experts differ strongly. Therefore these two applications are an ideal case to show the potential as also the limits of the reuse of tasks.

In the third section I show how the first application can be designed in a task-oriented fashion. The KADS-methodology (Breuker and Wielinga, 1991) is taken as a basis for modelling since the intention of its developers is to make it a European standard in knowledge engineering. Since KADS users (Überreiter and Voß, 1991) model mostly static applications some deficiencies can be seen if the methodology is applied to a dynamic process like reactive scheduling.

In the fourth section I show how parts of the first application can be reused for the second application, and in the final section I discuss the pros and cons of task-oriented design for scheduling applications and show which aspects shall be examined further.

TWO SCHEDULING APPLICATIONS IN STEELMAKING

I give a brief introduction to two scheduling applications in whose development I was involved. In both cases the application of an existing tool was not promising because the concept of *compatibility between jobs* neither exists in a commercially available system nor in a research prototype. Furthermore, we were confronted with the requirement to integrate the system into an existing software environment and to implement a user interface on a given display. A further problem that complicates the use of an existing tool is the intention to imitate the problem solving process of the present human experts. The latter process is advantageous because the solution is more intelligible and explainable for the user.

Both applications are situated in steelmaking plants. Producing steel from iron is usually a *flow-shop*. An amount of steel called a heat is treated on different aggregates and finally cast and delivered to subsequent plants like mills or forges. Usually, different kinds or qualities of steel are produced. For every quality a *process plan* exists that specifies the operations to be performed on heats in a fixed sequence and the required aggregates and materials. Since the operations are performed with hot steel it is important to have only short slack times between operations. A heat may consist of several orders for cast goods.

We have developed an expert system for the Böhler company in Kapfenberg (Styria) that schedules heats in the steelmaking plant for one week (Dorn and Shams, 1991). In the plant high-grade steel is made from ordinary steel and scrap iron. Both are melted together in an electric arc furnace before further refinement operations are performed. At the end of the steelmaking process is the casting of the steel into ingots or with an horizontal continuous caster into slabs. Afterwards the steel is delivered to the rolling mill. However, the milling process is not regarded in this application. Most of the heats are cast into ingots which requires space in the teeming bay. This teeming bay is usually no bottleneck resource. However, for special orders like very big ingots the capacity is restricted since they need specific places.

The main scheduling problem is the number of different steel grades. One grade may need a high amount of nickel and chrome whereas another needs a high amount of vanadium. The problem in scheduling is that residuals of one heat in the electric arc furnace may pollute the next heat. As a general rule it is said that 3% of the difference of the elements in two subsequent heats will be assimilated by the second heat. If a steel grade is restricted to a very small amount of an element and the heat takes a larger part up, the heat is destroyed. The compatibility rule is effective for 42 chemical elements, but usually only 8 main elements are considered.

Furthermore, it is important not to waste expensive elements. If one job demands a high percentage of an expensive element like cobalt the subsequent job should use as much of the residual as possible. The compatibility problem leads to the examination whether two heats may be produced one after another in the electric arc furnace. However, this compatibility is no crisp function.

Further temporal and spatial constraints exist, but for the human schedulers and the expert system the compatibility is the main criterion for sequencing. The main objectives are the high quality of steel and as few wasted heats as possible. In contrast to most described applications and theories *work-in-progress* (WIP), *just-in-time* (JIT) or *makespan* are no relevant goal or *evaluation* functions for schedules.

At the VA Stahl company in Linz a system was developed that schedules heats in a plant for mass steel production (Stohl *et al.*, 1991). In contrast to the first application, pig iron is delivered hot from the blast furnace to the steelmaking plant and the diversity of the steel grades produced is less. The refinement aggregates are almost the same as in the first application. Instead of electric arc furnaces, converters are used but this makes no difference from the scheduling view point.

One difference that has an influence on the scheduling strategy is the exclusive production on continuous casters. The compatibility of jobs in terms of steel quality and cast format must be observed with these casters. They are the critical aggregates that should produce continuously. If the molten steel is not delivered in time to the caster, the strand "breaks" and a longer set-up time is necessary. Usually, up to ten heats are scheduled in a group. After approximately eight to twelve heats the funnel of the tundish (a part of the caster) must be replaced. If a new tundish is prepared in time and the steel is delivered also in time, one can produce steel continuously for several days. Of course, this is of great benefit. However, the strategy to generate such groups changes as soon as the supply of pig iron from the blast furnace is too slow. In this case one tries to schedule single jobs that have unique characteristics and can not be produced so easily with other orders in a group.

The planner in the steelmaking plant gets a list of pre-ordered groups of jobs from the rolling mill. Every group should contain enough jobs for one continuos sequence on the caster. The main objective for the production is the maximal output. Work in progress is no evaluation function since the steel never waits for a longer time. There are no places where the steel could wait. The evaluation of work-in-progress becomes only meaningful if we regard steelmaking plant and rolling mill together. In another expert system project attempts have been made to minimize the waiting time between steelmaking plant and rolling mill.

The most difficult problem in the steelmaking plant is the reaction to unexpected events. Sometimes the funnel must be changed earlier than expected and *reactive scheduling* is necessary. Furthermore, often it is not known when and how much steel is delivered from the blast furnace. If it becomes apparent that the delivery slows down, reaction may be advisable. Consequently, revisions of the plan must be performed during the execution of an existing schedule.

Although both applications are flow-shops in the same domain, they differ in their applied scheduling strategies. Since the domains are too complex to solve the scheduling process without heuristics and strategies, we apply strategies used by human experts. While in the first application the scheduler regards the sequences of jobs on the electric arc furnace, the expert in the second plant generates groups of jobs that can be scheduled till the next maintenance interval scheduled for the caster.

Now it is a challenge to design one expert system with the objective to reuse as much knowledge as possible for the second one. With object-oriented representations it is easy to reuse descriptions of aggregates and of the physical and chemical knowledge about steel. Since this knowledge is only a small part of the necessary knowledge we need further representation techniques to support the reuse.

THE MODELS OF EXPERTISE

In knowledge-based systems a separation of domain and control knowledge is desired. Often a stronger distinction is made for different kinds of control knowledge. A common distinction is made between inference knowledge, task knowledge, and strategic knowledge. I demonstrate the task-oriented design of a knowledge-based scheduling system and the different kinds of knowledge that occur in the first application. In figure 15-1 the relations between the four levels of expertise are described.

The central model of expertise is the task model. In generic tasks it is described, how problems in a domain are solved. Since only *generic concepts* (meta-classes) are used in the specification of such a task, they may be used in different applications. Besides a specification language, concepts from two other models are used: the domain and the inference models.

In the domain model the objects and relations between objects of the domain are described. We distinguish between the *scheduling theory* that defines the meta-classes like order, job and schedule, the *domain theory* (steelmaking) that defines classes like steel grade and heat, and the assertional knowledge about a certain application that defines for instance the steel grade "M238" with its chemical elements. Objects of the application are classified in reference to meta-classes that are used in the tasks. Furthermore, knowledge about the actual situation has to be defined.

To enable such a task model, inference techniques that are described in the inference model are needed. These inferences are specified again in terms of meta-classes of the domain. Typical inferences in the scheduling domain are temporal inferences (Canzi and Guida, 1993).

The fourth model of expertise is the strategic knowledge. This knowledge is used to "tune" the problem solution. Since scheduling problems are often too complex to use general heuristics, domain specific heuristics are required. In the strategic model we can choose between different heuristics like e.g. *shortest-processing-time* (SPT) or *earliest-due-date* (EDD) that are used to select the next job to be scheduled. Moreover, in scheduling, often objectives like the minimization of makespan, work-in-progress or lateness are used to optimize schedules. These optimizing criteria must be specified, and accordingly a task can be chosen that supports this criterion. Strategic knowledge is used to select from different tasks dynamically in a certain application or as a criterion during the development of a system for the selection of a specific task.

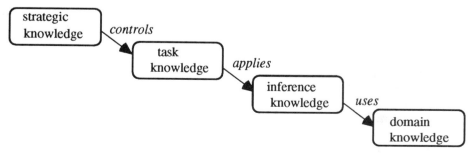

Figure 15-1: Models of expertise

Although it is advisable to design such a system top-down, starting from strategic and task knowledge, the four layers are described here in a reversed order starting with the domain layer, because the higher concepts are easier to comprehend if the concepts of the domain are known.

Domain knowledge

The *domain knowledge* embodies the conceptualization of a domain for a particular application in the form of a domain theory. Common primitives are objects, properties of these objects, and relations between properties or objects. Objects are partly physical objects like resources of the production process and partly virtual objects like the schedule. Using an *object-oriented representation*, machines, personal, tools, energy, and other materials can be represented as subclasses of resources and enable thereby the description of tasks that handle resources regardless of whether a machine or a tool is used. Nevertheless, specific tasks can distinguish between different subclasses.

Relations between objects which are usually "*is-a*"- or "*part-of*"-relations can also be interpreted as *constraints*. Important for scheduling applications are also quantitative and qualitative temporal relations.

To design the physical objects is quite easy. However, the design of the virtual objects like a schedule will have significant influence on the methods used later on. As a consequence, I recommend to design first the task and inference model.

Since we use the well known *temporal logic* of Allen (1983), a schedule is represented as a graph of *temporal intervals* with relations constraining the intervals (Dorn, 1991). We use a propagation algorithm based on the concept of sequence graphs that is more efficient for such applications (Dorn, 1992a) and that considers also quantitative temporal knowledge (Dorn, 1992b). Compatibility constraints between jobs are further relations in our domain that are modelled by fuzzy values (Dorn *et al.*, 1992). Some meta-classes for flow-shops are described in figure 15-2.

The classes for the steelmaking process in particular are described in a different graph. These are still not concrete objects but refinements of former class descriptions. Jobs in the steelmaking plants are usually called heats, a schedule is a casting plan, and the set of all used machines are called steel-refinement aggregates. Classes like "electric arc furnace" (EAF), "converter" (CNV), "ladle furnace" (LF), "vacuum oxygen degassing aggregate" (VOD), "teeming bay" (TB), "teeming crane" (TC) and "continuos casters" (CC) are defined, too. In both expert system projects it was essential to use during knowledge elicitation and representation exactly this vocabulary, which was used also by the experts. One task of the knowledge engineer is then to relate these specific notions as for example a casting plan with a schedule.

On the lowest level of the domain model we describe the assertional knowledge of an application that includes besides other facts the existing aggregates (e.g. EAF3, CC3, ...) and resources.

To schedule a job (heat) means to insert these intervals and interval constraints into an interval graph. A schedule (casting sequence) consists of an interval graph, a list of jobs already scheduled and a set of allocations. An allocation is like the engagement in (Canzi and Guida, 1993) a reservation of a resource for an operation of a certain job.

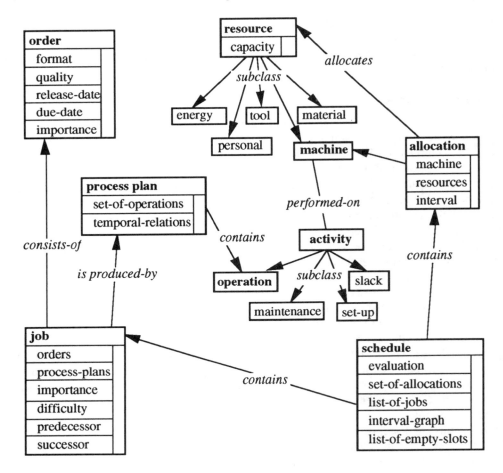

Figure 15-2: Generic domain theory

A typical *process plan* with temporal intervals and relations is given in the following two figures. It consists of operations that must be performed on certain aggregates. Furthermore, set-ups and other preparation activities are included.

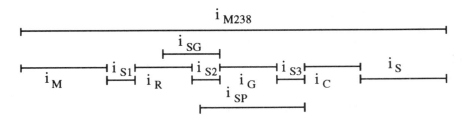

Figure 15-3: Temporal description of process plan

The process plan is formalized by interval logic. We use a syntax presented in (Dorn, 1990). An operation O takes place during an interval I is described by: $O @ I$. An interval in the following notation contains a lower and an upper duration in minutes. On the right side of the figure temporal constraints between intervals are given using the abbreviations introduced by Allen (1983).

heat(M238) @ i_{M238}				
melting(EAF)	@ $\langle i_M, 70..300\rangle$	i_M s i_H		
slack$_1$	@ $\langle i_{S1}, 0..30\rangle$	i_{S1} d i_H	i_M m i_{S1}	
refinement(LF)	@ $\langle i_R, 70..200\rangle$	i_R d i_H	i_{S1} m i_R	
slack$_2$	@ $\langle i_{S2}, 0..30\rangle$	i_{S2} d i_H	i_R m i_{S2}	
set-up(VOD)	@ $\langle i_{SG}, 10..30\rangle$	i_{SG} {< m o s d} i_H		
degassing(VOD)	@ $\langle i_G, 30..60\rangle$	i_G d i_H	i_{S2} m i_G	i_{SG} {< m} i_G
slack$_3$	@ $\langle i_{S3}, 0..5\rangle$	i_{S3} d i_H	i_G m i_{S3}	
preparation(TB1)	@ $\langle i_{SP}, 10..20\rangle$	i_{SP} {< m o s d} i_H		
casting(TC, TB1)	@ $\langle i_C, 15..45\rangle$	i_C d i_H	i_{S3} m i_C	i_{SP} {< m} i_C
solidifying(TB1)	@ $\langle i_S, 180..720\rangle$	i_S d i_H	i_C m i_S	

Figure 15-4: Process plan

In a generated schedule an interval graph exists whose intervals contain also earliest and latest start times and end times of intervals.

Inference knowledge

Inference knowledge describes how basic reasoning capabilities use domain knowledge to generate *control knowledge* for the task model. Control knowledge is e.g. an evaluation value for a schedule, the importance of a job or a sequence constraint between two operations.

Typical inferences are temporal inferences like these in interval graphs "transitive-constraint", evaluation of compatibilities "comp(job_1, job_2)", and many more. Temporal reasoning is used to check *temporal constraints* like due dates, allocation constraints (only one heat may be produced on the continuos caster at one time and a heat cannot be on different aggregates in overlapping intervals), and the correct execution of process plans. Most of the required inferences are complex and we do not have the space to specify them here. I give one inference that is needed in the tasks that will be defined later.

The input and output of inferences are specified with meta concepts of the domain theory. How the inference itself is performed is independent of a specific application. For the specific application the meta concepts in the input and output definition are substituted by domain concepts. The following inference looks for the most appropriate slot for a given job regardless of whether the slot is occupied. A slot is an interval in the schedule that depicts the time when the job uses the critical aggregate. In our first application this is the electric arc furnace. If a large slot is examined that could contain several jobs we have the possibility to generate a new slot at the edges of the large slot or in the middle of the slot. To divide a large slot into three slots is considered less desirable.

inference: search-best-slot(job, schedule, slot)
input: job → heat, schedule → casting-plan
output: slot → slot-for-furnace
    current-best-slot := slot := first-slot(schedule);
    best-compatibility = comp(job, job(successor(slot)));
repeat
    slot := next(slot);
    if empty(slot) **and** large(slot)
      then begin
        new-compatibility := comp(job(predecessor(slot)), job)
        if better(comp(job, job(successor(slot))), new-compatibility)
          then new-compatibility := comp(job, job(successor(slot)))
        if better(middle, new-compatibility)
          then new-compatibility := middle
      else new-compatibility := comp(job(predecessor(slot)), job) +
             comp(job, job(successor(slot)))
    end if;
    if better(new-compatibility, best-compatibility)
      then
        current-best-slot = slot;
        best-compatibility = new-compatibility;
    end if
until slot = last-slot(schedule);
if large(current-best-slot)
    then divide(current-best-slot, slot)
    else slot := current-best-slot

Algorithm 15-1: "search-best-slot"-inference

Task knowledge

Task knowledge describes how elementary inferences can be combined to achieve a certain goal. A task can be seen as a fixed strategy for achieving a goal based on some assumptions about the domain. One typical task is to schedule one job. Its goal is to get the job scheduled.

We assume a schedule already exists. Schedule and job are generic concepts that are substituted for the specific application with domain objects. There are two ways to schedule the job: either it exists an empty slot in the schedule that is appropriate for this job or an already scheduled job is removed from the schedule to enter the new job in this free slot. In order to perform this task some inferences are applied that generate control knowledge. Several intermediate schedules and evaluations for these schedules are computed. We assume that an evaluation inference for schedules exists. In (Dorn *et al.*, 1992) we have described an evaluation method based on fuzzy sets. The evaluation function considers the importance of jobs, the difficulty to schedule a job, and the quality of the schedule itself by measuring constraint violations.

Tasks may be defined on several abstraction layers. We design one task "schedule-job" that is called by another task. This task that is not described here schedules all orders of a given list. The task "schedule-job" applies a further task "allocate" that enters the complete process plan into the schedule and checks the temporal constraints.

task schedule-job
input: new-job → new-heat, actual-schedule → old-casting-plan
output: schedule → casting-plan
goal   scheduled(job)
control-terms
   old-job = job;
   $slot_1$, $slot_2$, $slot_3$ = slot;
   s_1, s_2, s_3 = schedule;
task-structure
   s_1 := actual-schedule;
   search-best-empty-slot(new-job, actual-schedule, $slot_1$);
   allocate(new-job, $slot_1$, actual-schedule);
   s_2 := actual-schedule;
   if better(evaluate(s_1), evaluate(s_2))
      then
         search-best-slot(new-job, actual-schedule, $slot_2$);
         remove(old-job, $slot_2$, actual-schedule);
         allocate(new-job, $slot_2$, actual-schedule);
         s_3 := actual-schedule;
         search-best-empty-slot(old-job, actual-schedule, $slot_3$);
         allocate(old-job, $slot_3$, actual-schedule);
         if not better(evaluate(actual-schedule), evaluate(s_1))
            then if better(evaluate(s_3), evaluate(s_1))
               then actual-schedule = s_3
            end if
         end if
      else actual-schedule = s_1
   end if

Algorithm 15-2: "schedule-job"-task

A further task used later is to look for jobs that could fill slots in a schedule.

task schedule-resource
input: slot → eaf-slot, list-of-jobs → list-of-heats,
         actual-schedule → casting-plan;
output: actual-schedule → actual-schedule-of-heats;
goal: filled(slot);

Algorithm 15-3: "schedule-resource"-task

The first task can be interpreted as a simple form of *order-based scheduling* and the second task as a form of *resource-based scheduling*. The described tasks can now be used by a task that schedules job after job as is necessary in our first application.

The abstraction level of our task is very high. The assumption that we have a flow-shop cannot be seen in this description. Also the existence of uncertain or vague knowledge is not assumed in this task. It would be no problem to apply this task also in a job-shop with very exact data concerning durations and compatibilities. For a new application the domain theory must be adapted and if necessary new inferences for exact data must be specified.

Strategic knowledge

The fourth kind of knowledge – the strategic knowledge – is used to determine which goals are relevant to solve a particular problem. How each goal is achieved is determined by the task knowledge.

An example of how strategic knowledge is applied to tune a problem solution can be illustrated in our domain. Typically for many scheduling systems is that they look for jobs that fit best into the first free slot of a schedule. The problem with this strategy is that jobs difficult to schedule will remain unscheduled. In order to prevent this, we start with scheduling difficult jobs. Since we search always for the best slot in the schedule, after a while some small slots between scheduled jobs occur. It became apparent in the expert system that it has to change this strategy after a while. When it has scheduled the most important jobs it tries to fill the gaps in the schedule. Consequently, it looks for jobs yet unscheduled that can be scheduled in the gaps. The following strategy implements such a behaviour.

strategy
determine-importance-of-jobs(list-of-Jobs, important-Jobs, other-Jobs);
determine-critical-aggregate(list-of-Jobs, critical-aggregate);
repeat
    remove(job, important-Jobs)
    schedule-job(job, actual-Schedule)
until empty(important-jobs);
for all jobs ∈ other-Jobs
    while exist-single-slot(critical-aggregate, actual-Schedule, slot)
      schedule-resource(slot, other-Jobs, actual-Schedule);
    remove(job, other-Jobs);
    schedule-job-by-exchanging(job, actual-Schedule);
end for all

Algorithm 15-4: "mixed-job / resource-based" strategy

This strategy is an example of using strategies in one application. However, another mode is possible. A strategy can be used to decide for an application which tasks are necessary.

REUSE OF THE TASK MODEL

The reuse of software is of fundamental importance for industrial development. If a company is specialized in the automation of production processes in a certain domain as for example the steel industry, they are interested to reuse as many software entities as possible to reduce the development costs as far as possible. However, this is not yet a standardized process.

I propose a task-oriented design to help in the process of reusing components of expert systems. In traditional software engineering object-oriented methods are proposed by several researchers. In the steelmaking process one could design objects like, for example, a continuos caster. This object could contain methods that describe different techniques and operations that are performed on the caster. For example, a method to decide the casting velocity.

For a scheduling problem it seems not so important to model methods of certain machines since we do not need methods of the caster for the scheduling problem. In scheduling, only the relations between the different objects (machines) in the production process are relevant. However, it is of outstanding interest to model the different objectives and solutions (strategies) to achieve schedules that fulfil this objective. On a more abstract level, however, I could imagine that a scheduling system is an object with its own data structures and methods. This object would communicate with other objects that implements a production planner or a production supervisor.

I have shown that the scheduler in the second application observes other objectives than those in the first one. The continuos caster is the bottleneck resource, and consequently the assignment of jobs to it is the main scheduling criterion. This can be achieved by giving the "schedule-resource" task instead of the "eaf-slot" the "cc-slot" as new argument.

Compatibility constraints must be regarded in both applications, but besides quality constraints, constraints on the casting format must be regarded in the second application. The compatibility of subsequent jobs must also be regarded in principle on every aggregate in a steelmaking plant in which different qualities are produced. However, the experts regard these constraints only on the critical resource (aggregate). The actual values for the compatibility constraints should therefore be modelled as a property of the aggregates. Thus, for every aggregate this property is modelled, but only the property of the critical resource is used in the scheduling task.

A further difference is the scheduling of maintenance intervals (change of tundish) and the generating of groups. The strategy of the human experts is to generate first groups of jobs that can be scheduled until the next change of the tundish. The generation of such groups can be supported by the "schedule-resource" task. The generated groups are then small schedules of about ten jobs. Afterwards these groups could be interpreted as jobs that can be scheduled by using the "schedule-job" task. To use both tasks we have to insert a new subclass of jobs into our class hierarchy. This job has the same properties as the already defined job, but it has also methods to combine properties of single jobs.

During the execution of the scheduled heats changes or failures often occur. Reactive scheduling is necessary. To achieve such a behaviour another task is necessary. However, it may be realized by a task to "repair" schedules that I have not introduced, because there was not enough space here. In (Dorn *et al.*, 1992) we have presented a repair method (task) to improve schedules that still violate some constraints. This task could be used also for the reaction to changes in the environment. This change or failure causes a constraint violation that should be prevented.

CONCLUSIONS

We have presented a methodology for designing scheduling systems in a task-oriented fashion. This methodology supports the design and maintenance of such a system, and we have shown how a task model can be adapted in a new application. Additionally, we assume that for a given scheduling tool it will be more likely that it can be reused for another applications if the "way" how the system finds its solution is given formally and, of course, if a user can define new tasks or strategies. We are on the way to develop a scheduling tool box in this direction.

The described examples are first experiments for a task-oriented design. There are still many open questions. We have oriented ourselves by the KADS methodology, but there are some problems with this methodology. First, there is no representational formalism provided for temporal information in the domain theory. We managed this with interval graphs. Second, if we want to specify tasks for reactive scheduling we have to state that something in the domain can occur simultaneously to the problem solving process. These problems exist, because the developers of KADS have only used static applications like diagnosis of men or machines or configuration of machines.

Another problem exists with the user interface. A scheduling expert system should support and communicate with the expert, but it should not replace him. Therefore a detailed specification of possible man-machine dialogues must be done. A KADS user has the possibility to specify a cooperation model with tasks like "obtain", "present", "receive", and "provide". However, such a set of tasks is not enough to my mind. In our application several experts work with the system and every expert has different preferences. Some want a system that schedules all jobs automatically, others prefer to give some first decisions to the system, and others want to use the system only as a tool for checking constraints. There would be many different tasks if we allow every possible kind of cooperation. Therefore the cooperation should be specified otherwise.

To achieve great benefits from task-oriented design it would be important to have task libraries. To find appropriate tasks for a given problem an indexing scheme for scheduling applications must be developed. Krueger (1992) has mentioned that the reuse of software entities is most successful were concepts can be described by single words. Cited examples are mathematical functions. Thus it seems important to find some commonsense scheduling concepts like job, order, resource, etc. to define an abstract scheduling framework that is accepted by everyone concerned with scheduling applications. If we can find such a commonsense framework it seems reasonable to have reusable scheduling software.

REFERENCES

Adams, J., Balas, E. and Zawack, D. (1988) The Shifting Bottleneck Procedure for Job Shop Scheduling, *Management Science* **34** (3), pp. 391–401.

Allen, J.F. (1983) Maintaining Knowledge about Temporal Intervals, *Communications of the ACM* **26** (11), pp. 823–843.

Berry, P.M. (1993) Scheduling and Uncertainty Reasoning, in *Scheduling of Production Processes*, Chichester: Ellis Horwood.

Bezirgan, A. (1993) A Case-based Approach to Scheduling Constraints, in *Scheduling of Production Processes*, Chichester: Ellis Horwood.

Breuker, J. and Wielinga, B. (1991) *KADS: A Modelling Approach to Knowledge Engineering*, Technical Report ESPRIT Project, University of Amsterdam.

Bylander, T. and Chandrasekaran, B. (1988) Generic Tasks in Knowledge-based Reasoning: The 'right' Level of Abstraction for Knowledge Acquisition, in *Knowledge Acquisition for Knowledge-Based Systems*, B. Gaines and J. Boose (eds), pp. 65–77, London: Academic Press.

Canzi, U. and Guida, G. (1993) The Temporal Model of CRONOS-III: A Knowledge-based System for Production Scheduling, in *Scheduling of Production Processes*, Chichester: Ellis Horwood.

Clancey, W.J. (1985) Heuristic Classification, *Artificial Intelligence* **27**, pp. 289–350.

Coad, P. and Yourdon, E. (1991) *Object-Oriented Design*, Computing Series, Englewood Cliffs: Yourdon Press, 2nd edition.

Dorn, J. (1991) Qualitative Modeling of Time in Technical Applications, *Proceedings of the International GI Conference on Knowledge Based Systems*, München, Springer Verlag, pp. 310–319.

Dorn, J. and Shams, R. (1991) An Expert System for Scheduling in a Steelmaking Plant, *Proceedings of the 1st World Congress on Expert Systems*, Orlando, Fla, Pergamon Press, pp. 395–400.

Dorn, J. (1992a) Temporal Reasoning in Sequence Graphs, *Proceedings of 10th National Conference on Artificial Intelligence* (AAAI-92), San Jose, CA, pp. 735–740.

Dorn, J. (1992b) *Hybrid Temporal Reasoning*, Technical Report, Christian Doppler Laboratory for Expert Systems, CD-TR 92/43.

Dorn, J., Slany, W. and Stary, C. (1992) Uncertainty Management by Relaxation of Conflicting Constraints in Production Process Scheduling, *Proceedings of the AAAI Spring Symposium on „Practical Approaches to Scheduling and Planning"*, pp. 62–67.

Dubois, D. (1989) Fuzzy Knowledge in an Artificial Intelligence System for Job-shop Scheduling, *Applications of Fuzzy Set Methodologies in Industrial Engineering*, Gerald W. Evans *et al.* (eds), Elsevier, pp. 73–89.

Filipic, B. (1993) Enhancing Genetic Search to Schedule a Production Unit, in *Scheduling of Production Processes*, Chichester: Ellis Horwood.

Fox, M.S. (1987) *Constraint-Directed Search: A Case Study of Job-Shop Scheduling*, London: Pitman.

Krueger, C.W. (1992) Software Reuse, *ACM Computing Surveys* **24** (2), pp. 131–183.

McDermott, J. (1989) Preliminary Steps Towards a Taxonomy of Problem-solving Methods, in *Automating Knowledge Acquisition for Expert Systems*, S. Marcus (ed.), Kluwer Academic Publishers, pp. 225–255.

Minton, S., Johnston, M., Philips, A. and Laird, P. (1990) Solving Large-scale Constraint Satisfaction and Scheduling Problems Using a Heuristic Repair Method, *Proceedings of the 8th National Conference on Artificial Intelligence* (AAAI-90), pp. 17–24.

Musen, M. (1989) *Automated Generation of Model-Based Knowledge Acquisition Tools*, London: Pitman.

Naur, P. and Randell, B. (1968) *Software Engineering. Report on a Conference Garmisch*, Brüssel: NATO Scientific Affairs Devision.

Ow, P.S. and Smith, S.F. (1988) Viewing Scheduling as an Oportunistic Problem Solving Process, *Annals of Operations Research* **12**, pp. 85–108.

Prosser, P. (1993) Scheduling as a Constraint Satisfaction Problem: Theory and Practice, in *Scheduling of Production Processes*, Chichester: Ellis Horwood.

Rumbaugh, J., Blaha, M., Premerlani, W., Eddy, F. and Lorensen, W. (1991) *Object-Oriented Modeling and Design*, Prentice Hall.

Sadeh, N. (1991) *Look-ahead Techniques for Micro-opportunistic Job Shop Scheduling*, Ph. D. School of Computer Science, Carnegie Mellon University, Pittsburgh.

Smith, S.F., Fox, M.S. and Ow, P.S. (1986) Constructing and Maintaining Detailed Production Plans: Investigations into the Development of Knowledge-based Factory Scheduling Systems, *AI Magazine*, Fall, pp. 45–61.

Stohl, K., Snopek, W., Weigert, T. and Moritz, T. (1991) Development of a Scheduling Expert System for a Steelplant, *Proceedings of the IFIP Conference on Expert Systems in Mineral and Metallurgy*, Espoo, Finnland.

Überreiter, B. and Voß, A. (eds) (1991) *Materials of the KADS User Meeting*, Munich, Siemens AG ZFE IS INF 32.

Zweben, M.; Deale, M.; Gargan, R. (1990) Anytime Rescheduling, *Proceedings of the DARPA Workshop on Innovative Approaches to Planning and Scheduling*, pp. 251–262.

Index